Tracing the history of your house

Part of a sale indenture from 1753, one of the most common forms of title deed that the house historian will encounter. (C 103/12/1)

Tracing the history of your house

Nick Barratt

PUBLIC RECORD OFFICE

Public Record Office
Richmond
Surrey
TW9 4DU

ISBN 1 903365 22 8

A catalogue card for this book is available from the British Library

Front cover (top to bottom): Headed notepaper showing houses at Cullercoats, Northumberland
– letter from Duke of Devonshire, 10 September 1845 (PRO 30/29/17/5).

Valuation Field Book entry for Castle Farm, Egglestone Abbey, North Yorkshire (IR 58/25622).

Doorway of Plymouth House, reproduced by courtesy of Mavis and David Yates.

'Anne Hathaway's cottage, Stratford-upon-Avon', photograph by James Lewis of Nottingham,
registered for copyright by Boots Pure Drug Co. Ltd., Nottingham, 6 August 1897 (COPY 1/431).

'Woodcutter's cottage, New Forest', photograph by Ernest Edwin Nofsiter of Tottenham,
registered by him for copyright on 20 May 1892 (COPY 1/408).

Front/back of cover: Part of valuation map of Northop, Flintshire, dated 1912 (IR 131/10/85).

Back of cover: Mortgage deed, contract of sale and indemnity, 1880/1 (J 90/1711).

Printed by Cromwell Press, Trowbridge, Wiltshire

Contents

Preface

Before you begin using this guide, I would like to offer a few words of encouragement. There is no great mystery to house history. It is something that anyone can do. I should know, as I basically taught myself from scratch. I have been lucky enough to investigate the histories of the properties featured in the last three series of the BBC's *House Detectives*, and each one has given me an insight into different sources and alternative approaches to the subject.

I wandered into house history by accident. However, I did have some experience from a school project, over fifteen years ago, when I was chosen to take part in an 'experimental' O-level course. It focused on local history, and the key element was a field trip to research the history of a street in the community. Luckily for me, the chosen site was a road adjoining my own, and consequently I was able to amaze fellow students with the casual way in which I assigned dates to houses that I had seen constructed as a child.

But it is rarely as easy as that. Each property will require you to follow a unique research trail – one that might be obscure or full of unexpected twists and turns, with dead ends lurking around every corner. This is all part of the fun, as you never know what secrets you will uncover; yet it makes trying to write a comprehensive guide to the subject all the more difficult. I have concentrated on the main sources that I tend to use when I begin investigating the history of a house, and ones that will yield the most fruitful results in the majority of cases. However, don't be afraid to experiment with other sources, and let the history of the local community guide your approach.

I would like to express my gratitude to several people who have contributed to this volume in various ways. First and foremost, to Stella Colwell, Paul Carter and Amanda Bevan for reading through the entire text for accuracy – I am eternally grateful to them for doing so and any errors that remain are mine alone; to the specialists at the PRO for your help and support (you know who you are); to Nicky Pattison, Tim Dunn and Basil Comely for giving me my initial opportunity at the BBC; to Dan Cruickshank, who will forget more about architecture than I will ever learn; to Mavis and David Yates, who kindly allowed me to feature their house as a case study; and to Martin Cross, who first introduced me to local history many years ago. Above all, I would like to dedicate this book to my wife, Sarah, a fellow house detective, for her constant support that allows me to pursue a career that is also a lifelong interest.

So take heart, and with a deep breath set foot on your own unique detective trail. Good luck!

Nick Barratt
April 2001

1 | An introduction to house history

1.1 House history

The communities that we live in today are products of one of humanity's most basic needs: shelter. Throughout the ages people have constructed dwellings to protect themselves from the elements, from the smallest peasant's hovel to the grandest royal palace. The United Kingdom is blessed with a rich architectural heritage, and historians have tended to focus their attention on the grander buildings of the past – castles, cathedrals and palaces. Yet there are thousands of equally fascinating buildings waiting to be discovered, with stories to tell about who used to live there, and what roles they played in their local community. In short, you can use your own house – or indeed any property you consider to be of interest – as the starting point for a voyage of discovery through the ages.

In general, most house historians are attempting to find out when their houses were built. This can be a difficult task, as records that are specific to house construction are few and far between. A house detective faces the task of reconstructing a chronology from a variety of sources in which dwellings have perhaps left a trace. Rather than focusing on the bricks and mortar, one of the best ways of finding out about a house is by researching its owners or occupiers. Thus the house detective needs to combine many techniques, such as elements of genealogy. Furthermore, you should try to investigate the way in which your house has evolved over the ages, not only in terms of its architecture, but also the way it would have been furnished on the inside – after all, the people you have found would have considered it their home as well, and would have gone to great lengths to make it comfortable. If you have a plot of land with your house, you might uncover broken pots or household rubbish; it is highly likely that these were left behind by previous occupants, and can sometimes offer clues for dating purposes.

Once you have produced your chronology, listing construction or alteration dates and the names of the people who owned the house or resided there, take the next step and put your house in a wider context. Try to find out about the way people used to live, and what the local community was like at key moments in your house's past. Ask yourself what made it a good time to build your house, or why there was a sudden need to add another storey or wing. How did local events impact upon the lives of past occupants? Was there an important local industry that might give an indication to employment histories? All are areas that can bring the past vividly back to life.

However, it is important to begin your research with realistic expectations – not everyone is going to find themselves investigating a house that can be traced back to the thirteenth century, or indeed be able to pinpoint a precise date of construction. You will encounter problems along the way, and you may well feel that you have come to the end of the road. Don't give up – it is always worth trying a slightly different approach, or a new set of documents.

1.2   About this guide

House construction over time has varied from region to region, and from age to age. This variance in style can often provide valuable clues about when your house was built. Indeed your house might even be the last of many that have stood on the same site, so always treat documentary evidence with care and remember to use other clues, such as architecture, to help date the property. Guidance on architectural style and building technique is not within the remit of this volume, but details of relevant literature to help you date your house through building styles and regional patterns of house building are given in **Useful publications** at the end of the book. Instead, the first purpose of this guide is to provide a basic introduction to the many and varied techniques required to trace the history of your house, and thereafter to explain and illustrate some of the main documentary sources that can be used to construct a house chronology.

Chapters 1–2 introduce house history as a discipline and suggest useful ways of beginning your research. Relevant skills and tools of the trade are explained, and guidance is given about where to look for particular types of documents. A word on archives in general is also provided, as they can be a daunting place for the uninitiated. Chapters 3–13 then examine the most relevant documentary sources, with additional search tips, explanations of how to use the material and where it can be located. Finally, a research plan has been suggested (Chapter 14) and a case study given (Chapter 15), based on an actual house that was featured on BBC television's *House Detectives*. The sources that are described throughout are primarily to be found at the Public Record Office (hereafter PRO) at Kew, although sources that exist in local archives are covered in some detail where relevant. Sources for Scottish and Irish house history are referred to in passing but are not covered in detail in this guide, which is written for properties in England and Wales.

Some houses will be easier to trace than others, and there are no sets of rules to follow – each house will dictate where you will look for clues. House history is an imprecise art, and houses from disparate regions, constructed in various chronological periods, will require you to examine many different sources. Consequently, this guide is not intended to be a comprehensive survey of all sources that you may encounter. Instead, they represent the main areas of research that will provide the best results most of the time, and taken together should provide you with sufficient material. However, each house will have its own unique story to tell, with a unique documentary path to follow – that is one of the joys of house history, as you embark on a real voyage of discovery. You can be amazed by the facts you uncover, and should find the discipline enjoyable and ultimately rewarding.

2 Getting started

2.1 Introduction

One of the most important tasks in any piece of research is deciding how and where to start. This chapter provides some advice on your first steps along the detective trail, and suggests some ideas about where you can look for initial clues before you even set foot in an archive. This will involve talking to neighbours, previous owners or estate agents who were involved in past sales, and the important task of familiarizing yourself with the local area. Once you have completed these background searches, and armed with any preliminary information you might have uncovered, you can consider moving on to researching primary source material. The next task will therefore be to locate the most relevant county record office (hereafter CRO) or national institution, as it is here that you will find documentary evidence that will hopefully contain information pertinent to the history of your house. Archives can be difficult places to work in, especially if you have never been to one before, so a few hints are offered which should make the experience seem less intimidating and ultimately more rewarding. Tips about reading the source material are also provided, as you will soon discover that the vast majority of sources require some degree of interpretation, or indeed translation, before you can extract useful information.

Given that the aim of this book is to introduce documents that are primarily held at the PRO, the chapter concludes with a more detailed introduction to the electronic catalogues, paper guides and indexes that you will need to use to obtain a PRO document reference. Advice on document ordering and Internet searches is also given.

2.2 First steps

2.2.1 Beginning local research: talking to people

House history can be a very sociable pastime, as one of the best ways of finding out a bit more about your house and the road and area that it stands in is to talk to neighbours or previous owners. They may well know some snippet of information or interesting story that can lead you a little further back in time, or give you an avenue of research to pursue. They may even have done some research of their own. But remember to exercise diplomacy – not everyone will share your enthusiasm, so please phone or, better still, write before marching in demanding to know about the time they spent in the house. However, the opposite is sometimes also true, and you may not always like the tales that you are told about your present home. Remember that oral information is not always going to be accurate, and that it is your job as a house detective to corroborate these stories with hard fact, especially if you are looking for clues to the date of construction.

You may also find that people are willing to show you old photographs of the house. These might contain images of previous owners or occupants that you can later identify; there may also be evidence of different structures or building styles. You can check your attic or basement (if you have one), as people have a habit of squirrelling away old photos, along with papers and files that get forgotten or left behind in a move. It may seem surprising, but it is also worth checking roof fillings on earlier houses, as all sorts of material were used as insulation – including clothes and personal papers that were no longer required, all of which can be dated. Don't just restrict your search to the interior of the house; the garden may also contain clues about the lives of former occupiers. For example, you may have uncovered items such as clay pipes, broken pots or other domestic goods, as in the days before organized waste disposal, people often used their gardens as personal rubbish dumps. Although dating objects can often be difficult, and there is no guaranteed link to your property, they can at least tell you something about the use of the site, and local museums may be able to provide further guidance. Furthermore, you may come across evidence of old foundations as you dig, which again can provide telling clues about outbuildings such as stables, stores or indeed an entire earlier dwelling. These are all avenues that can be explored in more detail when you progress to archives, and at the very least can shed light on the way people used to live.

Away from the house itself, you can always talk to estate agents or solicitors who handled previous sales of the property. You may be pleasantly surprised as to the amount of information they can provide about the house, from sale catalogues to commissioned reports and surveys, even down to old title deeds that have never been collected by previous occupants. Again, caution is urged when making your approach, as these people are busy professionals who might not have that much time to spare for enthusiastic house detectives.

2.2.2 Researching the history of your local community

Another important step to take before commencing archival research is to pinpoint precisely where your house is situated in the local community. Not only
will you need to know which street it is in, and feel confident enough to locate it
on older maps that might not contain modern landmarks, but also you will need
to find out about the administrative districts in which it fell, as many documents
are grouped or arranged by these districts. The easiest to identify is the name of
the parish, although modern parish boundaries might not equate to older ones,
and you will need to be aware of the dates of these changes. These boundaries
should be marked on modern Ordnance Survey (OS) maps. Similarly, you
should find out if your house once formed part of a larger estate, and more
importantly the name of the manor that it fell in. Other administrative units that
you will need to at least make a note of include the Poor Law union; urban, rural
or district council; and the county division (for example, the name of the hundred, rape, riding, etc.).

To find out this information you will need to do some preliminary reading.
Luckily there are some detailed publications to help you. Relevant *Victoria County
Histories* (VCH) volumes give a county by county guide to places, divisions and
events of note, although not all areas are covered. Similarly, English Place Name
Society volumes can give you some useful information about the origins of place
names, and where they appear in documentary sources, as do topographical
gazetteers, antiquarian studies and local history society publications. Local
directories are another good source of information that can provide details
about the administrative district of which your house was once a part. All of
these publications should be available at your local studies library or CRO,
which should be your first port of call, and a list of sources is provided under
Useful publications. At this stage it is advisable to make a working copy of a
map that shows your area and mark these boundaries on it for future reference.

It is well worth taking some time to research a bit about the history of your
community before focusing on your house, as you will often uncover social or
economic developments that may have provided the reason for its construction
in the first place. Major changes to the community will have influenced the way
people lived their lives and therefore built their houses. Some of these issues are
covered in more detail in Chapter 11, when the impact of national events on the
locality is considered. However, the following questions are ones that you can
usefully ask yourself as part of the process of putting your house in a wider
chronological context:

- What was the local industry, and was your house associated with it (for
  example, docks, canals, factories)?

- What impact (if any) did the railways have?
- Do street or house names reflect the name of a local major landowner?
- Does the house name reflect a previous use of the property (for example, Miller's Cottage)?
- Do you live in a suburb of a town or city that enjoyed a period of rapid expansion at some stage in the past?
- Was there any bomb damage caused in the Second World War?

All of these aspects of the social history of your area will help you to understand why your house was constructed at a particular time, or may even determine where you will need to look for a particular type of document. For example, the construction of the railways in the mid nineteenth century was coupled with the creation of dwellings for railway workers, and many other industries followed a similar pattern.

2.2.3   Use your house as your first document

Of course, one of the most obvious places to start dating your house is with the house itself. The way in which it was built – its architectural fingerprint – will often tell you a vast amount about the period in which it was constructed, although it will be difficult to pinpoint a precise date. Instead, you should use the building style of your property to provide a wider date period within which it was probably constructed.

It is not within the remit of this guide to outline the tell-tale signs that you should be looking for, but a reading list has been provided. However, there are pitfalls associated with over-reliance on architectural evidence that you should beware of.

- Many regions developed unique ways of building houses that remained unchanged for centuries, or 'bucked the trend' compared with building techniques employed by the rest of the country for the same period.
- In contrast, to the untrained eye it might be tempting to attribute an early construction date to a rebuild in a retrospective style.
- Salvage from older properties, or indeed an earlier house that once stood on the same site, can often provide misleading information as well.
- Beware of partial rebuilds due to fire, which were especially prevalent when thatch was employed as a roofing material.

It is worth bearing in mind that properties built nearer the centre of a community or town are often older than those on the outskirts, or were at least constructed on the sites of earlier buildings. Also look at neighbouring houses and compare their architectural features with your own – they may be markedly different, which suggests that they were not constructed at the same time. It might be worth doing some research into their history as well, as you never know where you will uncover relevant clues.

2.3   Research techniques

2.3.1   Where to begin your research

Bearing in mind the advice provided in section 2.2, the best place to begin your research is at the most 'local' level. This will often be a local studies centre, usually located at your nearest main library. This is where you will find many printed volumes that are directly relevant to your community, such as those listed in **Useful publications**. Not only will these provide useful information about the area in which you live, but the experience will also ease you more gently into some of the research techniques that you will require later when you start work in an archive. Furthermore, printed local history studies will often (though not always!) provide document references to relevant material located in CROs or national archives. This will immediately give you a 'way in' to the records, saving you time and hopefully giving you a degree of confidence; you know that at least there will be something that you can look at. You will also find that the local studies centre will often have its own collection of photographs, maps, plans and newspaper cuttings that you can consult, giving you a good platform from which to build some knowledge. It is likely that staff at the local studies centre will be able to give you advice about further reading and where to go next to continue your research.

In all probability you will be directed to the next level on the archival hierarchy, the local record office. For most people this will be the relevant CRO, but residents in cities or large towns might find that there are specialist record offices that collect and contain specific records that are equally relevant. London is a particular case in point, with the London Metropolitan Archives (LMA) and the Corporation of London Record Office to name but two, and a multitude of local record offices that also exist at borough level. It is at the CRO that you will find the largest collection of locally relevant documents and primary source material, plus a wider array of relevant publications for your local area.

This is where your local knowledge will be put to good use, as in addition to the thousands of private papers that were deposited by former residents of the county, you will find records generated by the various administrative bodies that existed through the ages – hence the need to know your parish, manor, Poor Law union and county division. Once again, there will be staff on hand to help you with this, but if you do have some pre-knowledge it will save you a great deal of time, and make searching for (and within) records much easier.

It might seem logical to look for material relating to your house in the CRO for the county in which it is built, and most of the time this will hold true. However, your property might once have formed part of a larger estate, and the landowner may have resided in a different county. For a start, there is no guarantee that private records relating to your house were ever deposited in the public domain; but where such material has been made public, you are more likely to locate it at the CRO in the county where the landowner was resident. Be prepared – the detective trail can lead you to some very unexpected places, as the case study in Chapter 15 proves.

At the top of the tree will be national institutions such as the PRO and specialist archives. These will not necessarily be the best place to begin your research, but will nevertheless contain crucial information. For example, as you will discover in the following chapters, the PRO contains a wealth of information from the documents produced by the interaction between citizens and the state. More detailed information on the PRO is contained below in section 2.5. However, by way of introduction, the PRO is often described as the national archives for England, Wales and the United Kingdom. If you live in Scotland you should contact the National Archives of Scotland (NAS) in Edinburgh; the National Library of Wales (NLW), Aberystwyth, fulfils a similar function for the Principality, whilst the Public Record Office of Northern Ireland (PRONI) is located in Belfast. In effect, these four institutions hold 'government' papers created by various departments, but you will be surprised and amazed by how many will be relevant to your local community. After all, the responsibility of government was, theoretically, to look after people's best interests, and relevant and accurate information was required to fulfil this task. Tax assessments, land surveys, local correspondence, commissions and reports all survive to paint a far wider picture than the locally generated records found at CROs.

You will find that private papers, correspondence and other related material appear in other 'national' places of deposit that are slightly less accessible, such as the Bodleian Library, Oxford, and the British Library (BL), London. Other institutions such as the Family Records Centre (FRC) have been set up to make life easier for researchers embarking on a specialist line of research, and professional organizations also exist to offer guidance and advice. A full list of places, publications, organizations and websites that will enable you to locate where to start your research are provided under **Useful addresses** and **Useful publications**.

2.3.2 Research techniques

The following research techniques are designed to give you some guidance about getting started. You will probably develop some of your own as you progress, but bear these points in mind when you do start to think about how and where to begin your research.

Realistic expectations

In BBC television's *House Detectives*, a different property is featured each week with some strange mystery that the owners would like investigated. After 30 minutes of architectural and documentary sleuthing, the mystery is invariably solved and the delighted owners discover when, and by whom, the house was built. Be warned – this is never the case in reality! House history can be a time consuming process that requires a disciplined and methodical approach to the research. Unlike the TV series, you have no time limits, so you should plan your research carefully. It may take you many months or even years of work to settle on a date of construction, and even then you may have only narrowed it down to a rough period, rather than an precise date. This can be highly frustrating, which is why it is important not to set your sights too high in the first place.

No evidence?

The houses featured in the TV series are chosen for a specific reason, as they have an interesting story to tell. Your house may not, or the documentary sources that you need to uncover its history might not survive; indeed, this is one of the most common obstacles facing every house detective. Even when the necessary documents do exist, they can be difficult to interpret or understand, particularly the further back you manage to research. However, it is not all bad news – sometimes the lack of evidence will tell you that your house had not yet been built, so you can search later and perhaps easier sources.

Following clues

One of the most common temptations in any line of research is to assume a link between clues just because it seems the most likely conclusion. It is far better to work backwards from known facts in a methodical manner than jump in feet first without any real substantive evidence. The research pro-forma in Chapter 14 contains a practical structure that details how to establish a framework of definite facts, which should then lead you to other lines of research. Never give up – if one line of investigation runs dry, go back to your framework, or indeed the earliest known fact, and pursue a different approach. You will probably need to do this many times during the course of your research, and as a result you may revisit an archive several times as new evidence comes to light.

Corroborating documentary evidence

Remember that no two houses will ever follow the same pattern of research, as they were constructed at different times; even houses built at roughly the same time in the same community may yield vastly different results, depending on the people who lived in them, and what records were generated and, more importantly, survive. You may need to corroborate at least two or three separate sources before you can rely on the results with any degree of certainty. Don't be afraid to explore sources that you might not consider to be relevant – you never know where the detective trail might lead. The sources listed in this book are the most likely to yield results for the majority of houses, but you will find other sources that are of particular relevance to you.

Potential pitfalls

Not all properties will be described in the same way as they are today. House numbers are a relatively new invention, and many houses are described in documents by their physical location, or with reference to properties next to them which may not now exist. Indeed, house names and numbers, as well as street names, are liable to change; and much of your research will be about the people who lived there or the land on which the house was built, rather than the house itself. Finally, it can never be stressed too many times that architectural evidence should be used in conjunction with the documentary sources to prevent you 'discovering' that your house was built far earlier than it really was.

The Internet

More material is made available on the Internet each day, and the house historian can usefully access its growing resources to obtain advice and identify sources. Of particular use are the official websites that many archives and professional organizations maintain, as they contain information leaflets and contact details, plus online research services. Many also provide online access to their catalogues, and increasingly key word searches are available. However, you will need to exercise caution when using some of these online research tools, as it is tempting to rely on the results they produce as providing 'all' the information you will need. This is rarely the case, as many search engines scan document descriptions as opposed to document content, and will therefore not provide full access to place names unless they are specified in the document description. Furthermore, it is tempting to accept material posted on 'unofficial' websites, in particular name indexes or databases. Many are compiled by enthusiastic amateurs and will rarely be comprehensive; if you do obtain information that you think will be of use in your research, it is always wise to double check the facts against the original source material. One of the most essential skills that a house historian needs to develop is the ability to cast a sceptical eye over material and check information for accuracy and relevance. A list of potentially useful websites is provided under **Useful addresses.**

2.4   Working in archives

2.4.1   Gaining entry to an archive

It is always a good idea to get in touch with a prospective new archive before you visit it. You may need to reserve a seat or microfilm reader, and in any case it is always wise to check opening times and document delivery restrictions. It is also likely that you will need to obtain a reader's ticket before you can gain entry, and at least one form of identification is usually required, which will vary from archive to archive. CROs usually require a document with your address on it, such as a recent utility or phone bill, plus another official document (passport, driver's licence or banker's card). Some CROs form part of a County Archive Research Network (CARN), and one CARN ticket will give you access to all archives on the network. Not all CROs have joined this scheme, so it is better to check than to assume. Some ways of getting in touch with your CRO or target archive are suggested in **Useful addresses** and **Useful publications**, but these days many CROs have their own websites which provide access requirements, opening times and information pages about the material they hold. You may also be able to email for research advice.

2.4.2   Rules and regulations: preserving the documents

Document preservation and conservation is an important part of archival work, and to ensure that documents are not damaged you will find that archives impose strict rules on what you can bring into the reading rooms with you, plus guidelines on document handling techniques. In general, the golden rule of archives is that you must work with pencils only – biros and pens are forbidden due to the potential harm they can cause to original material. Similarly, erasers and pencil sharpeners should not be used or placed near documents, as they can cause damage. There is usually a no eating or drinking rule in place for similar reasons, and this extends to cough sweets and chewing gum. If you are unsure about how you should be handling an item, or you feel it is delicate, please ask an archivist to assist you. Most archives have a store of foam wedges, supports and weights to help set the document out in a way that carries a minimum risk of harm. Try to limit your own contact with the item; for example, if reading a line of text, do not run your finger along the document, as grease from your skin can cause damage. Instead, place a piece of white paper under the line of text to help you keep your place. If you are having difficulty reading faded text, ultraviolet lamps can often help. Similarly, maps and plans are often covered under clear protective sheets, and you should always ask before you attempt to trace a document.

2.4.3   Language and old handwriting

If you are fortunate enough to be able to trace the history of your house beyond 1733, you may well encounter difficulties interpreting relevant material, as the language of official documents was Latin. So material such as manorial court rolls, a highly important source for a house historian, will need translating, as will any official record of deeds or land transfers that were enrolled in the central courts. The exception to this is the Interregnum period (1649–60), when the Parliamentary regime decreed that all official documents should be written in English, and in any case you will find that some types of document had already adopted the vernacular language before 1733.

Another potential problem will be that scribes tended to employ abbreviations when recording entries, so you will not necessarily be working from easily identifiable Latin words. Handwriting changed over the ages, and even if a document has been written in English, it may be difficult to decipher. Official sources can be easier, as scribal technique tended to change more slowly as writers adopted the handwriting of their predecessors. However, private hands varied widely, even within a relatively short period, often employing idiosyncratic shorthand techniques. Spellings also differed widely between authors, and it is not unusual to find variant spellings of the same word in a single piece of text. All of these problems can make interpreting documents difficult.

However, there are ways to make documents seem less intimidating. Most archives stock Latin dictionaries and aids to help you understand palaeography, which is the technical term used to describe the handwriting and abbreviations employed in the documents. Furthermore, there are specialist volumes written for local historians that provide translations and explanations of the formulae for the most commonly used documents that you will encounter. You will find relevant material listed under **Useful publications**.

If you are still unsure, try selecting a similar document from the Interregnum period, which will be in English. Most documents follow standard patterns, with only the details of individuals and places altering. This will enable you to decide where you should be looking in the document for key phrases, and assist with translation. In addition, some local history societies provide transcriptions and translations of important document series, with the added advantage that they are usually indexed. These too can be used to aid interpretation of difficult original material.

Finally, not everyone is familiar with the way documents are dated. Many dates are given in the form of a regnal year (for example, 15 Henry VIII covers 1523–4), and a large proportion of legal material also incorporates a legal term – namely Michaelmas, Hilary, Easter and Trinity – that signifies a particular part of the year in which business was conducted. Furthermore, you may come across dates such as 28 February 1700/01, which refer to the old-style dating technique employed by the church that started the New Year on 25 March, rather than on 1 January as we do today. The practice was dropped in 1752, the same year that the Gregorian calendar was adopted. The best guide to the many and varied ways of writing dates is Cheney's *Handbook of Dates*, as this provides tables giving regnal years, Easter days and Saints' days, which also occur as a way of giving a date.

2.4.4   Historical context

When looking at the material you have selected, it is very tempting to jump straight in to identify references to your house or house owners. This would be a mistake. Before you can usefully extract information from a document, you will need to understand why that document was created in the first place. If you do not do this, then you may be taking the information it contains out of its historical context and therefore run the risk of misinterpreting it. After all, documents were not initially created for the purpose of helping house detectives date their properties in the twenty-first century. The records might not easily lend themselves to modern research techniques – for example, indexes may not survive, or you may need to identify names of people rather than the property where they lived. Ask yourself why the document was created, and what information it was originally intended to provide. This will allow you to read it in its own context, and thereby understand why it is arranged the way it is. It may therefore be necessary to corroborate the source with one or more others before you can extract useful information. Most archives provide information leaflets about documents and why they were created, so set aside some time to read these useful articles so that you fully understand why you need to look at the documents.

2.5   The Public Record Office

2.5.1   Archival references at the PRO

In this guide, document references will be provided to material located at the PRO. Each document has its own unique reference, and the PRO has adopted a coding system to allow you to identify which item you need. The coding system is primarily based around the government department, institution or body that created or maintained the documents in the first place, and usually consists of three separate parts. You will need to make a note of the document reference and order it from the repository floors before you can see it. This in itself can be quite a challenge, given that the PRO holds an estimated 9 million individual items on 175 kilometres of shelving, with approximately 2 to 3 kilometres of documents being added at the start of each calendar year. Indeed, the holdings are so large that some material is stored in a repository at Hayes, which takes three working days to transfer and produce at Kew.

The first part of any document reference will always be a letter or series of letters which denote the government department or institution that created or maintained the record. This is known as the **Department Code**. Hence, records created or maintained by the Inland Revenue are assigned the department code **IR**.

Over the course of their working lives, each department created thousands of documents, in some cases hundreds of thousands. Instead of listing them in one long sequence, they have been sub-divided into logical groups, each of which contains documents of a similar type or theme. For example, the records generated by a particular section of a department have been grouped together, as have documents of a distinct type, such as maps. A number is then assigned to this sequence, called the **Series Number**, and the combination of Department Code and Series Number allows an archivist to quickly tell what type of information is contained within that series. For example, the Field Books produced by the Inland Revenue for the 1910 Valuation Office survey have been assigned the series reference **IR 58**. It is therefore your task to identify the PRO series that is going to contain material relevant to your research.

Once you have located your series, your next task is to identify which individual item within that series is most relevant. To provide a unique reference, every document within a series is given a **Piece Number**, and this forms the third part of a PRO reference. Some pieces have in fact been listed at a more detailed level – for example, individual letters in a bound volume of correspondence. Numbers at this level are called **Item Numbers**.

2.5.2 The *PRO Guide*, catalogue and finding aids

When referring to a particular type of document, this guide will provide a PRO series code such as **IR 58**. However, there are a number of additional aids that exist to help you with your research. One of the best ways to start your research is to access the PRO catalogue. The electronic version – PROCAT – allows you to undertake key word searches of document descriptions, although this does not search document content. Many documents do not have very good descriptions, but for a local historian the system can be of great use to identify references to places or people, especially in some of the more obscure parts of the catalogue. There is also access to the catalogue via the PRO's website (http://www.pro.gov.uk/).

You will also find that the on-site *PRO Guide* is a useful three-part index to the records. Part Three, identified by a yellow spine, is a subject index that links topics with departmental series. Relevant series can be checked for potential use in Part Two of the *Guide*, which has a green spine and tells you the date range of each series, plus a brief description of the content of the documents. Part One of the guide (which has a red spine) is not strictly relevant if you wish to find a document reference, but it contains useful information on the background history and function of the government departments listed in Part Two, and can be used to provide background context to the records. On occasion it will also provide relevant department codes and series numbers that are not always cross-referenced in Part Two.

Once you have identified a series that may contain useful information, you can then access the series list in the paper catalogue. These folders, arranged in alphanumerical order, contain the same information as the electronic catalogue, with two additional advantages. You will find introductory notes that provide information about the documents themselves, although not every series list contains them. You should also find a sheet of paper at the front of the series list that provides a worked example of a document reference, which is useful as not every series requires a simple three-part reference; sometimes a sub-series is required for particularly large series, such as the maps that accompany the 1910 valuation survey.

To help get you started, the PRO has produced leaflets that describe the most popular documents or topics that are researched. These are free, and are also available on the website. You will also find contemporary lists and indexes, published guides and other reference works available at each of the enquiry points. If you are in any doubt about what you should be doing, there are reader advisors at hand to point you in the right direction. Finally, if you are visiting for the first time, once you have registered as a reader you are asked to join a free induction that shows you how to find your reference and order documents via the computer terminals.

3 Maps, plans and land surveys

3.1 Introduction

If you are unfamiliar with archival material, a good place to begin your research will be with maps and plans, as they are relatively easy to interpret. Whilst they rarely provide details of owners or occupancy, they do at least give you a visual record of your local area. If you consult enough maps from a wide variety of dates, you can start to construct a chronological framework within which to base documentary research. Maps that do *not* show your house can be just as important as those that do, as you can start to narrow down your research to a later period. However, maps may depict an earlier building that has subsequently been demolished to make way for a later construction, and without architectural or corroboratory documentary evidence it can be very tempting to assume they are one and the same.

The PRO houses a vast collection of maps and plans, created as a by-product of the work of individual government organizations and departments. It is estimated that there are over 1 million maps and plans in the archive, but they are not fully catalogued, and new maps are discovered each day. In addition to these individual items scattered across a wide range of PRO series, there is a substantial, although incomplete, collection of OS sheets from various periods. Some of these form part of land surveys conducted by government departments, which are doubly important as they incorporate related assessment books. These can often give you names of owners and occupiers linked directly to property at a specific date.

However, it is important to remember that local archives will hold the majority of cartographic material that is relevant to your area, which often complements the holdings of the PRO. There are also specialist map collections, such as the BL's Map Department, which is a registered place of deposit for OS material (in contrast to the PRO, which is not).

The following sources are the most appropriate and easily accessible at the PRO. To gain familiarity with your local area, you should begin by consulting some of the OS sheets on open access. The next step will be to examine the valuation survey and tithe apportionments, as they can provide a snapshot c.1910–15 and c.1836–58. The results you obtain will form a framework that can be filled in by the detailed census returns at the FRC that exist in ten-year intervals from 1841–91 and are described in Chapter 9, section 9.2. If you have a rural property which you suspect formed part of a farm, then you can examine the records of the National Farm Survey from the 1940s. Once you have your framework, any of the other map searches listed below may yield useful information, especially enclosure awards, estate maps, military surveys and deposited plans that are often listed in the PRO's extracted map catalogue.

3.2   Ordnance Survey records

3.2.1   About the records

The work of the modern OS department originated in the Board of Ordnance section of the War Office in the mid eighteenth century, when their remit was to create a military map of the Highlands of Scotland. In 1791 a Trigonometrical Survey was commissioned to produce a military map and for the first time a map for general use. The first official map was published in 1801 at the scale of 1 inch to the mile. From 1841, under the Ordnance Survey Act the OS became a separate institution, primarily creating maps and plans for ascertaining and recording boundary changes, as well as publishing county sheets.

3.2.2   County maps

Although the PRO is not a registered place of deposit for OS maps, you will find many examples at the PRO that can help you pinpoint your house in its locality. Their primary function will be to provide an overview of your area and allow you to identify changes in the community over time.

The earliest series of published OS maps at the PRO date from 1801, and are on open access in the reading rooms. The scale is 1 inch to the mile, and therefore does not give a particularly detailed view of property in town and city centres. However, rural properties are easier to spot, and in any case they can provide an overview of an area and a point of comparison with later OS editions. The PRO also holds 5 inch to the mile London maps from the nineteenth century on the open shelves, plus twentieth-century 6 inch to the mile maps, arranged by county. It is far easier to see individual properties on these maps, and they can be a useful reference tool when trying to locate your property for other searches. These maps are currently on open access in the Map and Large Document Reading Room.

In addition to the PRO, the BL is a registered place of deposit for published OS sheets, and most CROs have relevant county sheets for various periods.

3.2.3 Boundary records

Boundary records can provide some information about property, as they record changes in public boundaries in Remark Books (PRO series **OS 26**) and Record Books (**OS 31** and **33**). Property situated on parish boundaries can frequently be found marked in these books, which are arranged by county in alphabetical order. Parish name books (**OS 23**) can provide supplementary information about local administrative names, and evidence presented in disputed boundary cases were recorded in Boundary Reports (**OS 32**). Sketch maps (**OS 27**) and Journals of Inspection (**OS 29**) provided official confirmation of any changes before 6-inch Deposit Maps were published with the final decision marked on them (**OS 38** for England and Wales, and **OS 39** for Scotland).

These sources will be of limited use unless your property falls near a county or parish boundary. As such, they should perhaps not be the first ports of call, but can be used to supplement existing information.

3.3 Valuation Office survey

3.3.1 About the records

The 1910 Valuation Office survey, also known as the Lloyd George Domesday, is one of the most useful sources for house history. Not only does the survey combine maps with assessment documents, but it also covers land and property in both urban and rural communities. The aim of the project was to assess the capital appreciation of real property that was attributable to the site itself, under the terms of the 1909–10 Finance Act (10 Edward VII c.8). A more detailed description of the history of the survey is provided in W. Foot, *Maps for Family History*.

As part of the assessment process, England and Wales were divided into 14 valuation regions (later reduced to 13) and further sub-divided into 118 valuation districts. Two sets of maps were compiled for each region and were used to detail all land or property that formed part of the survey. Each land unit – which varied in size from individual houses to large fields – was then assigned a hereditament (assessment) number, usually marked on the map in red, with the boundary for that property marked in red, or sometimes green, depending on the region. The official 'record' maps (*see* **Figure 1**) are deposited in the PRO in series **IR 121** and **124–35**, while working copies, where they survive, are in the custody of the relevant CRO. The financial data compiled during the course of the survey was recorded in Field Books, which are at the PRO in series **IR 58**;

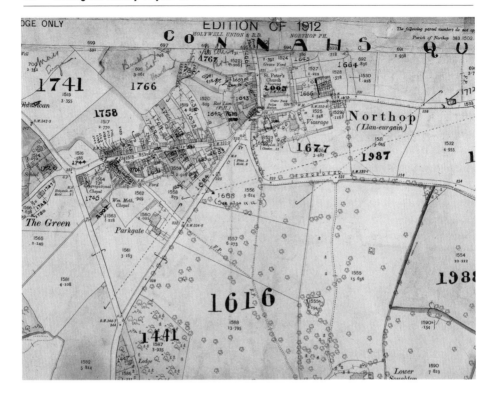

Figure 1 An extract from the valuation map for Northop, dated 1912. The property, formerly known as 'The Yacht Inn', is assigned hereditament number 1685. The distinctive shape of the property is clear from this map. (IR 131/10/85)

Revenue Books, often referred to as 'Domesday books' and which contain similar but less detailed information, are preserved in the CROs. It is the **IR 58**s that will be of most use to a house historian as they contain information about the property, whilst recording the names of the owners and occupiers, for the period c.1910–15.

Similar records for Northern Ireland and Scotland can be found in the PRONI or the National Archives of Scotland (NAS) respectively, and are described in more detail in section 3.3.4.

3.3.2   Accessing valuation survey maps (excluding London)

Before you can view the Field Books at the PRO you will need to identify and order the relevant valuation survey map on which your property is marked, as it acts as an index by providing you with the relevant hereditament number. There is a key sheet, or county diagram, for each county and they are arranged alphabetically in three folders, two for England and one for Wales. Remember to look

Diagram 1 This section of the Flint county key sheet has a grid reference 9. In Roman numerals, it is written as IX.

under Southampton for Hampshire, and be sure to consult the photocopied 'old series' index sheet for Essex (with the exception of the SW corner of the county, which uses the 'new series' index).

Each key sheet is divided into a series of numbered grids, which are in turn sub-divided into 16 smaller unnumbered rectangles, with each rectangle representing a map at the OS scale 1:2500 (or 25 inches to the mile). Your task is to identify within which of these smaller rectangles your property falls. At times this can be a tricky process; given the small scale of the key sheets, it is often difficult to identify the correct part of a township or city, and even some small villages might be hard to pinpoint with any degree of certainty.

Therefore you should start by making a note of the relevant larger numbered grid. You will need to convert the grid number from Arabic to Roman numerals, as the maps you will be ordering use this method of coding. To assist you in this conversion process, the PRO has produced a leaflet that shows the various Roman numerals used. (See **Diagram 1**.)

The next step is to locate within which of the smaller rectangles your property falls. You can make a judgement based on the key sheets, but if you are uncertain which rectangle is relevant there is an alternative method. As you have obtained the grid number (in this case IX), you can use this to search the 6-inch OS county maps that are on open access, as they contain individual maps that have exactly the same grid numbers, but at a scale that should allow you to locate your property with ease (1:10 560). It is then a case of comparing the OS sheet with the key sheet and judging which smaller rectangle is most appropriate. If you are still in some doubt, or think that your property might straddle the boundary between two rectangles, you should order both maps.

1	2	3	4
5	6	7	8
9	10	11	12
13	14	15	16

Diagram 2 If your property fell within map grid 9, rectangle 16, your map reference would be Flintshire IX.16.

To find the PRO reference for your chosen map, you need to assign a number to the relevant rectangle. As you will see on the key sheet, the rectangles form a grid, four across by four down. Simply count from left to right, assigning a number to each rectangle as you

Table 3.1 List of Valuation Office districts and relevant PRO series

Region	PRO series
South-Eastern	**IR 124**
Wessex	**IR 125**
Central	**IR 126**
East Anglia	**IR 127**
Western	**IR 128**
West Midland	**IR 129**
East Midland	**IR 130**
Wales	**IR 131**
Liverpool	**IR 132**
Manchester	**IR 133**
Yorkshire	**IR 134**
Northern	**IR 135**

go. Hence, the top row is 1 to 4, the second row 5 to 8, the third row 9 to 12 and the bottom row 13 to 16. (*See* **Diagram 2.**)

The next stage is to assign a PRO reference to your chosen map so that you can order it for examination. The survey is not arranged by county but by Valuation Office region, and the maps for each region have been allocated their own PRO series. A summary is listed in Table 3.1.

For administrative purposes, each region was sub-divided into separate districts, and each district has been assigned a PRO sub-series number. You will find the maps listed in the relevant section of the series list. The name given to each district is meant to reflect a geographical area but can often be misleading, and you may need to search through several districts before you find your map. A summary of the districts for each region is provided at the front of each series list, and in Appendix 1 (pp. 70–2) of Foot's *Maps for Family History*. Furthermore, this publication also provides a list of where you will find maps for each county (Appendix 2, pp. 73–9) and a list of map locations for a wide variety of places (Appendix 3, pp. 80–2). Copies are available on open access in the reading rooms.

You may find that the geographical area covered in your map crosses the boundary between two of these districts. In these instances duplicate maps were made, one for each district. You will probably need to order both copies, as they will contain information for the relevant district only.

NW	**NE**
SW	**SE**

In some cases you will find that the PRO copies of the maps have not survived. If this is the case, there is a chance that the working copy has been deposited at your local CRO, and this may give you the information you need to order out the relevant Field Book.

In general, the maps you will obtain are at a scale of 1:2500. To make it easier to mark properties in towns and cities, maps at scales of 1:1250 and 1:500 were

Diagram 3 If 1:1250 maps existed for Flintshire square IX.16, this is how they would be arranged. So if you wanted the south-east quadrant, you would need to locate Flintshire IX.16.SE in the series list.

1	2	3	4	5
6	7	8	9	10
11	12	13	14	15
16	17	18	19	20
21	22	23	24	25

Diagram 4 If 1:500 maps existed for Flintshire square IX.16, this is how they would be arranged. So if you wanted map 20, you would need to locate Flintshire IX.16.20 in the series list.

also created. There are four 1:1250 maps for each 1:2500 map, representing the northwest, northeast, southeast and southwest quadrants. (*See* **Diagram 3**.)

The 1:500 maps are even more detailed, and there are 25 for each 1:2500 map arranged in 5 rows of 5 (*see* **Diagram 4**). Where they exist, a reference to more detailed maps is usually found on the 1:2500 map, and generally they are listed in the series list after the 1:2500 maps.

Once you have located the relevant map in the series list, note the PRO reference for the map and order it out. When it arrives, you will see that each property or piece of land has been assigned a number, usually marked in red. Make a note of this, plus (if marked) the income tax parish (ITP) in which it falls. ITPs were created to group together small ecclesiastical or civil parishes, and are an important means of reference when locating the relevant Field Book that accompanies the map.

You may notice that land parcels are given a coloured wash to distinguish them from their neighbours. Sometimes detached parcels of land that form one distinct hereditament are indicated by the note 'Part' or 'Pt' next to the hereditament number. This is usually accompanied by a brace (usually in red) that joins separated land parcels, or a hereditament that has been divided by a feature such as a road. Detached or separated hereditaments may stretch across several maps.

3.3.3 Accessing valuation survey maps for London

The procedure for locating a map for the cities of London and Westminster, and the surrounding suburbs, is slightly different. There is a separate series of key sheets for the London area that divide large grids into 100 smaller rectangles, rather than the usual 16. The folder also contains larger scale inserts to allow you to identify your property in more detail, although the series is not complete. The procedure is exactly the same – you should make a note of which grid and rectangle is most appropriate to your property, remembering to convert the grid number to Roman numerals. The maps for the London region are in PRO series

IR 121, which is sub-divided into 19 districts, each with its own PRO sub-series number. Once again, the names assigned to these districts can be misleading, and you may need to search through several regions to find the most relevant map. Remember to look for duplicate maps that appear in different districts and order both.

The London region contains maps for property located in the surrounding counties, so you may need to search the relevant county key sheets as well to obtain map references. Further guidance is provided in Foot's *Maps for Family History*. London maps are at the OS scale 1:1056, while county maps are at the usual 1:2500 scale. You should be able to identify your property and make a note of the red hereditament number that has been assigned to it.

3.3.4   Accessing Field Books

Once you have obtained the hereditament number for your property from the map, you are ready to locate the relevant Field Book. Each Field Book contains the information for exactly one hundred hereditaments in numbered blocks, for example 1–100, 101–200, 201–300 and so forth, and each hereditament is assigned four pages in the book. This is where you will obtain crucial information about the property and its owner or occupier. Although the details will vary, you may be pleasantly surprised at what you uncover. You should at least get the names of the owner and the occupier, plus the full street address. It is not unknown for descriptions of the property to be included, with the possibility of finding sketch maps or inserts, descriptions of outbuildings, dates of previous sales, and even construction dates. These are all nuggets of information that can give you invaluable clues for later research.

Like the maps, the Field Books (*see* **Figure 2**) are arranged in valuation districts, and identifying which region can be complicated. You should first check for any clues on the map itself, such as the name of the ITP in which your property falls; ITP boundaries are usually marked in yellow at the edges of the map. If these are not marked, or an ITP name is not provided, you will need to use several finding aids that are located on open access in the reading rooms.

With the series lists for **IR 58** are place name indexes that link a parish or place name with the relevant valuation district under the column headed 'Valuation'. Make a note of the name of this district, as the main series list for **IR 58** is arranged by valuation district in alphabetical order, with the ITPs listed in alphabetical order under the main valuation district at the top of each page. There are separate indexes for London that are arranged by street name which then assign a valuation district and ITP.

If the place you are looking for does not appear in the list, you should consult

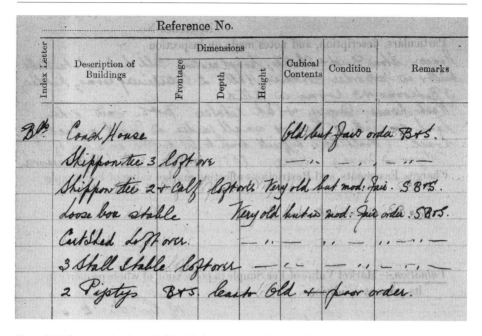

Figure 2 (a) The entry in the valuation Field Book for hereditament number 1685. The property is referred to as 'Plymouth House' and is in the possession of Edward Foulkes. (IR 58/94483)

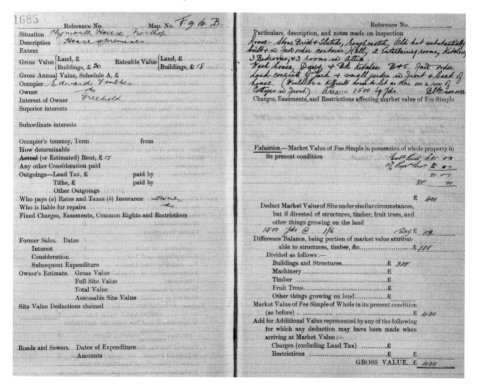

Figure 2 (b) A clue to Plymouth House's former use is given by the outbuildings, which include a 'Coach House'. (IR 58/94483)

the Board of Inland Revenue's *Alphabetical List of Parishes and Places in England and Wales*, which is also on open access, in two volumes. This will assign an ITP to smaller parishes, hamlets or townships that were not large enough to be granted ITP status, for which you can then search in the place name index for the **IR 58** series list. Even with this guide, you may still have to use your local knowledge and judge which is the most relevant place.

These series lists can be difficult to use, and there is no guarantee that you will always find the ITP in the relevant valuation district. However, the new PRO electronic catalogue allows you to search document descriptions by key word, while limiting your search to a single series. In this case you can often find your ITP by searching for it by name within series **IR 58**.

If you are still unable to locate your ITP in the **IR 58** series list, then you may need to look at the relevant Revenue Book at the CRO, as they contain a list of parishes that made up an ITP and give the range of hereditament numbers for each parish.

Field Books for Southampton, Winchester and Portsmouth, and an area around Chichester, were destroyed by enemy action in the Second World War. Many records for Chelmsford and all for Coventry are also lost.

3.3.5   Related records

The PRO holds Revenue Books for the City of London and Westminster (Paddington) in series **IR 91**. All other Revenue Books are at the relevant CRO, where you will also find the working maps. Where they survive, additional records created as part of the survey are largely stored at the relevant CRO as well. A summary of these are provided in Foot's *Maps for Family History*.

The Scottish valuation survey is available at the NAS. Record maps are in series **IRS 101–33** and Field Books are in **IRS 51–88**. Related valuation records are available for Northern Ireland at PRONI in a variety of **VAL** series. A survey of 1830 is available in **VAL 1B**, with maps in **VAL 1A**. A later assessment from 1848–64, known as the Griffith's Valuation, is found in **VAL 2B**, with maps in **VAL 2A**; there is an index available on CD. A householders index is also available for consultation. Thereafter, annual valuations were conducted from 1864 until the early 1930s, with returns stored in **VAL 12B**. A general revision was undertaken in 1935, with returns in **VAL 3B** and maps in **VAL 3A**.

3.4   Tithe apportionments

3.4.1   About the records

Tithes were originally payments in kind of a tenth of the annual produce of land by way of crops and animals, payable to either the parson of the parish, or an entitled lay person, or both. Payment of tithes had been in existence for centuries, and during this time individual arrangements had been made to commute the payment to a fixed sum of money, or in some cases a grant of land. Enclosures hastened this process, in particular the Enclosure Acts of the eighteenth and nineteenth centuries; more details are provided in section 3.7.

By the 1830s, tithes were highly unpopular amongst rural landowners, as they did not reflect the changing social and economic conditions of the dawning industrial age. Under the Tithe Commutation Act of 1836 (6 & 7 Will. IV, c.71), remaining payments in kind were to be commuted into fixed monetary sums based on a seven-year average of the price of wheat, barley and oats taken across the country. The process of commutation was primarily undertaken at a local level by negotiation, but a Tithe Commission was established to help parties reach agreement and arbitrate in disputed cases, in which case an award was produced. No matter which path was followed, the end product of the commutation process was a tithe apportionment that formalized the agreement or award. The apportionment consisted of a map that showed the properties that were liable to tithes, and an apportionment schedule based on the agreement or award that set out the liabilities for each landowner concerned. Under the terms of the Tithe Act an original and two copies of each record were made. The original was retained by the Tithe Commission, and subsequently these were deposited at the PRO in two series, **IR 30** (maps) and **IR 29** (apportionment schedule). One copy was sent to the parish church and the other to the relevant register of the diocese, and where these copies survive they have been deposited in the CRO. In general the mapping process lasted until c.1856, although most agreements and awards were settled by the mid 1840s.

As a source for house history, the tithe apportionments provide vital clues about property ownership and occupancy, although you will not obtain details about the property itself. The maps should allow you to pinpoint dwellings that existed before urban expansion changed the landscape later in the century. Even if your house was not yet built, you can discover who owned the land and what it was once used for. Coverage is not complete for England and Wales, as no apportionments were created for areas where agreements had previously been reached through other means. Tithe apportionments will also be of limited use for properties in towns and cities, although where tithes were still payable you will find detailed maps and assessments that provide an invaluable source. Similar records for Scotland and Northern Ireland survive at the NAS and PRONI and are described in section 3.4.4.

Tithes are a complicated topic, and the process did not stop with the Tithe Commutation Act of 1836. Further Acts followed, including the 1936 Tithe Act, which produced related documents. For more information you should consult the relevant PRO information leaflet on *Tithe Records*, and read some of the books listed under **Useful publications**.

3.4.2   Accessing the records

The best place to start looking for tithe maps and awards will be your CRO. In theory, they should have at least one of the deposited copies in their holdings. This potentially provides you with a choice of maps if one is of poor quality, and it may be possible to trace over the maps – something that is not recommended at the PRO. Furthermore, later amendments that affected the value of the apportionment, such as the subsequent use of land for railway cuttings, were attached to the apportionment; these are not always to be found on the PRO copies.

However, if you are planning to conduct some of the other searches mentioned in this chapter, or no copies are available at your CRO, there are approximately 11,800 maps and apportionment schedules available for you to consult at the PRO. The documents are accessed via a combined series list for **IR 29** and **30**, as the maps and apportionment schedules share the same piece number for each parish. The lists are arranged alphabetically by county, and thereafter by parish. Each county has been assigned a number, as has each parish, and these numbers combine to form your piece number, prefixed by **IR 30** if you wish to locate the map, or **IR 29** for the apportionment schedule.

Example

Days Farm, lies in the parish of Doddinghurst, Essex. The list informs us that the county number is 12 and the parish number is 109. The PRO references will be:

IR 30/12/109 (map)

IR 29/12/109 (apportionment)

Kain and Oliver's publication *The Tithe Maps and Apportionments of England and Wales* provides an easier means of reference, and is available on open access in the reading rooms. This volume combines a similar county and parish listing, assigning piece numbers to each parish. The entry for each parish contains a brief description of the documents you will be accessing, such as the date of the map, features covered, scale and surveyor (if known), and the date of the apportionment. Furthermore, there is an introduction for each county that provides a detailed description of tithe liability, with a map of the county that shows a general overview of how many parishes were liable to tithes and therefore produced documents as part of the survey.

Checking tithe liability is a popular line of research and is widely used for genealogical purposes. To help conserve these fragile documents, all agreements/awards at the PRO have been copied and are now produced on microfilm, whereas the tithe maps for English counties, running alphabetically from Bed-

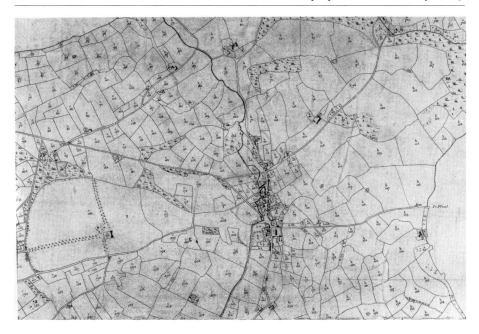

Figure 3 An extract from the tithe map for Northop, Flintshire. The date of the apportionment for the parish was 1838, and the map dates from c.1839. The 'Yacht Inn' is plot b.38 in the centre of the village. (IR 30/50/32)

fordshire to Middlesex, are available only on fiche; thereafter, from Norfolk to Yorkshire and for all Welsh counties, you will need to order the original maps.

3.4.3   Using the records

The first step is to view the tithe map for your parish (*see* **Figure 3**). It can be difficult to identify property on the maps, and you will probably need to use local knowledge or make a comparison with OS maps. Furthermore, the scale, scope and content of the maps will vary from region to region, despite the best efforts of the tithe commissioners to impose uniformity.

Each plot of land that was liable to tithes was assigned an apportionment number on the map, which will be unique to that parish. The apportionment number corresponds to an entry in the apportionment schedule in **IR 29** (*see* **Figure 4**). After a brief preamble that describes the means by which the apportionment was drawn up, you will find the apportionment schedule itself. It is divided into columns, listing the landowner, occupier, plot number (that corresponds to the plot numbers on the map), the name and description of the land and premises, the state of cultivation, quantities in statute measure, the names of tithe-owners, and other remarks. The schedules are usually arranged in alphabetical order by the name of individual landowners, rather than by plot

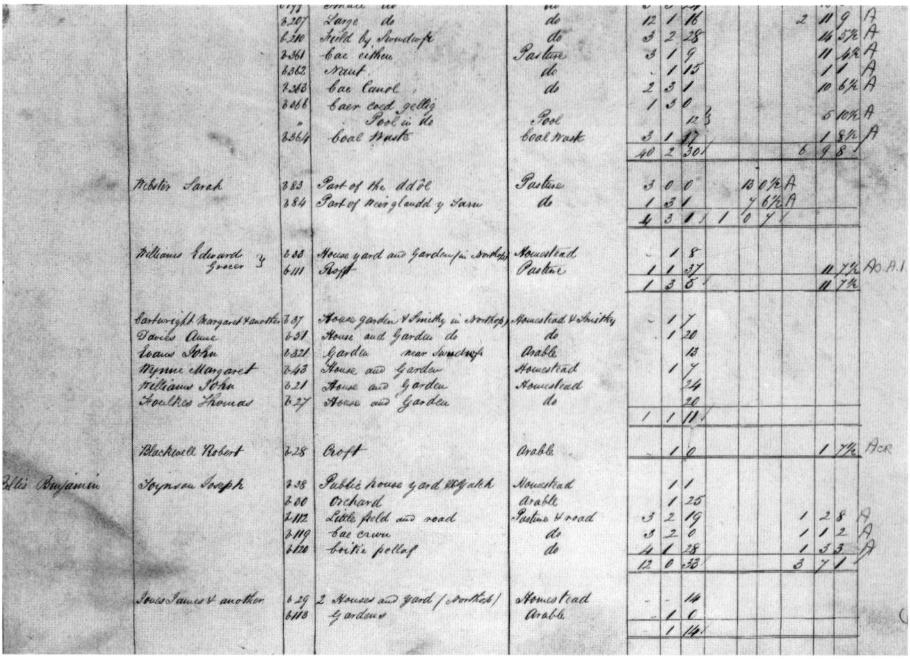

Figure 4 A section of the tithe apportionment schedule for Northop, Flintshire. It shows the lands owned by Benjamin Bellis, which include plot b.38 – 'Public house, yard etc. Yacht' – in the possession of Joseph Joynson. (IR 29/50/32)

number, but there is a key at the front of each apportionment book which you can use to find the page number on which each plot appears. You may need to ask for help in using the key, but it saves a lot of time.

It is the first three columns that are of most interest to the house historian, as you will find out the name of the owner or occupier and a description of the property, be it a cottage, house, outhouse, inn or shop. These names will allow you to conduct a search of other sources that exist for this period, such as the census returns discussed in section 9.2.

3.4.4   Related records

In addition to the maps and apportionment schedules in **IR 30** and **IR 29**, a whole series of related records were created that might contain some useful information, and the house historian should be aware of the following.

Tithe files in **IR 18** contain correspondence from commissioners who were investigating which areas had previously had their tithes commuted, and therefore can provide some information about places not covered in the apportionments. However, over the years these files have been heavily 'weeded' and thus survival of relevant material is not guaranteed.

Occasionally the commutation process brought to light disputes about boundaries, and where the commissioners were forced to make a judgement you will find a boundary award in **TITH 1**, with schedules and plans that contain information about owners and tenants.

Altered apportionments reflect changes of ownership of individual plots of land. Those before 1836 are filed with the relevant records in **IR 29**, but after this date they were filed as Orders for Apportionment, with maps, in series **IR 94**. These records can be of great use where later housing development took place in the area. Information about other records created under the 1936 Tithe Act can be found in the relevant PRO leaflet on *Tithe Records*.

In addition, your CRO will have duplicate copies of the tithe maps and apportionment schedules found in **IR 29** and **30**, so you may wish to start your research there (see section 3.4.2 for details).

The equivalent to tithes in Scotland were known as teinds, and were payable by owners of heriotable property within a parish, as opposed to being attached to the land itself as in England and Wales. As such you will find that there was no 'snapshot' commutation; instead, an Act of Parliament in 1925 ended the system of teinds. Records of the Teinds Court and Commissioners are found at the NAS in several series, such as **TE 1–6** (pre–1700) and **TE 7–9** (post–1700). You may also need to look in private and estate records.

Tithe applotment books for Northern Ireland are primarily held at PRONI in the series **FIN 5A**, with householder indexes on the shelves that provide surnames contained in the records. Some records are also held in the National Library, Dublin.

3.5   National Farm Survey

3.5.1   About the records

In an attempt to assist the war effort, the Ministry of Agriculture and Fisheries (MAF) set up County War Agricultural Committees to increase food productivity and ensure that there were sufficient supplies to feed the country. In 1940 an attempt was made to survey all working farms in England and Wales to identify the productive state of the land, assigning 'A', 'B' and 'C' grades.

A far more detailed survey was conducted between 1941–3, listing information on conditions of tenure, occupation, the state of the farm, fertility of the land, equipment, livestock, water and electricity supplies, weeds and general management. A plan of the farm, depicting boundaries and fields, was also produced as part of the process.

For the house historian, this is a particularly good source if you are tracing rural property, or suspect that your house once formed part of a farm. Not only will you obtain the name of the owner and address of the farm, but also details of the number of employees and the nature of the farm's produce, and this can provide background information on the way people lived. It complements the valuation and tithe surveys, and is obviously useful when the house in question was a farmhouse or building. However, the survey can also be helpful if you are researching an area that changed from farmland to housing after 1945.

3.5.2 Accessing the records

The documents of the 1941–3 survey are found in two record series at the PRO. The maps are in PRO series **MAF 73**, and are arranged alphabetically by county. You will first need to consult a key sheet that is available on open access. Each county has been assigned a number, which forms part of the PRO reference, and is stamped on the corner of the relevant county key sheet. Make a note of this number.

Each county map is sub-divided into numbered grids. Locate the grid in which your property falls, and make a note of this number as well. This forms the final part of the PRO reference, and you will be provided with all the maps within this grid.

Once you have obtained your maps, you will need to find the one that relates to your property. The maps you are provided with will cover the entire area in the grid. There will either be 16 maps at the scale 1:2500, which adopt the same grid system as employed on the county key sheets for the valuation survey (see section 3.3.2), or with four maps at the 1:10 560 scale. Once you have located your farm, you will see that the extent is marked using a colour wash, and has been assigned a reference; this usually consists of the abbreviated county code (a series of letters), the relevant parish number (the first number) and the farm number (the second number). The next step is to order the individual farm record that accompanies the map.

> **Example**
> Day's Farm, Doddinghurst, Essex (*see* **Figure 5**)
> Essex has the county number 13, and the property falls within the numbered grid 71. Hence, the PRO reference will be MAF 73/13/71.

The records are contained in PRO series **MAF 32** and are also arranged by county, and then alphabetically by parish. You should consult the series list, which contains an index that tells you where to find the records for each county. Work down the alphabetical list of parishes until you find the relevant one, and note the corresponding piece number in the left hand column. Also note the code that has been assigned to the parish, as this also forms part of the PRO reference.

You will be provided with an envelope containing the records for all farms that lie within the requested parish, and your farm can be identified by the

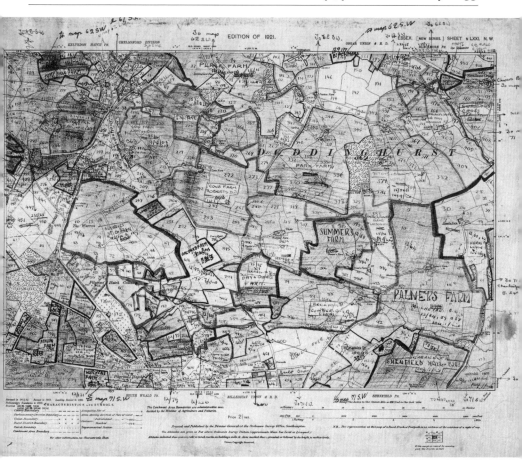

Figure 5 The National Farm Survey map for the parish of Doddinghurst, Essex. Property 15/18 is Day and Gent's Farm, in the possession of A.J. Harris. (MAF 73/13/71)

number assigned to it from the map. The individual farm record consisted of four parts. The first was completed by the farmer, and contained details of small fruit, vegetables and stocks of hay and straw; animals are also listed. The second surveyed agricultural land, also completed by the farmer, whilst the third was a similar survey completed by inspection and interview.

The final part is the most useful for house historians, as it contains details of utility services, farm labour, motive power, rent and length of occupancy. It also bears the final grade assigned to

Example
Day's Farm lies in the parish of Doddinghurst, which has been given the code reference 15 and is listed within piece number 837 in the left column (*see* **Figure 6**). The full PRO reference is therefore MAF 32/837/15.

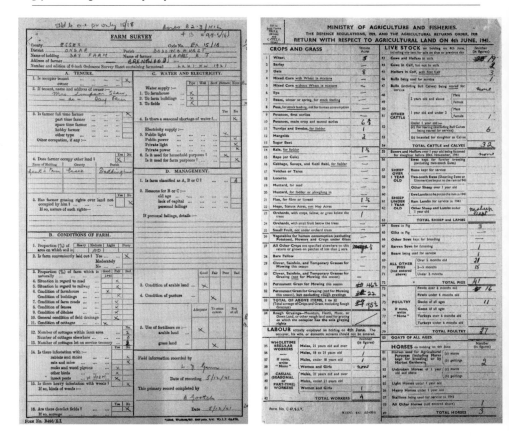

Figure 6 (a) Form B496 for Day's Farm shows that Gent's and Day's farms should be treated as one unit. It gives the name and address of the owner, Mrs Simpson Shaw, and mentions that two cottages form part of the farmstead. (MAF 32/837)

Figure 6 (b) Form C47 gives an indication of the way in which the farm operated. (MAF 32/837)

the farm. All documents contain the address of the farm and the farmer's name, and taken as a whole can provide a great insight into the extent of farming communities in the mid twentieth century.

3.5.3   Related records

Similar local committees were established during the First World War to assess and improve food production. Surviving records are to be found deposited in the relevant CROs, but will not contain the same level of detail as the records described above.

Minutes of the County War Agricultural Executive Committees are held in

MAF 80, some of which contain detailed indexes that include farm names. Furthermore, parish lists for June 1941 in **MAF 65** provide the names and full postal addresses for the occupiers of all agricultural holdings in each parish. They are arranged in county order, and an index is provided in **MAF 65/81**. However, all records are closed for 100 years, and the MAF should be approached for access.

A more limited survey was undertaken for Scotland. Farm boundary plans are stored at the NAS in series **RHP 75001–285**, but no individual farm records survive.

3.6   PRO extracted maps and plans catalogue

In addition to the OS material and the various land surveys and related records described above, the PRO contains many thousands of individual maps. Some were deposited with central courts as part of legal proceedings, others were created by government departments through their daily work, and were filed with the main documentation; or indeed once formed part of private estates that came into the possession of Crown administrators. No matter what their origin or final location in the PRO, whenever these maps have been discovered they were noted and extracted from their parent documents, thus forming a rudimentary map catalogue. Each extracted map was then assigned a new PRO reference, which usually consisted of the letter 'M' followed by a series of other letters to denote which part of the main catalogue it came from. A full list is available in the PRO leaflet *Maps in the PRO*.

At present, the map catalogue for England and Wales consists of three distinct parts. The first is a published volume entitled *Maps and Plans of the British Isles 1410–1860*, and represents the earliest collection of maps and plans that were found, extracted and catalogued. The process of noting extracted maps was continued by a card index, arranged in county order and presently available in the Map and Large Document Room. Generally the maps in this section postdate those listed in the printed volume, although you will find maps that are earlier but were identified only after 1860. The new references for the maps are provided, plus a reference for the document from which they were extracted. However, the PRO has altered its reference system since the original compilation of the catalogues, and to obtain a modern PRO reference you will need to insert a 'I' between the letters and the numbers.

The final section is the Blue Card catalogue, contained in a series of folders and arranged in county order. This contains references to maps that have been identified, but not extracted from their parent documents. It is still being added to as new maps are found, and these are recorded on the blue cards that give this section its name. In addition, there is a supplementary series of indexes to the unextracted map catalogue, arranged and cross-referenced by subject and place. This will allow you to quickly identify relevant buildings or property, although there are only a limited number of private or residential dwellings listed.

You will find most of the maps described in sections 3.7 to 3.10 listed in the general PRO map catalogues. In addition, the PRO's electronic catalogue allows you to conduct a key word search of document descriptions, which now includes all sections of the map catalogue. This means that, in theory, you will be able to identify any of the maps listed in the catalogue, although it is always wise to double check the sources described above.

3.7   Enclosure maps and awards

3.7.1   The enclosure movement

The way in which land has been managed and cultivated in England and Wales has altered through the centuries, and one of the most important methods of change was the enclosure movement. The term 'enclosure' is employed by social and economic historians to describe a variety of mechanisms of change associated with the consolidation of smaller plots of land into larger units (engrossing or encroaching). However, it also covers land in communal use that was altered to a state of private property for the exclusive use of a single owner. The process of enclosure throughout England and Wales was piecemeal, gaining momentum from the sixteenth century onwards. Most early enclosures were arranged through private agreement between landowners and tenants, and have left no formal record, although you might find references in court cases or special commissions where the process was disputed.

3.7.2   Records of enclosure awards

Enclosure awards are legal documents that record the subsequent ownership of land, and were commonly enrolled by decree of one of the equity courts, or were enrolled in other courts of law to provide a legal basis for the award. Advice about searching for legal material at the PRO is provided in Chapter 8, but a brief summary of the most likely place to start looking is provided in Table 3.2.

Table 3.2 Enclosure records at the PRO

Private enclosures	
Commissions of Enquiry	**C 47/7, 205**: Chancery commissions
	E 178, 134: Exchequer commissions and depositions
	DL 44: Duchy of Lancaster
Petitions to the Privy Council	**PC 1, 2**: Privy Council correspondence and registers
Licences to enclose	**C 66**: patent rolls
Enclosure by enrolled decree	
Chancery	**C 78**: decree rolls (with some place and name indexes)
Exchequer	**E 159, 368**: memoranda rolls
	E 123–31: entry books
Duchy of Lancaster	**DL 5**
Palatinate of Durham	**DURH 26**
Other sources	
Extracts of non-enrolled awards	**CRES 6**: Constat Books, Crown Estate Commissioners; also **CRES 2**

3.7.3 Enclosure by Act of Parliament

From the mid-eighteenth century an increasing number of enclosures were affected by private Acts of Parliament; copies are now stored at the House of Lords Record Office, with some duplicates at relevant CROs. Their popularity prompted General Enclosure Acts to be passed in 1836, 1840 and 1845. Enclosure commissioners oversaw the process, and their records from 1845 survive in the PRO series **MAF 1**. Parliamentary enclosure awards were also enrolled and can sometimes be found in the PRO series **CP 43, C 54, DL 45, DURH 26, E 13** and **KB 122**, although most awards and the accompanying maps are to be found in the CRO. A fuller description of these sources is provided in the PRO leaflet *Enclosure Awards*, and further reading has been suggested under **Useful publications**.

3.7.4 Using enclosure awards

In general, enclosure maps and awards will be of limited use to the house historian, as it is rare to find individual properties marked or listed in the documentation. However, they do provide a visual snapshot of the local area at a given time, as well as information on the names of local landowners involved in the process and the land they owned; furthermore, this land may even be where your house stands today. A typical award (*see* **Figure 7**) usually describes the boundaries of land that forms part of the enclosure Act, followed by a list of changes to ancient rights (if applicable), and a description of the allotments to landowners made under the terms of the Act, distinguishing between copyhold

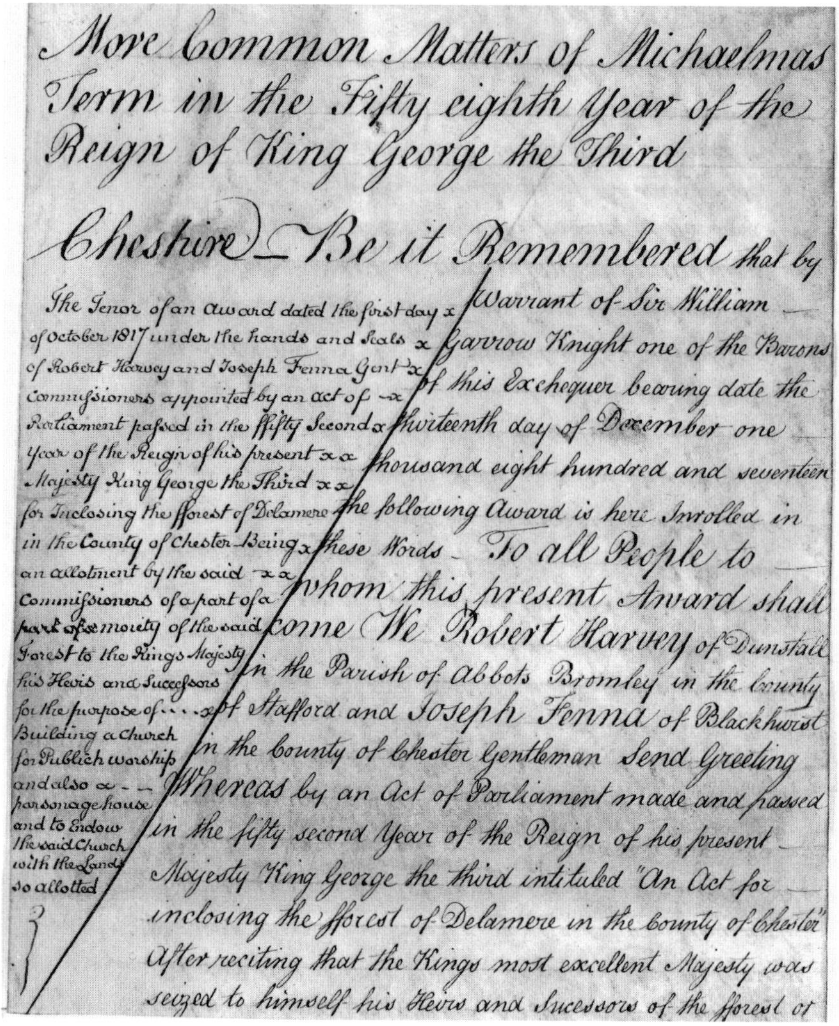

The Tenor of an Award dated the first day of October 1817 under the hands and Seals of Robert Harvey and Joseph Fenna Gent Commissioners appointed by an Act of Parliament passed in the fifty Second Year of the Reign of his present Majesty King George the Third for Inclosing the fforest of Delamere in the County of Chester Being an allotment by the said Commissioners of a part of a part of the moiety of the said Forest to the Kings Majesty his Heirs and Successors for the purpose of Building a Church for Publick worship and also a parsonage house and to Endow the said Church with the Land so allotted

More Common Matters of Michaelmas Term in the Fifty eighth Year of the Reign of King George the Third

Cheshire} Be it Remembered that by Warrant of Sir William Garrow Knight one of the Barons of this Exchequer bearing date the thirteenth day of December one thousand eight hundred and seventeen the following Award is here Inrolled in these Words To all People to whom this present Award shall come We Robert Harvey of Dunstall in the Parish of Abbots Bromley in the County of Stafford and Joseph Fenna of Blackhurst in the County of Chester Gentleman Send Greeting Whereas by an Act of Parliament made and passed in the fifty second Year of the Reign of his present Majesty King George the third intituled "An Act for inclosing the fforest of Delamere in the County of Chester" After reciting that the Kings most excellent Majesty was seized to himself his Heirs and Sucessors of the fforest or

Figure 7 Enclosure award for Delamere Forest enrolled on the 1817 memoranda roll. It stipulates that a parsonage house should be constructed as part of the process. (E 159/704)

and freehold tenure. This in itself can be of great use if you wish to search manorial documents but require additional information on the layout of the local area. A detailed schedule then lists the owners and provides a number for each plot, and therefore acts as a means of reference to any surviving map.

Although enclosure awards are scattered across a range of archives and in a variety of sources, a volume entitled *A Domesday of Enclosure Acts and Awards* by W. E. Tate summarizes the details for the most common areas. The volume is

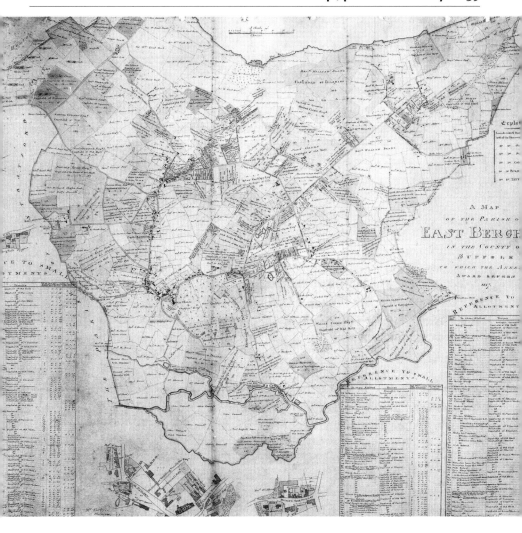

Figure 8 Map accompanying enclosure award for East Bergholt, Suffolk, in 1817. As well as defining the allotments to be made, it serves as a guide to the type of holding (freehold, copyhold) for lands and property in the parish. Furthermore, names of owners are assigned to each plot, providing a virtual survey of the parish. This type of information can be crucial in determining how land was passed between members of a family or transferred to new owners. (MR 1/247)

arranged in county order and lists the type of award, the date the award was granted and where the documents can be found. A copy is available on open access in the reading rooms, along with a series of supplementary lists of awards in the PRO that also provide references. Furthermore, a large number of enclosure maps (*see* **Figure 8**, on p.39) are separately listed in the extracted map catalogues, with links to the parent awards.

3.7.5   Related records: apportionment of rentcharge

The term 'rentcharge' refers to rent that was charged on a particular piece or unit of land, and the need for apportionment of rentcharge arose when large land-units were sub-divided into smaller units, usually a consequence of the enclosures of the eighteenth and nineteenth centuries. Under the terms of the Enclosure Act 1854, Law of Property Act 1925 and Landlord and Tenant Act 1927, it fell upon various government departments to equitably distribute the rentcharge between the new plots of land.

The records generated by these apportionments can provide information about how the charge was divided in a particular area, and will give details of individual streets and properties. There are three main types of record – orders (**MAF 17** for the period 1854–1965, **HLG 61** for 1965–7), certificates (**MAF 19** for the period 1854–1965, **HLG 62** for 1965–7), and certificates of redemption of rentcharge (**MAF 21** for the period 1843–1965, **HLG 63** for 1965–7). The records are fairly easy to access, and are arranged by the street or district that was affected. You should be able to obtain an idea of the individual who made the application for an apportionment, plus the person or persons who held the lease of the land.

3.8   Estate maps and plans

Private estates owners periodically conducted surveys of their property, usually to introduce new estate management procedures. Maps were often produced, sometimes linked to assessment books that can be cross-referenced to surviving manorial material. These provide an invaluable snapshot of landholding and property, and seem to occur most frequently when an estate changed hands. The most likely place to find such material is at the relevant CRO, but the PRO does have a collection of estate maps that are listed in the map catalogues. In addition, the PRO is the logical place of deposit for maps, plans, rentals and surveys relating to Crown estates and property, plus areas of autonomous jurisdiction. These can be found among the papers of the Office of Land Revenue Records and Enrolments (**LRRO**) and the Crown Estates Office (**CRES**), with maps for the Duchy of Lancaster in **DL 31**. Estate maps and plans are described and listed in more detail in Chapter 6.

3.9   Deposited maps and plans for public schemes
3.9.1   Railways

Many public schemes involved the creation of maps and plans to depict the potential impact of the scheme on the local community, especially if compulsory purchase orders of land were involved. The most dramatic event that triggered large-scale map making was the construction of the railways from the 1830s, which changed the face of many local communities. With the arrival of the railways, construction of new dwellings often occurred, along with the removal of older properties that were in the way of the proposed routes. Many of these changes are depicted on maps that formed part of individual railway company archives, and are now deposited at the PRO as part of the former holdings of the British Transport Historical Records section (BTHR). For the pre-nationalisation period the records are arranged by local railway company, so you will need to identify which company operated along the line nearest to you. A PRO leaflet has been written to help you with this process, and there are finding aids available on open access in the reading rooms.

The records are primarily in series **RAIL 1029–37** and **1071**, plus some in **MT 54**. Photographs of railways are contained in **AN 14** and **31**, and **RAIL 1057** and **1157**. Other material will be located with the administrative papers of the individual railway companies, including papers on accommodation and other related property that may have eventually found their way into private hands, and are described more fully in Chapter 11.

3.9.2   Roads

In a similar manner, road building through the ages necessitated the creation of maps, plans and associated documentation. One of the earliest methods of road management was via turnpike trusts. These organizations, which were locally administered and funded, were responsible for the maintenance and upkeep of the roads in their care. Records of the trusts will be found either at parochial level, or among quarter sessions papers whenever the trusts failed to adequately maintain the roads and were therefore liable to prosecution. Where such cases were recorded, you may well find that the area of road that required repair was linked to the property or properties outside which it ran, and the names of the owners are sometimes listed. Quarter sessions records are not stored at the PRO, and are usually found at the relevant CRO.

Royal Commissions were often appointed to enquire into the state of roads administered by the turnpike trusts, and the maps produced as a result of this process can depict property. Relevant material can also be found in Ministry of Transport files – for example, series **MT 27,** which relates to the Holyhead and Shrewsbury roads – where many useful maps can be found. After the dissolution of turnpike trusts, the responsibility for road building and maintenance was passed to local authorities, and many road building or improvement schemes can be found among the Ministry of Housing and Local Government files in the HLG series. However, the most likely place to find maps and plans relating to turnpike trusts and roads will be the relevant CRO, where local authority maps and plans for road improvement schemes will have been deposited.

Private roads and streets developed out of the turnpike trusts, and in addition to the maps and plans referred to above, you may wish to explore various files on their maintenance and development. Earlier records can be located with material on turnpike trusts in **MH 28**, while more modern records are in **HLG 51** and **MT 149**. Correspondence regarding conflicts of interest between private roads and railway companies can be found among the records of the individual railway companies, for example **RAIL 1057**. You will also find references to private roads in enclosure awards, although county archives will be the best place to begin searching.

3.9.3   Rehousing plans after public schemes

You will also be able to find references to planning or building proposals in a range of PRO series, in particular with regard to twentieth-century housing development schemes. Most of these schemes have plans attached to them, but these are not usually noted in the document descriptions. There is a wealth of cartographic material in a variety of HLG series that are described in detail in Chapter 12. Of particular use will be the records in **HLG 24**, which include rehousing schemes under the terms of statutory instruments, with sealed plans and schemes on the provision of accommodation for persons displaced from working-class dwellings as a result of undertakings including railway, gas, tram, school, harbour, road and other improvements, under the terms of the Housing of Working Classes Act 1903.

3.9.4   Geological Survey maps

You may also find some useful information from the records of the Geological Survey. Although their main work from 1835 was involved in geological science, many of the functions included survey work and map making, and will be of use if your property is situated on a place of geological value. Indeed, many geological surveys were conducted before building commenced, and therefore the maps and associated documents can provide information about when a property was built. Some records are at the PRO in series **DSIR 9** and **ED 23** and **24**, while the remainder will be found at the British Geological Survey. The Geologists' Association is also worth contacting (see **Useful addresses**).

3.10 Military maps

In addition to the early Ordnance Survey maps, the War Office maintained its own cartographic section, primarily for mapping military terrain. The house historian can often use military maps to locate houses that were formerly built as, or used for, military instillations such as hospitals, barracks, fortifications or bases. The record series **WO 78** is the best place to look for military maps and surveys, and these often include civilian property in the vicinity of a proposed military site. Maps in series **WO 78** are listed in topographical county order in a series of folders on open access in the reading rooms. Most of these have been noted in the map catalogues, while the subject indexes to the unextracted map catalogue include many references to military installations.

It is also possible to locate Ministry of Defence buildings that later passed into private possession, and in addition to **WO 78** there are Army establishment maps and plans in **WORK 43**, with Air Force establishments in **WORK 44**. If you have the time, it might also be worth scanning through the files of the Board of Ordnance, who were responsible for the construction of many stores, barracks and depots. You will, however, need to be armed with some prior information, as there are few indexes available to the letter books and accounts that provide details of places.

Although the PRO has a large collection of military maps, the best place to begin your research will be the Ministry of Defence map library at Tolworth, and you could also try the Imperial War Museum (*see* **Useful addresses**).

3.11 Maps and plans in the Office of Works

The remit of the Office of Works included responsibility for maintaining public buildings and national monuments in England and Wales. Although these will be of little use or interest to the house historian, it is not unknown for government property to eventually pass into the hands of private individuals. Indeed, the Office also maintained files on what it considered to be historic buildings, some of which were private residences. Included with the thousands of documents created or maintained by this department are two series of plans and drawings in **WORK 30** (public buildings) and **WORK 31** (ancient monuments and historic buildings). There are rudimentary indexes to these classes on open access in the reading room that list the buildings by place.

If you do manage to find an item that is of use, registered files can be found in **WORK 12** and **14** respectively. Miscellaneous plans and drawings are listed in **WORK 38**. Similar material for Northern Ireland can be located in **WORK 42** (maps and drawings) and **WORK 27** (registered files).

3.12 Architectural drawings

Most government departments made no differentiation between architectural drawings and other maps and plans. Where they have been identified or extracted you will find them listed in the PRO's map catalogues, as described in section 3.6. However, the vast majority will be among registered files and papers, and still await discovery. The papers of the Office of Works (**WORK**), Office of Land Revenue Records and Enrolments (**LRRO**) and the Crown Estates Office (**CRES**) are rich sources, although they largely relate to public buildings. These may be of use if your property once formed part of a Crown estate, or was owned by a government department. However, you will find that files created by local authorities are of more use, in particular those that relate to building schemes. These are often listed in files created by the Ministry of Housing and Local Government (HLG), and are treated in more depth in Chapter 12.

In addition to the PRO map catalogues, and the sources referred to above, a card index to drawings by individually named architects has been compiled, and the 'blue card' index of unextracted maps described in section 3.6 also contains a similar list. There is also a list of signed drawings found in the Office of Works. However, as with most searches for maps and plans, the best place to start will be at the CRO. The National Monuments Record holds plans, drawings and aerial photographs for buildings of historic value, including many architectural plans. There are separate sites for England (with a search room in London), Wales and Scotland. In addition, you may find relevant paperwork and plans in the Royal Institute of British Architects (RIBA) Library, while the Victoria and Albert Museum holds a collection of architectural drawings (*see* **Useful addresses**).

3.13 Photograph catalogue

In addition to the map catalogues, the PRO has compiled a separate list of photographs that have been found among parent documents. Indexes, arranged by place and subject, are available for consultation in the reading rooms and will contain some images of houses and private property. In addition, there are distinct series that solely contain photographs, along with series of extracted photographs that begin with the prefix **CN**. The most relevant series include **INF 9** (Dixon-Scott collection of towns and villages c.1925–48), **INF 11** (British Council collection of London scenes, 1935–45), **CN 1–19** (extracted photographs from various series), **BD 11** (Welsh local authority files that include housing), **BD 28–29** (Welsh local authority files, Town and Country Planning), and **DT 21** (properties acquired by the General Nursing Council in London). **COPY 1** also contains many photographs, and a surprising number are of individual properties. It is, however, important to remember that you may find related photographs of property almost anywhere in the PRO's holdings, and that these series will be of limited use to the house historian; in any case, the best place to begin your search for photographic material will be at your local studies library or CRO.

4 Land law and conveyancing

4.1   Introduction

One of the most important sources for any house historian will be the records generated by the transfer of the property from owner to owner. This is a complicated area to research, as property transfers took many forms over the centuries and usually involved the creation of legal documentation, which can often be difficult for the beginner to understand or interpret. Collectively, these documents are known as 'title deeds', and their whereabouts are discussed in Chapter 5. However, it is important for the house historian to grasp the basic ways in which land itself was held, as the type of tenure determined the method of transfer. There were basically two main groups of tenure – 'free' (freehold) and 'unfree' (copyhold) – and this chapter should be regarded solely as an introduction to the common ways in which freehold property was held and transferred. One of the most important methods of transfer was by a process known as 'conveyancing', technically defined as the 'legal transfer of ownership of property from one party or parties to another'. The transfer of copyhold land was restricted by the regulations of the manorial system until the late nineteenth century, and is described in detail in Chapter 6.

The main period to be examined in this chapter runs from the Norman Conquest to 1925, when a series of statutes were passed to regulate land law and conveyancing. This guide is clearly not the place to describe the evolution of land law in great detail, as the house historian will need to know only the basic forms of tenure and associated legal terminology to understand the documents that were generated over the centuries; however, if you wish to explore this topic in greater detail, see the relevant section of **Useful publications** (p. 208).

You will find that in this chapter reference is made to land rather than to houses as such. This is because in the eyes of the law the term 'land' included any buildings that were built upon it.

4.2   Landholding under the 'feudal' system

4.2.1   The feudal pyramid

The establishment of the 'feudal' system in England and parts of Wales in the aftermath of the Norman Conquest, in the eleventh century, shaped the way in which land was held for centuries to follow. In its simplest terms, the basic structure can be described thus: the king held all land, but granted some of this land to reward his followers, who held the land direct from the Crown as tenants-in-chief. In turn they granted land to their supporters, who continued the process to create a pyramid structure of landholding. This method of land grant was known as 'subinfeudation', and with the exception of the Crown at the top, left everyone who held land as the tenant of an over-lord.

4.2.2   The manor

The main unit of land was known as the 'manor', and was probably based on an Anglo-Saxon system of land division. It is important to grasp the concept that manors were not always compact geographical land units, but instead were often spread among the lands of other manors, and it was the unifying bonds of allegiance to a single lord of the manor that defined the unit in social and economic terms. Furthermore, the boundaries of the manor should not be confused with those of the local parish, as they were separate administrative units. A single manor may stretch across several parishes, or conversely one parish may contain more than one manor.

4.2.3   Land tenure

Each manor had a 'lord', who in turn granted strips of land within the manor to tenants in return for service, usually a combination of rent, military obligation or work on the lord's land. Any surplus land retained by the lord was known as the 'demesne'. The terms by which tenants held land from the lord of the manor was called the 'tenure', and determined whether the tenant was free or unfree. Free tenants could hold land by either military or socage tenure. In the case of the latter, free tenants were required to perform an agreed amount and type of work on the lord's demesne each year. However, unfree tenants, or villeins, had only the amount of work set, and were instructed by the lord's representative as to the nature of the work when the time came. More information on manorial tenants can be found in Chapter 6.

4.3   Freehold land

4.3.1   Types of freehold tenure

As the previous section has demonstrated, in essence no-one 'owned' land since it had all been originally granted by the Crown. However, the terms by which land was granted throughout the feudal chain were of vital importance in determining how it could be transferred in future. The following are descriptions of the three main ways in which freehold land could be granted to an individual. They are technically known as 'estates', which means a period of time that the land would be held by the recipient.

In addition to the three freehold estates, a fourth type of estate, namely lease or a 'term of years', developed and is also considered here. As it was possible for leases to be made on copyhold land as well as freehold, it was deemed a non-freehold estate. There was a further important distinction between freehold land and lease. In the eyes of the law, freehold land was deemed as real property, or realty, and could not be 'devised' (or bequeathed to another) by will until the Statute of Wills was passed in 1540, and more specifically after the Tenures Abolition Act of 1660. However, leases were considered to be personal property, or personal, and therefore could be included in a will. This distinction is considered in more detail in Chapter 7.

Fee simple

Land that was granted to an individual 'and his heirs' was deemed to be fee simple. In essence, this meant that on the death of the recipient it would pass to his immediate heir at law, unless the fee simple had already been granted (or 'alienated') to another by a previous agreement. When the line of heirs of the recipient finally died out, then the land would return to the original grantor or his heirs. Thus the word 'fee' indicates that the land was inheritable. However, as a fee simple was realty, it could not be devised by will to another until statutory developments in the sixteenth and seventeenth centuries.

Fee tail

Land granted in fee simple guaranteed only that it would be passed to the heirs of the recipient as long as it was not alienated. This was inconvenient to landowners who wished to keep their landed estates within the family for future generations. A solution was created by the 1285 Statute de Donis Conditionalibus, which stipulated that land granted to a recipient and 'the heirs of his body' would pass to all future issue of the recipient without the possibility of alienation. This was known as a fee tail, and only when all future issue had died out would the land revert to the original grantor or his heirs.

Life interest

As the name suggests, the grant of a life interest in land would last only as long as the lifetime of the recipient, who became the 'life tenant'. This meant that the heirs of the recipient could not inherit the land. However, a recipient of a life estate could grant the land to others, but the new recipient was said to hold the property 'pur autre vie', or for the life of another. This meant that the interest of the new recipient could last only as long as the life of the original recipient, at which point it would revert to the original grantor.

4.3.2   Leases

If an individual wished to grant land to another for a limited period of time but did not want to grant a life interest, since the recipient could live for an uncertain length of time, he leased the land for a 'term of years' (or 'demised' it). The following are the most common forms of lease that you will probably encounter, although you should bear in mind that it was possible to lease both freehold and copyhold land. This type of tenure was also referred to as fee-farm.

Fixed leases

Fixed leases were for a set period of time (for example, six months or ninety-nine years), and usually involved the payment of a fixed sum at the beginning. At the end of the agreed term the original lessor would reclaim the land, or renegotiate another lease with the tenant.

Periodic leases

Periodic leases were also for fixed periods (for example, weekly, monthly or yearly), but would be automatically renewed for the duration of another period of time unless either party provided a period of notice. Rent was paid on a regular basis (for example, per week, per month or per year).

Other forms of lease

In addition to these 'terms of years', other forms of lease were possible.

- Tenants at will were created when an agreement was made between the lessor and the lessee that either could determine, usually on the expiration of a fixed or periodic lease. Although no rent was payable, the tenant was due to pay some form of compensation to the lessor.

- Leases for life were tenable for the duration of the tenant's life, as were leases that were curtailed by the marriage or death of the tenant.
- Tenancies at sufferance came into being at the expiration of a lease when the tenant remained on the land without the lessor's permission.
- Renewable leases contained a clause that allowed the lessee to request a new lease to be granted on the same terms as the old, as long as the request was made within a stipulated period before the expiry of the original lease. Perpetual renewable leases were possible before 1925.

4.3.3   Terminology used in grants of freehold land

The following are the main terms with which house historians will need to familiarise themselves when attempting to decipher the types of grant of freehold land.

Possession, reversion and remainder

When a landholder, A, made a grant of land that was held as 'fee simple' to another individual, B, for life, B was deemed to be in 'possession' of the land. On B's death the land would eventually revert to A (or his heirs if he predeceased B), as the life interest in possession had thus ended. Therefore, during B's lifetime, A still held the fee simple 'in reversion', even though he did not actually possess the land.

However, if A had specified that the land should pass to a further individual, C, for life at the death of B, then C was said to hold a life interest in the land 'in remainder'. At the death of B, then C would take on the life interest in possession. Therefore, the grant would be 'to B for life with remainder to C for life'.

Conditional and determinable grants

If a grantor wanted to specify various terms to a grant, he would make it either conditional or determinable. A grant of 'conditional fee simple' meant that there was a condition attached to the grant. Phrases such as 'on the condition that', 'provided that' and 'but if' were commonly used to frame such a grant. There were two types – a precedent condition, which stipulated that the grant could not be received until the condition was fulfilled, and a subsequent condition, which would end the grant if the circumstances described in the condition ever arose.

Alternatively, a grant of 'determinable fee simple' meant that a limiting restriction was imposed, and this type of grant commonly contained the phrases 'until', 'during', 'while' and 'as long as'.

Conditional and determinable grants could also apply to grants of life interest, but were not permissible for grants of fee tail. If a grant was not conditional or determinable, then it was called 'absolute'.

Various types of interest

A future interest in a grant is one that has yet to be enjoyed by the recipient. As we have seen above, the grant of land, held in fee simple by A, to B for life, with remainder to C for life only resulted in B taking immediate possession of the land. C could claim to have a future interest in the grant, as it was dependant on the death of B.

A contingent interest was where a condition had yet to be fulfilled before the grant took effect, or when the identity of the recipient was still unknown. Contingent interests were most commonly associated with future heirs to a property, either because they had not attained the age of 21, or were not yet born. If an interest was not contingent, then it was said to be vested, as no conditions had to be fulfilled before the grant could take effect, or when the identity of the recipient was already known.

Therefore a grant of land, held as fee simple by A, to B for life, with remainder to C for life when he attained the age of 21, gave B a vested interest and C a future contingent interest.

Trusts

Trusts, also known as 'uses', were originally designed to grant the legal possession of land to one individual while permitting another individual to enjoy the actual benefits of possession, such as any rents that were collected from the land. Usually two or more trustees were named in the original grant, and they were bound to hold and administer the land under the terms of the trust. Therefore, if A made a grant of land in fee simple to B and C 'for the use of D', then A would no longer be the legal possessor of the fee simple – it would now be the trustees, B and C.

D also had an interest in the estate, but not in the eyes of the common law. Instead the interest was deemed 'equitable', as the law of equity compelled the trustees to carry out the terms of the trust for the benefit of D. Hence, if trusts were disputed, cases would be heard in the courts of equity, whereas property transfers made solely under the principle of common law ought, in theory, to end up in one of the common law courts. Advice about tracking down such disputes in the law courts is provided in Chapter 8.

The trust would end only when the trustees transferred the legal fee simple to D. Trusts were normally set up that transferred the fee simple to the trustees, but in theory they could hold either life interests or fee tail. The trust would end only when the legal estate was transferred to the beneficiary of the trust, provided he was of full age and that his equitable fee was not conditional or determinable.

Settlements

A settlement was the term given to a land grant that involved the creation of a succession of interests in the land, either by direct grants or via trusts. Settlements became especially important in the nineteenth century when the owners of large landed estates created chains of inheritance that bound land to their families, known as 'strict settlements'. These are considered later in this chapter.

4.3.4   Changes to land law under the 1925 legislation

In 1925, a series of statutes were passed that altered English land law. The main components were the Settled Land Act (1925 c.18), the Trustee Act (1925 c.19), the Law of Property Act (1925 c.20), the Land Registration Act (1925 c.21), the Land Charges Act (1925 c.22) and the Administration of Estates Act (1925 c.23). This guide is not the best place to investigate the impact of these pieces of legislation, but you will find that they have been referred to when relevant. Some suggested reading material on the subject is listed under **Useful publications**.

4.4   Methods of transfer

The previous section has outlined some of the basic ways in which freehold land, and therefore the houses that were built on the land, could be granted or held by an individual. The way in which land was held therefore determined the method by which property could be transferred from one party to another. These are outlined below, with information on where to find relevant material within the PRO. In addition, advice about searching for title deeds – the combined record of previous transfers – is provided in the next chapter.

4.4.1   Feoffment

Enfeoffment was the term used to describe the conveyance of land held by fee simple from one party to the other within the confines of a manor. The seller physically passed a sod of land from the property to the buyer, a process known as 'livery of seisin'. Once the transfer had been completed, the purchaser was then a tenant of the manor and subject to its rules and regulations. Although no written evidence of the transfer was legally required until the Statute of Frauds in 1677, both parties, as well as the lord of the manor, found it expedient to produce a record of the transaction. The result was a 'feoffment', known as a deed of gift, and was in effect a private charter that described the transfer from one party to the other. You will find that the format of the document tends to give the names of the people or parties concerned and a description of the property involved, with a summary of the feudal terms and conditions under which the property was held from the lord of the manor. The grant was permanent, signified by the Latin clause *habendum* which in full usually reads *Habendum et tenendum . . . in perpetuum* (to have and to hold . . . for ever). The date of the transfer is usually provided at the foot of the text.

Feoffment originated in the eleventh century, and had lapsed as a form of conveyance by the mid nineteenth century. No official enrolment in a court was required, and so there are no logical places at the PRO to start looking. Feoffments will turn up as part of title deeds, but the best place to begin your research will be at the CRO.

4.4.2   Deeds of lease

Documentation was also created when land was leased to individuals by one of the means described in 4.3.2. The *habendum* clause defined the period of the lease, and the rent is stipulated by a *redendum* clause ('yielding and paying'). The PRO will not be the main place of deposit, and any surviving records will probably be stored in the relevant CRO. However, you may well find deeds of lease for copyhold property enrolled on the official manorial court rolls, described in Chapter 6.

Of particular use will be leases that were used to convey building rights to a plot of freehold land. These allowed the builder to construct a property and then rent it out, while the freeholder enjoyed rent from the leaseholder. Building specifications can often be found in the terms of the lease, and may include a description of the intended property with measurements and proposed room layout.

4.4.3   Final Concord or Fine

From the late twelfth century until 1833, one of the most popular methods of land transfer that generated an official record of the process was the Final Concord, or Fine. The conveyance was achieved through a fictitious legal dispute between the purchaser, or querent, and vendor, or deforciant, which was usually resolved in the Court of Common Pleas. A final agreement, known as the concord or fine, was reached between the two parties. The concord was written in triplicate on a sheet of parchment, two copies side by side and the third along the foot of the parchment. This was then split into three parts by means of an indented or wavy cut as a preventative measure against fraud. One part was given to the vendor, another to the purchaser, while the court retained the final part, the 'foot'. This gave rise to the popular name by which surviving documents at the PRO are known – the 'feet of fines'.

From the fifteenth century, fines were commonly used to convey land held in fee tail, as the process partially broke (or 'barred') the entail; a 'base fee' was created that was similar to a fee simple, except that it lasted only as long as the original fee tail would have done. Thus the new possessor of the land would need to check whether the original entailed interest had expired, as that was when the land would revert to the original grantor, usually the lord of the manor in which the land was situated.

The text of each fine is formulaic, beginning with the phrase 'this is the final agreement', followed by the date of agreement and the names of the judges. The document then provides the names of the parties, identified by the word INTER (between), with the querent listed first, followed by the deforciant. A description of the land or property in question is then provided, although you will find that there is no great detail given. A 'purchase price' is usually recorded, although this was a standard sum as early as the fourteenth century and did not reflect the actual purchase price. The documents are written in Latin until 1733, with the exception of the Interregnum period 1649–60, and if you are unfamiliar with the language, this standard pattern will allow you to identify enough key words and phrases to extract useful information about your property.

Feet of fines at the PRO are in series **CP 25/1** for the period 1195–1509, and **CP 25/2** for the period 1509–1839. Many feet of fines for individual counties have been published, and a list is available on open access. The means of reference to feet of fines is through a series of contemporary indexes from 1509–1839 that are arranged by legal term and then by county or city in **IND 1/7233–44** and **1/17217–68**. These will provide you with the names of the county, querent and deforciant, and the location of the property.

Another series of contemporary repertories from 1623 to 1734 are kept in **IND 1/7182–9**, and annotated entries that correspond to numbers stamped on the fines can be found in **IND 1/7191, 7192** and **7195–232**. Indexes to these repertories that list entries by county and number are located in **IND 1/7190** (1731–2), **1/7193** (1743–5) and **1/7194** (1745–7).

Supplementary material related to the feet of fines also survives. The concord of fine files, stored in series **CP 24/1–13**, and the notes of fine files, stored in series **CP 26/1–14**, contain legal documentation surrounding the compilation of

Table 4.1 Records of fines

Jurisdiction	Feet of fines	Concord of fines
Palatinate of Chester	**CHES 31** 1280–1830 **CHES 32** (enrolments) 1585–1703	**CHES 31** 1280–1830 **CHES 32** (enrolments) 1585–1703
Palatinate of Durham	**DURH 12** 1535–1834	**DURH 11** 1660–1834
Palatinate of Lancaster	**PL 17** 1377–1834 **PL 18** (enrolments) 1587–1834	**PL 17** 1377–1834

the feet of fines themselves. You may find draft texts, annotations and background information on the agreements in these series, which are arranged in regnal years. There are indexes for the notes of fines in both **IND 1/7233–44** and **IND 1/17217–68**, which double up as indexes to the feet of fines themselves, and can be used as a rough guide to the location of the concord of fines. However, it should be noted that some documents were filed in legal terms different from those described in the indexes.

A summary for feet of fines and related material for semi-autonomous jurisdictions is provided in Table 4.1.

Feet of fines for Wales are in series **WALE 2, 3** and **6**, but have been transferred to the NLW.

4.4.4   Common recovery

The common recovery was developed in the fifteenth century as a permanent means of barring entailed property, as long as the tenant in tail was in possession of the land, or had obtained the permission of the tenant in possession. In effect, it was another fictitious legal dispute brought in the Court of Common Pleas, designed to convert the fee tail to a fee simple.

The potential purchaser brought an action against the tenant in tail, claiming that the land was his all along and that he wished to 'recover' it. The tenant in tail appointed a third party, known as the common vouchee, to effectively represent him in court. The common vouchee was therefore required to appear in court to defend the suit on behalf of the tenant in tail. However, he would default, thereby providing the justices with the opportunity to make a judgment against the tenant in tail in favour of the original plaintiff. The entail against the land was thus broken through legal judgment and the land passed to the plaintiff as fee simple. In reality, the land would have been sold before the court case on pre-agreed terms.

The documents can appear quite complicated, given the complex legal process involved in effecting the conveyance. However, you will find that they tend to follow a fairly common format, and are once again in Latin until 1733, with the exception of the period 1649–60. As it was a court judgment, the record begins with a royal greeting, followed by the names of the justices and the relevant county. You will find that the description of the property is fairly brief, but you will obtain the names of the two main parties. Usually the name or names of the common vouchee relate to court officials, but occasionally they can refer to parties that had a vested interest in the case.

Until 1583 these judgments were originally recorded in the plea rolls of the Court of Common Pleas, which are in PRO series **CP 40,**. Contemporary indexes exist in the form of docket books in **CP 60**, which will provide the names of the parties, the county and the relevant membrane number within the roll. The process proved to be so popular that from 1583 separate Recovery Rolls (*see* **Figure 9**) were kept, which are in series **CP 43**. Indexes for the period 1583–1835 again provide the names of the parties, the county and the membrane number, plus varying amounts of information on the property itself, and are to be found in **IND 1/17183–216**. Related material can be found in the Alienation Office entry books **A 9**, which record writs of entry intended for use in conveying land by common recovery.

A summary of locations for common recoveries and related material for semi-autonomous jurisdictions is provided in Table 4.2.

Table 4.2 Common recoveries for semi-autonomous jurisdictions		
Palatinate of Chester	**CHES 29**	Plea rolls 1259–1830
	CHES 30	Plea rolls (Flint) 1284–1820
	CHES 31	Recoveries files 1280–1830
	CHES 32	Recoveries enrolments 1585–1703
Palatinate of Durham	**DURH 13**	Plea rolls 1344–1845
Palatinate of Lancaster	**PL 15**	Plea rolls 1401–1848

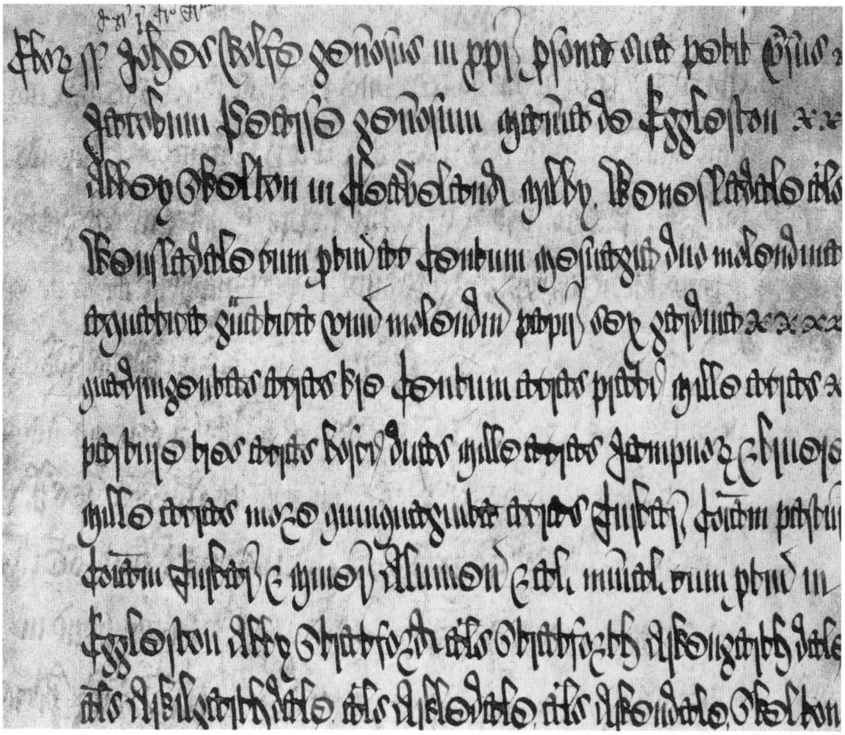

Figure 9 The transfer of the lands and possessions of Egglestone Abbey, Startforth, is recorded in an entry on the recovery roll from 1717. Its mill is described as a paper mill (*molendini paperii*). (CP 43/537)

4.4.5   Bargain and sale

One of the most important developments for conveyances and land transfers came with the Statute of Uses (27 Henry VIII c.10) in 1536. As we have seen, realty could not be devised by will before this date. However, the tenant was able to set up a trust, or 'use', by making a grant of the land to trustees 'for the use and behoof' of himself for the duration of his lifetime, and then on trust to the use of whoever he designated in his will. This was possible because the trustees would be the legal possessors of the realty, while the tenant continued to enjoy the benefits and rents due from the land, which were considered personalty and thus could be devised. On the death of the tenant, the recipient would then direct the trustees to dissolve the trust and transfer the legal fee simple to him.

This arrangement benefited all except the lords of the manor in which the property was situated, as they were in danger of losing track of the rights and services due to them – the trustees legally owed these services to the lord, but as they were administering the land on behalf of another they did not enjoy the benefits, and so could not perform the services; whereas the tenant was no longer under legal obligation. The Crown was one of the biggest losers under this system, and the Statute of Uses was designed to rectify this by giving the beneficiary the legal estate of the land, thereby restoring the lord's ability to exact service from him. One of the most important consequences was that tenants with a life interest in the land were often created. In response, a device called the 'bargain and sale' was employed to convey uses from one party to the next.

In essence the bargain and sale was an indenture between two parties, whereby the first party bargained and sold property to the second. The first party remained the legal possessor of the fee simple, and conveyed the use of the land to the second party, who was liable to perform services to the lord of the manor under the terms of the Statute of Uses. To enable people to legally identify the correct person to perform these services, the Statute of Enrolments (27 Henry VIII c.16) was also passed in 1536 that required all bargains and sale of freehold property to be enrolled, either with the county Clerk of the Peace in the quarter sessions, or with one of the central courts at Westminster. The PRO does not hold quarter sessions records, but where they survive they will be found at the relevant CRO. However, a large number of bargains and sales were enrolled on the Chancery close rolls in **C 54**, and are described in the next chapter.

The documents will contain the following information that will be of use to the house historian. First, the date of the transaction and the names of the parties are given, followed by details of the financial transaction and, most importantly of all, a description of the property. The terms of the use are then defined, followed by the names of the witnesses. You may find that some enrolled bargains and sale contain recitals of earlier transactions, giving you a unique link to past transfers and the names of previous owners.

4.4.6   Lease and release

From the seventeenth century onwards, a new form of conveyance was introduced that developed the principle of bargain and sale and took advantage of the lease to create a means of conveyance that removed the need to enrol the transfer in court. The vendor drew up a bargain and sale of a lease of the property to the purchaser, usually for a term of one year, with the rent on the land being a nominal amount, typically one peppercorn. Under the Statute of Uses, the purchaser became vested in the lease without entering into possession, hence avoiding feudal dues. However, the lease was not enrolled, as only direct transfers of freehold property were subject to the Statute of Enrolment. The second part of the deed took place the following day and was a release that, on payment of a sum of money, removed the terms of the original lease and therefore vested the freehold interest with the purchaser.

As the requirement to enrol the transfer had been effectively bypassed, there are no court records in the PRO. Surviving examples of deeds of this nature may survive in one of the places listed above, but you should start your search for surviving deeds by lease and release in the relevant CRO.

4.4.7   Disentailing assurance

Under the terms of the 1833 Fines and Recoveries Act, the need to undertake a fictitious lawsuit to bar the entail to land was replaced by a document known as a disentailing assurance. This permitted the holder of the fee tail to bar the entail as long as he was in possession of the land, or had the permission of the tenant who was in possession. It was a legal requirement to enrol these documents in Chancery, and examples can be found on the close rolls in C 54.

4.4.8   Strict settlements

By the nineteenth century, nearly half of all land was regulated by 'strict settlements'. To ensure that land was passed within a family, landholders had combined various forms of conveyance to establish a restricted, or 'strict' settlement of their land to certain named successors and 'the heirs of their body legally begotten'. At the heart of the settlement was a series of life interests for the current tenant and his son, followed by an entailed remainder to unborn future heirs, whose interests were known as 'contingent remainders'. Since it was possible for an existing life tenant to destroy a contingent interest at any point, from the mid seventeenth century onwards trusts were used to protect any contingent remainders. This was made easier after 1660 when realty could be devised by will. By the nineteenth century, the format of a typical strict settlement was as summarised below.

- The first clause was the premises of the deed, which set out the date and the names and occupations of the parties involved in the settlement.
- This was typically followed by recitals of previous transactions that related to the current deed, which will allow you to trace the title of the property; this clause began with 'WHEREAS'.
- Next came the testatum, which outlined the purpose of the deed and began with 'WITNESSETH'. You will find out the reason why the deed was being created; a description of the property, introduced by the phrase 'ALL THAT'; and any exceptions to the property under settlement.
- The habendum clause, 'TO HAVE AND TO HOLD', set up the trusts contained in the deed, which related to the settler and often included an annuity for the heir until he inherited; pin-money to the settler's wife; jointures

(money after the death of the husband) to his widow; and portions to any younger children. The property was then conveyed to the trustees for a term of years or in fee simple.

- The crucial section was the entail, which set up a series of life tenancies in the land for those already born, and a series of fee tail for those unborn. The trustees would be granted the fee simple, or a term of years, to protect the contingent remainders, and a final remainder was included to the settler and his heirs. This section would also include any conditions that might be attached to the grant to future heirs.

- The trustees were then given various powers that allowed them to administer the estate.

- Finally, the testemonium clause, 'IN WITNESS THEREOF', concluded the deed and stated that the parties had signed and sealed the deed in the presence of witnesses.

Under the terms of the 1925 Settled Land Act, two documents were required to draw up a strict settlement. The first was a vesting deed, which described the settled land, conveyed the legal estate to the tenant for life, and stated the names and powers of the trustees. The second was a trust settlement, which essentially described the trusts concerned in the settlement and appointed the trustees.

Strict settlements were therefore complicated documents, and this section has provided only a very brief introduction to their format and potential use. If you wish to explore this topic in more detail, suggestions for further reading are provided in the section on land law and conveyancing in **Useful publications**.

5 Title deeds

5.1 Introduction

Today, when you purchase a house the legal documentation affecting the purchase will be added to the existing title deeds for the property, and a solicitor will assist with the formal registration of the transaction with the Land Registry. To finance the purchase, most people apply for a mortgage, and the title deeds for the property are then deposited with the mortgage provider or solicitor acting on their behalf as security against the loan until the mortgage is paid off, or the property is sold on.

However, there was no systematic registration of land or property transfers until the formation of the Land Registry in 1862; and even then, registration remained a voluntary process for most areas outside inner London until late into the twentieth century. Before the creation of the Land Registry, transfers and title deeds were often enrolled in courts of law; but as we have seen in Chapter 4, the rules, restrictions and regulations that governed land transactions and sales varied across the centuries, and subsequently resulted in different forms of transfer. This often presents the house historian with a myriad of potential places in which to look for evidence.

It is also important to stress that the very nature of the records can cause confusion, as the documents contain legal jargon and can be lengthy and repetitive. Many of the legal terms are defined in the **Glossary** at the end of this book, although relevant expressions will be explained in the context of the records they relate to. Furthermore, many records created before 1733 will be written in Latin, with the remainder in old-fashioned English or even French. Do not let this deter you, as you will be primarily searching for names of previous owners and dates of transfers, and therefore it will not always be necessary to transcribe the material in full.

Following the description of the various forms of freehold tenure in Chapter 4, the aim of this chapter is to present a summary of where to look for title deeds at the PRO and elsewhere. However, it is important to remember that title deeds also contained transfers of copyhold and leasehold property, plus details of devises through wills. These are topics that are covered in more depth in Chapters 6 and 7 respectively.

5.2   Title deeds

5.2.1   A definition of title deeds

Defined in its strictest terms, a 'deed' is a legal document. Title deeds (*see* **Figure 10**), also known as muniments of title, are therefore the collected legal documentation for past transfers of a particular piece of land or property, and should perhaps be more accurately described as the 'deed package'. In effect, they represent legal proof of ownership through previous transfers. As such, a variety of different types of document might be included in the deed package, such as

Figure 10 A selection of documents from the late nineteenth century – mortgage deed, contract of sale and indemnity – found among the title deeds for 'The Wilderness Club', Richmond, Surrey. (J 90/1711)

indentures, mortgages, wills, manorial records and court papers. In theory, title deeds can stretch back for many centuries, and until 1925 this was often the case. However, under the terms of the 1925 Law of Property Act, the requirement to prove descent of land as far back as possible was removed, with a new period of proof limited to only 30 years. This period was further reduced to 15 years in 1970. In consequence, older title deeds became redundant, and often no longer formed part of the deed package that was passed from one purchaser to the next.

Therefore, title deeds will differ from property to property, depending on how previous sales or transactions were conducted. You may find that there are no title deeds for your property more than 15 years old, or you may strike it lucky and find deposited deeds that stretch back many years. You will usually be able to identify from the documents the names of the vendor and purchaser; a description of the property in question, along with its boundaries and abutals; the date of transfer; and the sums of money involved. Tenants and occupiers are also occasionally listed in the body of the text, and you may also find that the dates of previous sales are recited. If you are lucky, the date of construction may even be specified, particularly if the original building lease for the plot of land is included. No matter what form the paperwork takes, the house historian will be able to extract enough information to construct a detailed chronological framework.

5.2.2   Where to look for title deeds

Trying to locate old title deeds can be a difficult process, as there is no logical place of deposit. Modern title deeds are usually retained by the mortgage provider as security, given that in technical terms a 'mortgage' is a pledge of land as security against a loan of money. Banks, building societies or solicitors acting on behalf of a mortgage provider are the logical place to begin your search, although you will find that most mortgage providers will charge a fee before they allow you to view the title deeds. Once the loan has been paid off, the need for this security ends, and you are entitled to claim your title deeds. This raises the problem that previous title deeds may well be in private hands, and consequently there is very little chance of tracking them down unless you can identify where the previous owners might now reside.

The alternative is that old title deeds were deposited in the public domain. When the 1925 Law of Property Act was passed, many solicitors and mortgage providers took the opportunity to dispose of title deeds that had accumulated over many years, and presented them to either current owners or, more usually, the relevant CRO. These are usually listed either by place or by the name of the family or business collection within which they were deposited.

However, a large proportion of old title deeds were simply thrown away and ended up in skips or rubbish tips. Nevertheless, it is still worth approaching solicitors that operate in your area on the off chance that they still have old title deeds squirrelled away in cupboards. It might also be worth talking to local estate agents, as they can often provide information about where and when previous sales occurred.

5.3   Deposited title deeds at the PRO

Although your CRO will be the best place to begin your search for deposited title deeds, the PRO also has a surprisingly large collection. The documents have accumulated for several reasons. Some properties had become part of the Crown estates through purchase or forfeiture, which meant that the legal proof of ownership was deposited with the relevant administrative body. Alternatively, property disputes that ended up in court often required the litigants to provide evidence of title; sometimes the documents were left behind and remained within the holdings of the court.

However, there is no overall index to title deeds at the PRO. The remainder of this section outlines some of the main areas where you should consider looking for existing deeds, and a full list of PRO series is provided at the end of this book.

5.3.1   Private title deeds

Large collections of title deeds for private properties have come into the hands of the Crown and can be found in a variety of PRO series, depending on which institution or government department handled the transfer. Similarly, in the aftermath of the suppression of the monasteries, many more deeds for monastic land and properties have also been collected. No matter what their origin or final location within the PRO, the deeds are described as Ancient and Modern, depending on their date; Ancient deeds usually pre-date the seventeenth century, whereas Modern deeds date from the seventeenth century to the early nineteenth century.

The list of PRO series containing private deeds that commences on p. 197 links them to any relevant finding aids and indexes that exist. In summary, the main series in which to look for deeds are **C 146–9, E 40–44, E 132, E 210–14, 326–30** and **354–5**. Deeds for areas that enjoyed semi-autonomous jurisdictions, such as the Duchy of Lancaster and the Palatinates of Durham, Lancaster and Chester, can be found in **DL 25–7, DURH 21, PL 29** and **WALE 29–31** respectively. Some of the deeds in the largest series, **E 40, C 146** and **E 210**, have been transcribed and indexed in *A Descriptive Catalogue of Ancient Deeds in the Public Record*

Office, 6 volumes (HMSO, 1890–1906), which is on open access in the reading rooms. There is a key sheet in the front that provides PRO references for each deed.

These deposited deeds will be of most use if your property once formed part of a large private estate, as the vast majority of the material relates to principal landowners or tenants-in-chief who fell foul of the Crown and escheated their property. Most of the records will also be very early, so you will be highly unlikely to find title deeds to a specific modern property; most will relate to land on which houses were later built, rather than to the transfer of a building itself. Even if you are looking for earlier records of land transactions, the sources may be limited in use unless you know the names of the individuals who took part in the exchange. However, if you do not have this information, the indexes do include references to places, and most of the items are now available to search by key word via PROCAT, the PRO's electronic catalogue.

5.3.2   Title deeds to Crown lands

In addition to private property deeds, there are also areas where you can look for deeds to Crown property that may later have been sold into private hands or which were leased out to private individuals. These are also listed at the end of this book but, in summary, you are most likely to find records in series **CRES 38**; **LR 14–16**; **LRRO 13–18**, **20**, **25**, **37** and **64**; **IR 10**; **TS 21**; and **WORK 7–8**, **13** and **24**. Many of these series have registers or card indexes that can aid identification of people or places, and these are also indicated in the list commencing on p. 197. Furthermore, a key word search of PROCAT will also yield results.

As with private deeds, it is important to remember that it will be unusual to find references to individual properties, and you will find that much of your research will focus on prior usage of a site, rather than identification of your current house. Records generated by the management of Crown estates should provide more relevant information about individual properties built on Crown land, and are described in Chapter 6.

5.3.3   Deposited deeds as evidence

In addition to title deeds to private or Crown property, the records preserved by central law courts can prove to be a rich source for the house detective. In cases of disputed property ownership, litigants were required to provide evidence of title to support their case. Quite often the litigants failed to collect this evidence, and the courts retained these papers to form a wonderful archive that is rich with private records. This topic is covered in more detail in Chapter 8, but a summary of where to look is provided below.

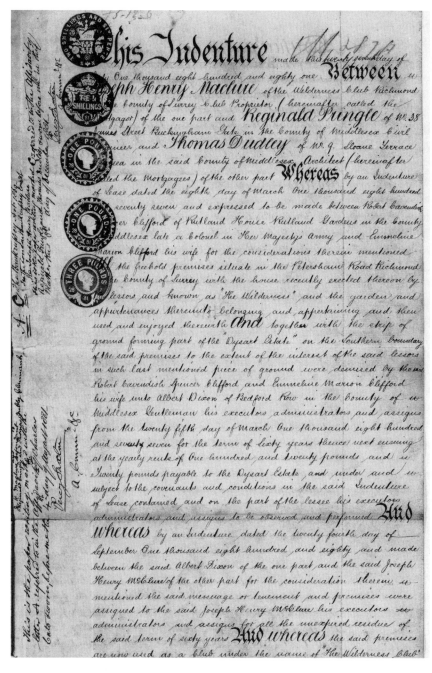

Figure 11 First page of indenture concerning 'The Wilderness Club', Richmond, Surrey, mortgaged by Joseph Henry McClure to defendants Reginald Pringle and Thomas Dudley, who were trustees of settlement on his marriage to Miss Ellen Bottomley. The dispute concerned coal rights in Whiston and Huyton, Lancashire, the plaintiffs being Joseph Crossland McClure and Elaine McClure, infants. (J 90/1711)

The best place to begin your search will be amongst the Chancery Masters Exhibits, which contain evidence produced during Chancery disputes. The records are arranged in PRO series **C 103–115** and **171**, with a composite index in the series list for **C 103**. Masters documents, which contain similar records, are also contained in series **C 117–126**. Exhibits from Exchequer court cases can be found in series **E 140**, and later records from the Supreme Court of Judicature are in series **J 90** (*see* **Figures 10–11**), which are stored at Hayes and currently require three working days' notice before they can be produced at Kew. You may also find deeds among the Court of Wards and Liveries records in **WARD 2**, as well as in the Chancery court of the Palatinate of Lancaster in **PL 12**, and exhibits in the Exchequer of Chester that include deeds and other land documentation relating to the city of Chester and surrounding villages are in **CHES 11**.

If you are able to identify relevant material within any of these areas, you should, in theory, be able to track down records of the court case itself, which should provide even more information about the litigants and potential owners. This type of research is described more fully in Chapter 8.

5.4   Enrolment of deeds

5.4.1 Land Registry

In 1862 the national Land Registry was established to provide a means of recording land transfers across England and Wales. Before this date, certain types of land transaction were required by statute to be enrolled in a variety of courts, depending on the type of transaction that took place.

Initially, there was no legal requirement to enrol land transfers at the Land Registry, and compulsory registration was introduced by the Land Transfer Act 1897 on only a gradual basis, county by county, with particular importance given to urban areas. Technically, compulsory registration for all counties has existed since 1990, although for most counties this has been the case since the 1970s. This means that presently only about 70 per cent of all eligible properties are actually covered by the records of the Land Registry, although this will increase as more properties come onto the register.

The records maintained by the Land Registry will contain information on the sale, plus maps or plans that depict boundaries of the land or property in question. The register of a property contains details of the current ownership only, as well as details of any registered mortgage or deed affecting the land, which might contain references to previous sales. Anyone can order a copy of the register and most documents referred to in it, as well as a copy of the title plan. Application should be made on the appropriate form to the office that deals

Table 5.1 Local deed registries

Name	Date range	Location
Middlesex	c.1709–1940	LMA, 40 Northampton Road, London EC1R 0HB
Bedford level	17th century onwards	Cambridgeshire Record Office, Shire Hall, Cambridge CB3 0AP
West Riding Yorkshire	1704–1972	West Yorkshire Archives Service, Newstead Road, Wakefield WF1 2DE
East Riding Yorkshire and Hull	1708–1976	East Riding of Yorkshire Archives and Records, The Chapel, Lord Roberts Road, Beverley *Correspondence to:* County Hall, Beverley HU17 9BA
North Riding Yorkshire (not including City of York)	1736–1972	North Yorkshire CRO, Malpas Road, Northallerton DL7 8TB

with that area. There is a fee charged for this service. Copies of the application forms and further details are available from any Land Registry office, or via its website (http://www.landreg.gov.uk/).

The Land Registry may also hold historical records of an individual property from the time when it was first registered. These are only available at the discretion of the office concerned, and application should be made in writing, explaining why the records are needed. Again, a fee would be charged. Alternatively, you can normally purchase copies of any register in person at the headquarters of the Land Registry in Lincoln's Inn Fields, London, or at any district Land Registry, although it is advisable to telephone in advance of a visit.

5.4.2 Local registries

Before the Land Registry was set up, registers of deeds were already in existence in some parts of England. They were established by statute in an attempt to prevent fraud, as the possession of the deeds conferred legal ownership. The statutes also defined the type of transaction that was eligible for registration. Usually these were leases over 21 years; freehold transfers; mortgages and wills. They do not contain deeds as such, merely a memorial of the deed and a date of enrolment in the register. Details of the relevant archives that hold local registries are provided in Table 5.1.

In addition, registration of property or land transfers for the City of London occasionally occurs on hustings rolls. A search of the records located at the Corporation of London Record Office at the Guildhall, Aldermanbury, might yield some results. Similar registration occurred for property in other cities or

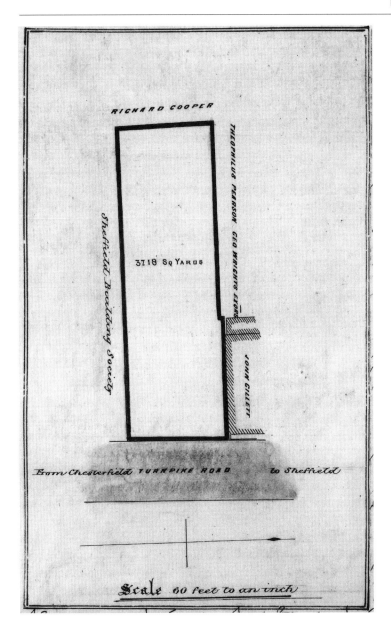

Figure 12 Plan from enrolled trust deed for the construction of a schoolhouse in Newbold, Derbyshire, in the close roll for 1872. (C 54/17354)

boroughs in municipal courts, and the records can usually be found in the relevant CRO or at municipal record offices. Some counties have collections of deeds enrolled under the Statute of Enrolments 1536. In addition, from 1715–91 Roman Catholics and non-juror Anglicans had to register their estates and changes of ownership. These records are to be found both in CROs and at the PRO in series **E 174** and **FEC 1**.

5.4.3   Enrolment of deeds and conveyances at the PRO

In addition to the deed registries described above, other statutes regulating the conveyance of land stipulated that the transfers must be enrolled in a court of law. Furthermore, many individuals voluntarily enrolled their title deeds so that it was clear who was the legal owner of the land. The PRO holds many records of these courts, and the most useful series that contain enrolled transcripts of title deeds are listed below.

Enrolments in Chancery

One of the most accessible places for deed enrolment was in Chancery. For a fee, private individuals had memorials of property sales or land transfers copied onto the back of the close rolls, contained in series **C 54** (*see* **Figure 12**). From 1536 this practice gained in popularity when it was decreed that the enrolment in a court of law of a particular type of land conveyance known as bargain and sale was a statutory requirement (described in section 4.4.5). Once the Land Registry had been established and continued to grow in popularity, the close rolls were used less frequently as a place of enrolment. From 1903, when the close rolls were discontinued, the Supreme Court Enrolment Books in **J 18** served the same purpose, although you are unlikely to find any title deeds enrolled much beyond the middle of the twentieth century. Indexes to the enrolments in these sources survive in a variety of forms, and a summary is provided in Table 5.2.

Close rolls are especially useful if the land was formerly owned under a chari-

Table 5.2 Indexes to Chancery close rolls

Date	Finding aid	Location
1227–1509	*Calendar of Close Rolls*	Open access (listed under **C 54**)
1509-1837	Index to grantees (buyers)	Open access (**C 275/12–85**)
1837–1848	Index to grantors (sellers)	Open access (**C 275/86–8**)
1573–1902	Index to grantors (sellers)	Open access (**C 275/89–169**)
1903–	General indexes (annual)	Open access (listed under **J 18**)
1559–1567	Calendar of enrolled deeds	**IND 1/9455–7**
1689–1820	Deeds enrolled for safe custody	**IND 1/16936–7**

table trust. There are separate indexes by place available in the reading rooms.

Grants of land made by the Crown were initially recorded in charter rolls in series **C 53.** You can find information about who owned a plot of land before your house was built, although they tend to be an earlier source (ending in 8 Henry VIII) and therefore less useful for a modern house historian. Later grants, along with enrolments of Crown leases and other methods of bestowing land onto individuals, were recorded on patent rolls in series **C 66,** and between 1483–1625 confirmations of previous grants were enrolled separately on confirmation rolls in series **C 56.** Patent rolls are of particular use in the Reformation period and beyond, when grants of land and property formerly belonging to monastic institutions were enrolled.

Published calendars to charter rolls exist for the entire period and are on open access. Patent rolls are also calendared for the period 1 Henry III–24 Elizabeth I, with a transcript in existence for 1201–16, and additional indexes in various Deputy Keepers Reports (DKRs). The *List and Index Society* has published later indexes for the remainder of Elizabeth's reign, and Palmer's Indexes, which also cover close rolls and other chancery series, continue the series beyond the Elizabethan period. These can now be found in the PRO index series **IND 1/17276–428** and are listed in the Catalogue of Index Volumes and Obsolete Lists and Indexes (*List and Index Society, vol.* 232).

Enrolments in the Exchequer

Although primarily a financial institution, the Exchequer served as a court of common law and equity where deeds and land transactions were also enrolled, and the house historian will find relevant records in one of three main areas.

Memoranda rolls originally developed to allow the officials of the Exchequer to make written notes about debts and financial issues. They were kept in duplicate, known as the King's Remembrancer in series **E 159** (1218–1994) and as the Lord Treasurer's Remembrancer in **E 368** (1217–1835). Enrolments of legal business, fines and conveyances developed during the sixteenth century as part of the Exchequer's equity jurisdiction, and from 1927 separate enrolment books, recording conveyances and associated plans, can be found in **E 159** alone.

Finding aids for **E 159** between 1543 and 1884 exist among the PRO's index series **IND 1/17051–79** and **1/6724–32,** the last two of which are called 'indexes to enrolments'; you will need to refer to *List and Index Society, vol.* 232, to determine which index you should consult for a particular period. Similarly, repertory rolls for **E 368** have also been transferred to the PRO's index series and provide the name of the county, a brief note of the subject of the entry, and the rotulus number on which it is found. Relevant volumes are **IND 1/6909–35, 6993–5, 7016–28** and **7031–51.** Other indexes include Tayleure's in **IND 1/16898,** which covers various dates up to the reign of Charles I (1625–49); and an index of char-ters and grants in **IND 1/17043**.

The plea rolls in **E 13** (1236–1875) are, as the name suggests, enrolments of common law pleas, often relating to land transfer and usually by private liti-gants, into the Exchequer of Pleas. Repertory rolls, which act as indexes, are in the series **E 14** and cover the periods 1412–99, 1559–1669 and 1822–30. There is also a selection of calendars in two series, one chronological and one alphabeti-cal, to 1820 on open access.

Finally, miscellaneous books of the Exchequer in **E 315** (1100–1800) cover a disparate range of material bound up in the 527 surviving volumes. A huge amount of information relating to land transactions after the Reformation is stored in these documents, including enrolled deeds and leases. An index to some of the enrolments of Crown leases in the series is in appendix 3 of DKR 49 (pp. 209–360), and there are a number of manuscript calendars and indexes on open access in the reading rooms.

Civil pleas in the court of King's Bench

Apart from dealing with Crown pleas relating to criminal issues, the court of King's Bench also heard civil pleas. Due to the documentation generated by the court, it proved a popular means of registering deeds or conveyances. Coram rege rolls exist from 1273–1702 in series **KB 27**. Lists of deeds enrolled during the reigns of Edward I and Edward II, and for 1656–1702, are in **KB 173/1**. Enrolled deeds from 1390 to 1595 and from 1649 to 1655 may be traced through the Docket Rolls (which from 1390 to 1656 are in **IND 1/1322–84**) or Docket Books (which from 1656 to 1702 are in **IND 1/6042–96**): and from Michaelmas 1595 to Hilary 1649 only, via the special Remembrance Rolls in **IND 1/1385–7**. However, these are not searchable by place and therefore will be of limited use to the house historian.

After 1702, Judgment Rolls were maintained in series **KB 122**. A repertory of deeds and wills enrolled in the Judgment Rolls down to 1805 is available, although the series is difficult to use.

For earlier enrolments, you will occasionally find details of title deeds to land in the records of the itinerant justices, also known as eyre rolls, in series **JUST 1**, with the earliest coram rege rolls located in series **KB 26**.

Court of Common Pleas

One of the most popular courts where deeds and conveyances were enrolled was the Court of Common Pleas. Civil pleas were entered onto plea rolls, which are in **CP 40** (1273–1874), which became used so frequently for a particular form of conveyancing, the common recovery, that a separate series of Recovery Rolls was created in 1583, in series **CP 43** (1583–1838); these were also used to enrol deeds. Feet of fines were also stored with the records of the Court of Common Pleas, in series **CP 25/1** and **25/2**, and along with the common recovery have been described in more detail in Chapter 4.

The plea rolls were composed of distinct sections, one of which was usually reserved for the enrolment of writs, deeds and charters. There are no indexes as such, but you can obtain rotulus numbers of particular cases from the pro-thonotaries' docket rolls in **CP 60** for the period 1509–1859.

Many means of reference survive for the recovery rolls, mainly removed to the PRO index series. **IND 1/17183–216** is a series of contemporary repertories from 1583 to 1835. From 1583 they are in the precise order in which the recoveries are arranged in the rolls, but from 1705 they are arranged alphabetically by county and then in entry order. You can use these rolls to obtain the county, the names of the parties, and the number of the rotulus on which the recovery is enrolled, although in some cases you may find additional details about the property involved in the case. A separate index to deeds enrolled in the recovery rolls between 1555 and 1629 is in **CP 73/1**, and from 1629 to 1836 in **IND 1/16943–9**.

Semi-autonomous jurisdictions

Enrolled deeds and records of conveyances can be found in similar court records for the semi-autonomous jurisdictions. The Duchy of Lancaster maintained its own Chancery, and enrolments are in the PRO series **DL 37**. In addition, many title deeds and records of legal transfers were recorded in the Cowcher of the Duchy. Records are in **DL 42**, and an index to the series exists on open access. Plea rolls for the Palatinate of Lancaster can be found in **PL 15**, where conveyances and further deeds will be located. You can use Imparlance or remembrance books in **PL 24** as a means of reference.

The Palatinate of Durham also operated a Chancery, and the records of its main administrative official, the Cursitor, are in series **DURH 3**, which includes Chancery enrolments 1333–1854, plus registers of private deeds enrolled in Chancery 1544–1616. The Cursitor's and Registrar's miscellanea in **DURH 8** also contains an enrolment book of deeds for 1879, and judgment rolls in **DURH 13** contain material similar to the plea rolls in the Courts of King's Bench and Common Pleas.

The Palatinate of Chester maintained an Exchequer, where deeds and other legal material were enrolled, which are in **CHES 2** (1307–1830), although there are large chronological gaps in this series. Three alphabetical calendars exist in DKRs 36, 37 and 39 under 'Welsh Records'. Plea Rolls for the Palatinate of Chester can be found in **CHES 29**, for which a calendar of the deeds, inquisitions and writs of dower on the rolls from Henry III to Henry VIII can be found in the appendices to DKRs 26–30. Similar material can be found in **CHES 30** as well, although the rolls for the period after 1541 have been removed to the National Library of Wales.

Crown lands

Enrolments of deeds relating to Crown lands are usually to be found among the records of the offices and government departments responsible for managing the Crown estates. The most important areas in which to look will be **LR 1** and **LRRO 13–18, 20** and **25; LRRO 64** and **66** are indexes to enrolments.

5.5   Searching for a sale or property transfer

Unless you are in possession of title deeds that provide details of when a sale occurred, it can be difficult to track down how and when a property changed hands. However, there are various areas where you might start to look for property transfers, or even details of leases to tenants.

Local newspapers are probably one of the best places to begin searching for details. You will find that more and more papers survive from the eighteenth century onwards, and they usually carry details or notices that advertise property for sale, rent or lease. Searching the papers may be a time-consuming task, as there are no internal indexes. Some CROs have compiled their own indexes to names, events and places, but although they act as a good starting place, they are rarely complete. However, where advertisements do survive, you are likely to find a detailed description of your house, plus the name of the sale agent or vendor. It is then possible to approximate a date of sale, and then search for evidence for the method of transfer. You could also try the British Newspaper Library, Colindale.

Alternatively, sale catalogues and estate agents' prospectuses can be discovered among the deposited business records of the relevant company. These will also provide you with a rough date of the sale, and possibly information about the interior of the property. The PRO has a collection of estate agents' sale catalogues among records deposited as evidence with the Supreme Court of Judicature in series **J 46**. These are arranged by place and can be searched on PROCAT.

Documents such as electoral registers, census and rate books can also be consulted to determine a change of ownership or occupancy, as they can exist in a series for many years. These are described in more detail in Chapter 9. The valuation records of c.1910 might also be of use, as the Field Books can contain details of recent sales, and some books are known to record subsequent sales.

5.6   Scotland and Ireland

Although the main focus of this chapter has been on enrolled deeds and land transfers in England and Wales, there are different sources and methods of land transfer for Scotland and Northern Ireland as well. Furthermore, deeds for property in Wales can also be found at regional archives, and at the NLW.

Land transfers and registration in Scotland generated documents different from those in England. An important means of transfer of ownership of a piece of land or building was via sasines. A register of sasines exists from 1617 onwards, arranged in counties and by royal burgh; and detailed transcripts known as abridgements begin in 1781. The records are stored at the NAS in Edinburgh, where you can obtain further information about the nature of the records and the evidence for house history that they contain. The NAS also holds registers for deeds in the various courts, such as the Register of Deeds in the Court of Sessions known as the Books of Council and Session (NAS series **RD**, from 1554), the Sheriff Courts (NAS series **SC**, generally from the nineteenth century onwards), Royal Burgh Courts (NAS series **B** for varying dates), Commissary Court (NAS series **CC**), and Local Courts (NAS series **RH 11**, before 1748).

The Irish government passed an act setting up the Irish Registry of Deeds in 1708, which is located at the National Archives in Dublin. In addition, PRONI holds microfilm records in **MIC.7**. The registry contains memorials that are much more detailed than those in England and usually comprise a complete copy or a fairly full abstract of a document. Furthermore, copies of the memorials known as Transcript Books are also available on microfilm, from 1708–1929, in **MIC.311**. Indexes to these series also exist, and after 1832 the townland or street, the county, city or town, and the barony or parish in which the lands are situated are given.

6 Manorial and estate records

6.1 Introduction

The aim of this chapter is to introduce some of the records that were generated by one of the oldest units of land in England and Wales – the manor. The PRO has a wide collection of manorial material for manors that were already in Crown hands, or had fallen into the hands of the Crown through forfeiture, for example. In general, manorial records will be of enormous importance if your property was built on copyhold land, as the manorial court had sole responsibility for the transfer of copyhold land between individuals until the mid nineteenth century.

The Crown was also the largest landowner in England and Wales, and generated administrative records for its many estates that were retained by a wide range of government departments, all of which can yield important information for the house historian. Records generated by private estate owners are also discussed, although the PRO is not going to be the best place to start looking for relevant material.

6.1.1 Manorial administration

We have seen in Chapter 4 how land law evolved after the Norman Conquest, and that the manor was the basic unit of land. It was also stated that manors were not always compact geographical entities, and were often united only by the social and economic ties that bound each individual to the lord of the manor. Collectively these social and economic ties – the terms of tenure, various bonds of obligation and general rules of the manor – were known as the customs of the manor, and would vary according to each manor and region. It is, therefore, worth making sure that you know which manor your property is located in before you begin your research.

The administration of the rules and regulations of the manor generated many types of record. Some will be of greater use to the house historian than others.

The most informative series are the official records of the manorial court, where the lord of the manor, through his appointed deputy, the steward, regulated tenants' entry into land and collected revenue generated by the feudal ties. These records are described in some detail, along with other documents generated by the day to day running of the manor, such as rentals, surveys and accounts. Survival of manorial records can be patchy, and advice about where to start looking is also provided, although if you are very lucky you may find records for some manors that stretch back from the twentieth century to the thirteenth century or earlier. It should also be noted that some parts of England and Wales were not subject to the 'feudal' system, and thus manorial records would not have been created.

6.1.2   Estate records

In addition, manorial documents formed part of larger collections of documents generated by private estate management, of which the manor may have formed an important constituent part. Aside from the court rolls, estate owners produced a variety of other documentary sources to assist them with the management of their financial arrangements. It is important to remember that these were private documents created for a private purpose. Sometimes this material has been deposited in the public domain, usually the relevant CRO. However, estate owners sometimes lived many miles from the property they possessed, in which case material would be deposited in another CRO. There is no guarantee at all that these family papers have been made public, or they may be stored in private archives. In either instance, you should exercise extreme caution and diplomacy if requesting access – after all, how would you feel if a stranger asked to look through your family's private records?

One of the largest landowners in the UK was the monarchy, owning vast swathes of land in its own right and often taking control of private estates. The PRO is the natural place of deposit for records relating to the administration of Crown lands, as well as areas outside normal county jurisdiction, such as the Duchy of Lancaster and the Palatinates of Chester, Durham and Lancaster.

6.1.3   Searching for houses in manorial records

The principal house in the manor was the lord's house, known as the capital messuage. In theory there was one per manor (the 'manor house'); but if a lord held more than one manor as part of a larger estate, he would have required only one capital messuage at his main place of residence, so there may not even have been a 'manor house' in existence. It is also important to remember that it was the land on which a house was built that was usually recorded in the manorial records; and most plots of land did not have property built on them. Where houses are listed, you will find the dwellings of the main tenants described as messuages or tenements, which tended to be more substantial buildings that can often form the basis of modern property. At the lower end of the social scale, cottages were usually inhabited by the poorer members of the manor and are less likely to have survived in their original form.

A final note – many manorial documents were written in the official language of government, which prior to 1733 was Latin, so you may need to take a bit of time to interpret and translate the material, and you will also need to become accustomed to the different handwriting of the stewards who compiled the records. No matter how difficult the material may appear to be, it is worth sticking to your task, as manorial records can be a wonderfully rich source for house history, often providing a sequential link for many generations.

6.2   Manorial tenants

The following are the main forms of tenure by which an individual could hold land in a manor. It is important to determine which of these would have been applicable to your property, as each form generated different records.

6.2.1   Freehold tenancy

As we have seen, land held by a tenant on fixed terms was known as 'freehold'. In effect, this land could be disposed of without recourse to the lord of the manor, although freehold property could not be devised by terms of a will until restrictions were eased under the provisions of the Statute of Wills in 1540, the Tenures Abolition Act of 1660 and the Statute of Frauds in 1677. Freehold tenants were expected to attend the manorial court, where they were often enrolled as jurors. Furthermore, they were liable to pay certain dues to the lord. These included a heriot payable on the death of the tenant, and a relief when an heir or purchaser of land wished to enter into possession of the land. As rents were fixed and the lord had minimal involvement in land or property transfers, freeholders rarely appear in the 'official' records of the manor, so you will be less likely to find details of property transactions. Instead, you should look in the areas described in Chapter 4.

6.2.2   Copyhold tenancy

More accurately described as customary tenants, copyhold tenants formed the majority of manorial tenants and held their land under the terms of the prevalent customs of the manor. In return for land, the customary tenant was required to work for a fixed number of days on the lord's land. However, in contrast to freeholders, the nature of work was not fixed in advance, and would be decided by the lord's steward only when the appropriate moment arrived.

The lord of the manor regulated entry into copyhold land through the manorial court, which produced a record of its business known as a court roll. This is where the origin of the name 'copyhold' lies, as the recipient of land was also given a copy of the relevant court roll entry as proof of title. Descent of land varied from manor to manor, depending on local customs, but there were two main types.

Land held by 'customary holders of inheritance' passed on the death of the tenant to an heir decided by the custom of the manor. There were various types of inheritance, such as primogeniture, partible inheritance or gavelkind (which was mainly found in Kent and parts of Wales). Alternatively, land held by customary tenants for life received only a life interest in the property. On the expiration of the interest, the land reverted to the lord. He was free to re-grant it to anyone he liked, although it was often the heir of the original tenant. Some manors accepted tenants for succeeding lives, a typical example being successive life interests for the tenant, his wife and one of his children. Copyhold land could be sold, but until 1815 was not regarded as inheritable and so could not be devised by will.

Copyholders were also required to pay a heriot, plus an entry fine when entering into a property. Default of payment could, and often did, result in loss of land. Other causes for default include the failure to repair the property or keep it in a good state, and such entries in the court rolls can often provide the house historian with crucial evidence about the date of rebuilds or extensions to a property.

6.2.3   Leasehold tenancy

Demesne land was the personal property of the lord of the manor, but it was frequently leased out to tenants at variable rates of rent, as it was not subject to the customs of the manor in the way copyhold land was. Furthermore, new land brought into cultivation – known as extents – was also leased out. Freeholders and copyholders alike were able to take advantage of leased land, while the lord benefited through the flexibility of a system that allowed him to review terms and conditions and set the lengths of the leases. You are more likely to find details of leases for demesne land amongst the private estate papers of the lord of the manor, or the steward who administered the land on his behalf. However, you may find some enrolments on the court rolls.

6.2.4   Related forms of tenancy

At the bottom level of society were the tenants at will, or cottars, who worked as labourers on the lord's land and held a cottage with a small strip of land or garden on which to cultivate food crops. They often occupied the waste of the manor, namely the land that was not under cultivation by any of the other tenants. They also rarely appear in official court records, unless they were subsequently charged rent to stay on the manorial waste.

Furthermore, tenants were allowed to sub-let their land, creating a situation whereby an official tenant might not be the actual occupier of a house or plot of land. However, the period of the sub-lease could only be 'pur autre vie', and would end with the death of the original tenant. Sometimes, 'uses' were employed to transfer land that created fictional legal tenants while the land was actually in the possession of other individuals. It is something that you will have to bear in mind if you do find names of individuals connected with your house in manorial documents, and you will probably need to consult corroborating sources, such as records of occupancy, described in Chapter 9.

6.3   Records of the manorial courts

6.3.1   Manorial courts

There were essentially two types of manorial court. The view of frankpledge and court leet were held twice a year to try minor offences and inspect tithings, which were groups of ten men who had mutual responsibility for their good behaviour. However, the most important type of manorial court was the court baron. The court was held on a regular basis to conduct and regulate the routine business of the manor, and court rolls are the written record of this process. The business varied from session to session, but generally included financial punishments for offences against the manorial rules; issues relating to the administration of the manor; the deaths of tenants and changes of occupancy since the last court meeting; and surrenders of land and admission of new copyhold tenants according to the custom of the manor. The lord of the manor's appointed steward or deputy officiated at the sessions. All free tenants were required to attend, and usually acted as jurors for the court. Customary tenants were also required to attend, and were amerced (penalised) if they failed to do so without paying an essoin (excuse).

6.3.2   Court rolls

If your property was originally held as copyhold, then you can start your research within the manorial court rolls (*see* **Figures 13–15**), which can be the

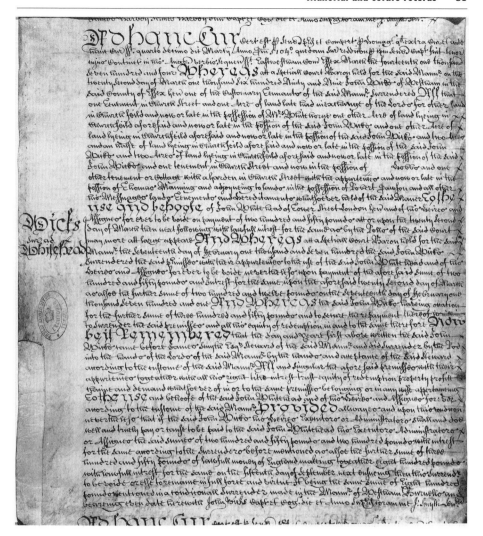

Figure 13 An extract from the court roll of the manor of East Ham, 1704. The entry relates to the discharge of a mortgage on a property in Church Street, originally made in 1639, worth £800. (SC 2/172/20)

most useful series of documents available to the house historian. These are the written record of the court baron, and usually follow a standard format. The heading of the roll details the type of court, the names of the manor, lord and steward, plus the date of the session in progress. The names of the jurors will be provided, which can give an indication of who the freehold tenants of the manor were. Customary tenants who paid an essoin not to attend the court are also listed.

The first section of the roll concerned presentments of all matters that the

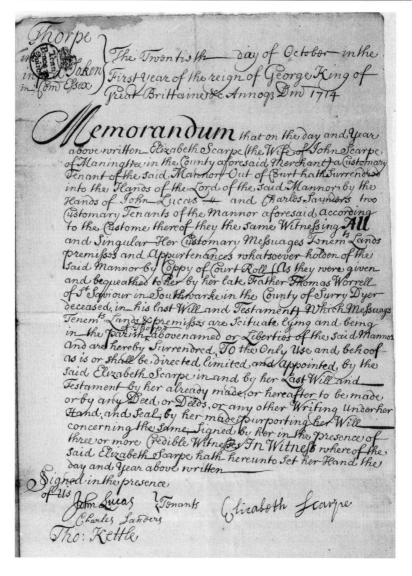

Figure 14 Part of the title deeds for a property in Thorp-le-Soken, Essex, dated 20 October 1714. It is a memorandum from the manorial court that the copyhold property has been surrendered to the use of the possessor's will, so that it can be legally devised. (C 103/12/1)

court would subsequently deal with. These were usually minor matters, such as disputes between tenants, but will occasionally feature repairs to property ordered by the lord of the manor, and references to property can be made in boundary disputes.

However, the most important section of the court rolls concerns the adminis-

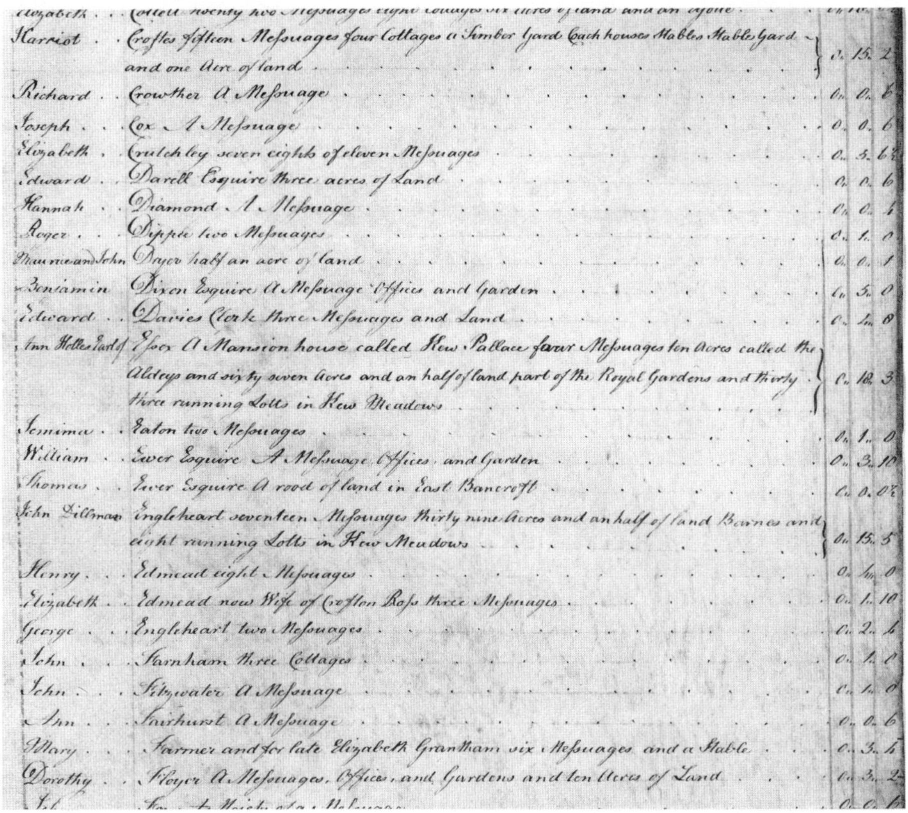

Elizabeth . . . Collett twenty two Messuages eight Cottages six acres of land and an eyote . . . . 0. 15.

Harriot . . . Crofts fifteen Messuages four Cottages a Timber Yard Coach house, Stables Stable Yard and one Acre of land 0. 15. 2

Richard . . . Crowther A Messuage 0. 0. 6

Joseph . . . Cox A Messuage 0. 0. 6

Elizabeth . . Crutchley seven eights of eleven Messuages . . . 0. 5. 6½

Edward . . . Darell Esquire three acres of Land 0. 0. 6

Hannah . . . Diamond A Messuage 0. 0. 4

Roger . . . Dipple two Messuages 0. 1. 0

Thomas and John Dyer half an acre of land 0. 0. 1

Benjamin . . Dixon Esquire A Messuage Offices and Garden . . 0. 5. 0

Edward . . . Davies Clerk three Messuages and Land 0. 1. 0

Ann Holles Lady of ? for A Mansion house called Kew Pallace four Messuages ten Acres called the Aldeys and sixty seven acres and an half of land part of the Royal Gardens and thirty three running Lotts in Kew Meadows 0. 12. 3

Jemima . . . Eaton two Messuages 0. 1. 0

William . . . Ewer Esquire A Messuage Offices and Garden . . 0. 3. 10

Thomas . . . Ewer Esquire A rood of land in East Bancroft . . 0. 0. 0¾

John Dillman Engleheart seventeen Messuages thirty nine Acres and an half of land Barnes and eight running Lotts in Kew Meadows 0. 15. 5

Henry . . . Edmead eight Messuages 0. 4. 0

Elizabeth . . Edmead now Wife of Crofton Ross three Messuages . 0. 1. 10

George . . . Engleheart two Messuages 0. 2. 6

John . . . Farnham three Cottages 0. 1. 0

John . . . Fitzwater A Messuage 0. 1. 0

Ann . . . Fairhurst A Messuage 0. 0. 6

Mary . . . Farmer and for late Elizabeth Grantham six Messuages and a Stable 0. 3. 6

Dorothy . . . Floyer A Messuages Offices and Gardens and ten Acres of Land 0. 3. 2

Figure 15 An extract from the steward's rental for the manor of Richmond (alias West Sheen), Surrey, from 1786. The names of the tenants are provided, with a brief description of the property for which they were liable. (SC 11/1011)

tration of the copyhold land. Land transactions concerning copyhold property were permissible only with the consent of the lord of the manor through the jurisdiction of the court. All new copyhold tenants were required to undergo a process of entry known as admission and surrender. First, the death of the old tenant would be announced in court and recorded in the court roll. Technically the land was 'surrendered' back to the lord, and the heir would then seek 'admission' to the property. A ceremony would be conducted in court whereby the tenant would grasp an official rod in the possession of the steward to mark his formal admittance to the property, and a record of the admittance would then be made in the court roll. A copy of the entry was provided to the tenant as proof of title. The entry usually contained a description of the property or piece of land in question, the name of the deceased tenant, the relationship with the new tenant, plus details of any longer terms of lives that might be involved. The property is usually referred to with reference to property on either side, or by the names of previous owners, although specific property names are occasionally provided.

Yet it is important to remember that the tenant might not be the occupier of a property. Tenants often leased their property, but required the permission of the lord first, and a written record is provided in the court rolls. Sales of customary land grew increasingly common, and were also recorded in the roll as an admission and surrender, the only difference being that the tenant was still alive.

Customary tenants increasingly followed the practice of freeholders by taking out mortgages on their property to raise loans, and these were entered into the court rolls. The practice was known as making a conditional surrender, as the tenant would surrender the property at court. The terms of the mortgage would then be entered onto the roll, so that if the mortgage was not repaid within the specified period then the tenant would default the property to the mortgage provider, who would become the new tenant and therefore be admitted. However, if the mortgage was paid in full, then the payment was recorded on the roll and the conditional surrender would be declared void.

'Surrenders to the uses of a will' was a device used to bypass the descent of land through the customs of the manor. The land was surrendered to the court, and then the use, in this case defined by the terms of the tenant's will, was recorded in the court roll to be honoured on the death of the original tenant. This method of transfer became increasingly popular following a sale of copyhold land, to ensure that the purchaser retained the right to pass the land to his heirs without the restriction of the customs of the manor.

Many court rolls contain internal alphabetical indexes to admissions and surrenders, which will be of use if you already know the name of a tenant who possessed your property. These become more common in later court rolls, and in addition separate index books, or even registers of admissions and surrenders, sometimes survive. Where they do, they can provide the date of the previous admission, and can often instigate a chain search back to the earliest surviving court roll or book.

6.3.3   Related records produced at the manorial court

In addition to the official court rolls, the steward created subsidiary documents to assist him with his duties. Minute books and draft court rolls usually contain notes taken during the court sessions, and provide details of admissions and surrender. As they were working documents, they were hastily written and contain many abbreviations, and as such they can be difficult to interpret. However, they serve as a useful substitute where official court rolls have not survived.

Estreat rolls contain records of amercements and fines made during the course of a court session. These can include financial penalties for not repairing houses, as well as details of entry fines for new tenants. You will usually find lists of names of the tenants who were due to pay, plus a note of the reason why they owed money.

Suit rolls and call books contain the names of all tenants who owed suit to the court, and in effect doubled up as court attendance registers. Although they will not contain details of property as such, they were amended and dated on the death of tenants and can serve as a useful means of reference to the court rolls themselves when trying to trace property descent.

6.3.4 Locating the records

The majority of court rolls and related records will be found in the relevant CRO. The obvious place to start looking will be at the CRO of the county in which the manor is located, but this will not always be the case where the lord of the manor was not a local resident. To assist researchers to find court rolls, the Manorial Documents Register (MDR) was established from 1926 with the sole aim of listing the location of such records in the public domain and private hands. The MDR is now maintained by the Royal Commission for Historical Manuscripts (HMC), and is located at the National Register of Archives (NRA). Furthermore, the list for some counties is now available on the Internet via the HMC website. At present, the relevant areas covered are Hampshire and the Isle of Wight, all three Yorkshire Ridings, and all counties within Wales. Work on Norfolk has begun, and plans for other areas are in hand.

Secondary sources such as the *VCH* may provide clues as to the whereabouts of manorial material, and often give detailed descents of manors that can help you to locate relevant archives or collections. You may also like to examine the records at the PRO in **HMC 5/6–8** that provide lists of owners of manors in 1925, or try to track down the last known steward as registered at the HMC.

Court rolls at the PRO are to be found in several series. There is a union index to manors in **SC 2**; and for properties within the remit of the Duchy of Lancaster there is **DL 30**, which is published as *Lists and Indexes VI*. There is also a separate union index covering (mostly) Crown manors in **ADM 74; C 104–9, 111–16 and 171; CRES 5; DL 30/351–587; E 140; F 14; J 90; PRO 30/26; TS 19; SC 2/252–350 and 2/506–92; LR 3 and 11; and MAF 5**. In addition, you will find references to material in **E 315; DURH 3; WARD 2; E 36; SP 2, 14, 16, 17, 23 and 28; LR 11; DL 42; SC 6 and 12; E 137; C 54; and E 106**.

6.3.5 Enfranchisement of copyhold tenants

By the nineteenth century, the conversion of land tenure from copyhold to lease-hold meant that less land was subject to the customs of the manor, making the process of admissions and surrender increasingly obsolete. Where the practice still existed, changing ways of life, increasing urbanization and more tenants who resided many miles from the manor itself meant it was inconvenient to perform the ritual admission via a court and to attend sessions that were increasingly irrelevant. In consequence, the enfranchisement of copyhold land was introduced in 1841.

Enfranchisement is the term used to describe the legal conversion of copyhold land to freehold. The process was started at the request of either the lord or tenant, but once it had been initiated the other party was required to give his or her consent; compensation for loss of manorial income was granted to the lord, and where disputes arose the Ministry of Agriculture and Fisheries became involved as an arbitrator. The 1922 and 1925 Law of Property Acts abolished all copyhold tenure, and all outstanding copyhold land was made freehold from 1 January 1926.

The records of enfranchisement are now stored at the PRO in the archives of the Ministry of Agriculture and Fisheries. Voluntary agreements and awards for compulsory enfranchisement from 1841–1925 are in series **MAF 9**. The records are arranged in county order, and thereafter by the name of the manor, and you will obtain the date of the award and the name of the tenant, plus evidence of title supplied from the court rolls by the lords from 1900; earlier evidences are in series **MAF 20**. Correspondence and papers can be found in **MAF 48**, while registers to enfranchisement records relating to **MAF 9** are in **MAF 76**. It will also be worth investigating the records in **MAF 13** and **27**, which contain agreements and certificates of compensation.

6.4   Related manorial records

Aside from the records generated by the manorial courts, which tend to be of most use if your property was copyhold, there is a wealth of related material that can provide useful data for all forms of manorial tenure. The most common areas that will be of use to the house historian are described below.

6.4.1   Manorial surveys

Various subsidiary documents were created to assist the steward with the administration of the manor, in particular to keep track of who owed manorial dues to the lord. Some of these can provide supplementary information for the house historian, even though properties themselves may not feature.

One of the most important types of manorial survey was the extent. This typically listed all the tenants for the manor, regardless of tenure, which meant that freeholders and leaseholders were recorded, as well as the copyhold tenants

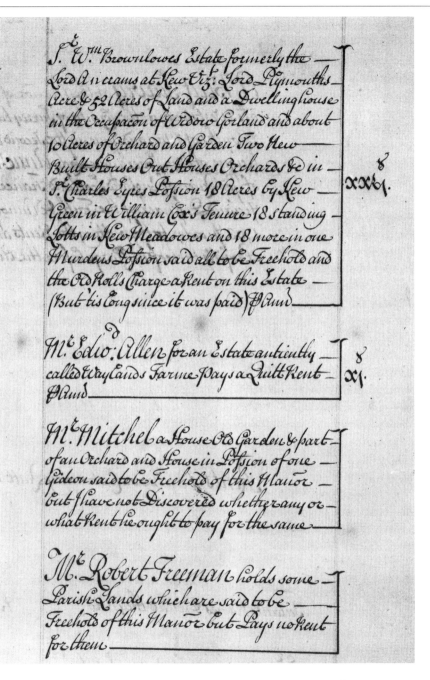

Figure 16 An extract from a survey of the manor of Richmond, Surrey, c.1703–4. A full description of each property is provided, along with a note about the type of manorial holding (freehold or customary) and the amount of rent due. (LR 2/226)

who appeared in the court rolls. The documents will typically provide the date that the extent was made, and then describe all land and its rent value to the lord, assigning the type of land to the name of a tenant, with a brief description of the property. However, extents were created only at the whim of the lord of the manor, usually when a manor changed hands. They became less popular by the fifteenth century, and were gradually replaced by rentals, which tended to be less detailed but still covered all types of manorial tenants. They were created on a far more regular basis, and were often annotated with details of deaths or changes of occupancy. You will find an increasing number of quit-rents included in the rental relating to labour services that had been commuted to monetary payments. These were the most prevalent form of survey until the sixteenth and early seventeenth centuries. You may also encounter custumals, which provided details of the customs of the manor. These may be of use if you are researching any customary requirements to maintain a house built on a plot of land, and you will also be able to identify the precise terms by which the tenants held their property.

Later surveys from the sixteenth century onwards (*see* **Figure 16**) took on new and varied forms, and included far greater detail than earlier list-based surveys. They were more formal, often the product of special manorial courts of survey, and conducted by survey commissioners. Tenants would be asked a series of questions so that the commissioners could compile a detailed assessment that commonly included a description of the boundaries of the manor; the customs of the manor; and a rent roll or rental. Boundary surveys can refer to property that lay on the outskirts of the manor, as natural features and fixed items such as large tenements were used as points of reference for the surveyors. However, the rent rolls are the most important section for the house historian. As with the earlier forms of survey, the rent roll will list all tenants who held property in the manor, plus a note of the rent they paid. Houses are commonly featured in the rent rolls, with any house names that might have been given, and outbuildings are sometimes listed too; although you are unlikely to find a detailed description or a location, unless it is with reference to neighbouring properties.

Maps were often produced to accompany survey documents. These provided a visual aid to the lord of the manor, and often contained a separate reference book that would list all the tenants for each holding. This can be an invaluable source, as not only are the properties depicted for a given date, but also they are linked specifically to the names of the tenants that were responsible for them. However, the survival rate of these associated reference books is not good, and the location of maps can be very diverse. They are usually found among CRO cartographic collections, or have passed into private hands and thus appear in some unlikely places, such on the walls of offices or private houses.

Records of manorial rentals and surveys in the PRO have been listed in a union index on open access entitled *Lists and Indexes XXV*. This includes material found in the following series: **SC 11** and **12**; **DL 29** and **42**; **SP 10–18** and **46**; **E 36**, **142**, **164**, **315** and **317**; and **LR 2**. A key sheet in the front allows you to convert entries to a PRO series reference. In addition, there is material in **ADM 79**, **C 47/37**, **CRES 34**, **35** and **39**, **F 17**, **LR 13** and **LRRO 12**, and you will need to search the series lists or undertake a key word search on PROCAT to identify relevant material. Maps are scattered across a wide range of series, and the extracted map catalogue is the best place to begin your research. Two distinct series are **DL 31** and **LRRO 1**. However, as with court rolls, you should probably expect to find the bulk of rentals, surveys and maps at the relevant CRO.

6.4.2 Manorial accounts

In addition to surveys, the records generated by financial transactions can contain information about individual properties. Stewards' account books (*see* **Figure 17**) are a good place to begin looking, as they record money owed in rent and can contain information about property as well, especially if expenditure has been ordered on behalf of the lord. The records are arranged according to the 'charge and discharge' system, which first lists all revenue accruing to the property and then details expenses and payments made from this revenue. The balance was the amount paid to the lord of the manor. Collectively, these records are known as ministers and receivers accounts. Other material that can be of use will include rent-rolls or rentals, not to be confused with the survey version, which provide lists of tenants who had paid money to the lord, as opposed to how much they owed.

Ministers and receivers accounts at the PRO are listed in *Lists and Indexes V, VIII* and *XXXIV*, and *Supplementary Series II*. Most of the records are in series **SC 6** and **DL 29**, although records in **E 315** and **36** are covered as well. Other records can be identified in series **LR 7–9**. Much of this material relates to Crown lands, and the bulk of ministers and receivers accounts for private manors will be in the relevant CRO.

6.4.3 Private estate records

Entire manors may once have formed part of far larger estates, and in addition to the sources listed above, documents relating to the administration of private estates can yield even more information on individual properties. As most of this was once the personal property of the estate owner, the deposit of relevant material into the public domain depends entirely on chance; but where family estate papers do survive, they can provide supplementary evidence. Building accounts, correspondence and personal papers can contain crucial clues about

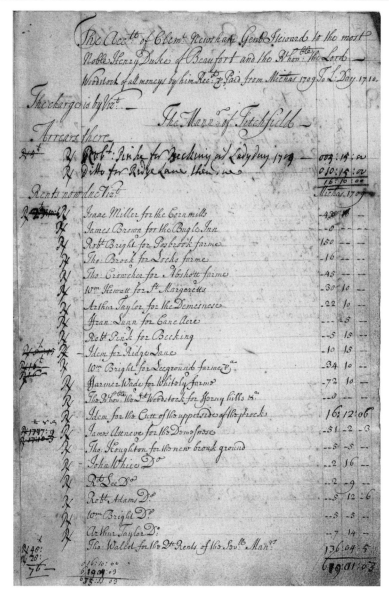

Figure 17 An extract from Clement Newham's book of accounts for the period 1709–10. The volume was compiled as part of his role as the steward for the Duke of Beaufort and Lord Woodstock, who enjoyed joint ownership of the manor of Titchfield. (C 108/45)

the construction of estate property, and separate rent and payment books that survived can add to our knowledge of who resided in the property. The PRO is not the best place to start looking for such material, although surviving estate papers can be found listed under the names of previous owners. In particular, the series with the prefix **PRO** contains private documents deposited by gift, or acquired due to their national importance, many of which relate to the administration of private estates. Other collections, including abstracts of title, can be found among court exhibit series, described in sections 5.3.3 and 8.6; a particularly rich series is **C 115**, the Duchess of Norfolk's Deeds, which contain a huge array of correspondence, accounts, deeds and manorial material. You can also obtain information about private property descent from wills and death duty registers, which are described in the next chapter.

When looking for estate papers, it is important to bear in mind that they are likely to be deposited in the CRO of the principal seat of the family, and so you may find related material in surprisingly distant archives. The case study in Chapter 15 clearly demonstrates this, as estate papers for the manor in question are located in the Huntington Library at San Marino, California, USA.

6.5   Records of the Crown estates

One of the largest landowners in England and Wales was the monarchy which, just like any private estate owner, generated administrative records as part of the management of its lands and manors. These can be a rich source of information for houses that were originally built on the Crown's extensive estates. The survival of records tends to be far greater than for most private estates, as separate government departments were created to assist with the management, in particular relating to the financial aspects. Consequently, there are many more places in which to start your research.

In addition to the published finding aids for court rolls, rentals and surveys and ministers and receivers accounts listed above, records of Crown estate management (*see* **Figure 18**, and also **Figure 26** on p. 164) are to be found in three main areas – the Crown Estates Office (**CRES**), the Office of Auditors of Land Revenue (**LR**) and the Office of Land Revenue Records and Enrolments (**LRRO**). The most important series are **CRES 2, 5, 6, 7, 34, 35, 39, 40, 45, 49** and **60**; **LR 1–3, 6–9** and **11–13**; and **LRRO 1–3, 5, 11, 12, 27** and **67**. Most will contain leases, papers and correspondence, of which many will relate to domestic houses and buildings. If you are unsure whether your property once formed part of a Crown estate, then you can try looking at **CRES 2/1613**, which includes a list of Crown manors in 1827; and **CRES 60** contains annual reports from all bodies that administered Crown estates between 1797 and 1942.

In addition to the administrative records listed above, certain Exchequer

Claims

...32...

No. of Claims as delivered.	In what Township or place.	Names of Proprietors.	Names of Occupiers.	No. of Acres claimed for.	Observations.
313	Willington	John Egerton	Joseph Reece	153　0　23	
	do.	do.	do.	33　2　4	
178	Woodhouses	Daniel Ashley			
204	do.	John Wrench	Elizabeth Gregory		
253	do.	Thomas Ashton	Samuel Yarwood	65　0　0	
255	do.	William Antwis	See this Claim in Frodsham Township		
271	do.	Earl Cholmondeley	Daniel Ashley	37　1　4	
		do.	Samuel Mason	20　2　39	
		do.	William Sandbach	0　1　0	
		do.	George Wilbraham	83　3　37	
284	do.	John Edwards, and others	Thomas Norcross	23　0　0	
			Mary Jones	1　0　0	
29	On the Forest	George Rutter And right of Warren on 287 Acres	John Lewis	8　3　32	Called the Forest House.
31	do.	Samuel Wilkinson And right of Warren on 700 Acres	Samuel Wilkinson	23　0　0	Called Wilkinson's Lodge.
32	do.	George Pugh And right of Warren on 300 Acres	George Pugh	28　2　0	
34	do.	Joseph Junion, Claims the right of keeping 60 Sheep and 25 Lambs			
72	do.	John Winpenny, ditto ditto ditto 60 Sheep			
	do.		For Common Land	3　0　0	
108	do.	Mary Hornby And right of Warren on 1,270 Acres and 24 Perches	John Wright	73　2　32	Called Massey's Lodge, and Massey's Meadow,
117	do.	Samuel Hornby And right of Warren on 528 Acres and 2 Roods	John Bull	128　3　0	Called Hornby's Lodge
	do.	John Lewis, Claims the right of keeping 600 Acres, and the right of keeping 300 Sheep			
164	do.	Robert Watson	Robert Watson, for Common Land }	2　0　0	
276	do.	John Arden	For Birkets Pool		
280	do.	do.	John Merrick for the Old Pale Lodge or the Chamber		
	do.	do.	William Brock for Eddisbury Lodge		
		do.	John Burgess for Utkinton, or High Billinge Office		
	do.	do.	George Pugh for New Pale Lodge		
		do.	Samuel Hornby for Hornby's Lodge		
	do.	do.	Peter Massey for Massey's Lodge		
		do.	George Rutter for Clotton Office, or Walk		
		do.	James Wright for Kelsall Walk, or Office		
		Ditto, for Young's Office and Janion's Office.			
		Ditto, for all the Conies and Pasturage of Conies, and Sheep, and for all Fishing, and the Titles of Chief Forester, Bowbearer and Forest Bailiff.			

ALL Persons are desired to take Notice, that a more particular Abstract of these Claims is left at the Swan Inn, in Tarporley, and another at the Bear's Paw, in Frodsham, for the inspection of all persons interested, their respective Agents or Attornies, and the Original Claims may be seen at the Office of Messrs. Lecke and Potts, in Chester, and that by the said Act, the Commissioners are empowered to settle, assess, and award such Costs, as they shall think reasonable to be paid, to the Party or Parties in whose favor any determination shall be made, by the Persons whose Claim or objection shall be disallowed or overruled, or against whom the said Commissioners shall determine.

ROBERT HARVEY,　}Commissioners.
JOSEPH FENNA,　}

Chester, 8th March, 1813.

Chester, printed by J. Fletcher.

Figure 18 A statement of claim from a bundle of papers relating to the enclosure of Delamere Forest, Cheshire, c.1796–1819. The forest formed part of the Crown estates, and was administered by the Office of Woods, Forests and Land Revenues. The department kept files on other administrative matters relating to Delamere Forest, such as abstracts of title, leases of lands and even the erection of workers' cottages. (CRES 2/127)

Table 6.1 Manorial records of semi-autonomous jurisdictions

Jurisdiction	Material
Palatinate of Durham	**DURH 3** court rolls **DURH 20** estreats, ministers accounts and rentals
Duchy of Lancaster	**DL 30, 42** and **49** court rolls **DL 29** ministers accounts **DL 29** and **42–4** rentals and surveys **DL 31** maps **DL 28** various accounts **DL 32** parliamentary surveys **DL 41** miscellanea **DL 50** estreats

series will also contain records of forfeitures of land to the Crown, such as leases, deeds and manorial material generated in the aftermath of the dissolution of the monasteries in the Augmentation Office. Furthermore, the English Civil War also saw widespread forfeiture, this time from the Crown and its supporters to the new Parliamentary regime. The records generated by these events are described in more detail in Chapter 11. Other areas worth investigating include the **FEC** series, relating to forfeited estates, while **WO 32/21803** contains a list of manors and deeds dated 1951 where the War Office had obtained manorial interests.

6.6   Records of semi-autonomous jurisdictions

Distinct series of manorial and estate records at the PRO have been created for the Palatinate of Durham and the Duchy of Lancaster, and are summarised in Table 6.1.

6.7   Scotland and Ireland

Scotland and Ireland developed a different system of landholding, and the best place to begin your research will be to contact the relevant national archives – NAS and PRONI. A brief summary of the type of material you will encounter is presented below.

In Scotland, the feudal system took a form different from that in England. 'Retours', or services of heirs, were used to pass land from one individual to the next, and can be found in a variety of places. Retours for superior subjects, the equivalent to the English tenant-in-chief, were recorded in Chancery and can be searched from 1530. Further down the manorial chain, lower vassals were granted a simpler 'precept of clare constat', that tend to be deposited in private or estate papers. From 1700, there are printed indexes to services of heirs, and some printed abridgements are available.

Legal challenges to this system tended to end up in the Court of Chancery and verdicts are recorded in the NAS series **C 22** and **C 28**. The inquisitions themselves can appear before sheriffs or burgh courts and, between 1821–47, can also be traced in NAS series **C 27** if they appeared before the court of the Edinburgh sheriff on commission. From 1847, all inquest papers appear in NAS series **C 29**. In addition, records of large estates can be found in NAS series **GD**, to which there are several name and place indexes available. This is where you may pick up account books and rent details similar to the material for England and Wales. Further estate material will be deposited in the relevant regional archive.

PRONI has a wide collection of landed estate records, and a guide to the holdings is available, arranged by the name of the estate; an index to landholders' names is also available. You will find rent rolls, rent ledgers, leases, wage books, maps and land agents' notebooks among the records. There are also records generated under the Encumbered Estates Acts of 1848 and 1849 that provide details of tenants and their houses through Encumbered Estates Rentals in PRONI series **D.1201**.

7 Records of property inheritance

7.1 Introduction

Chapters 4–6 have dealt with transfers of freehold conveyance, title deeds and copyhold land within the manorial system. Another important method of passing property, either within a family or alienating it to a stranger, was by making a legacy in a will. Similarly, death duty registers can also provide useful information about property descent, especially where the valuation of the estate was concerned. These sources are described below, and you will find them easier to search if you know the name of the owner, and a rough idea of the date of his decease. Further reading on the subject is suggested in **Useful publications**.

7.2 Property transfers in wills and administrations

7.2.1 The legality of bequests in wills

Legacies in wills that bequeathed property can be one of the most important ways of tracking the movement of property, and supplement legal sources for the transfer of land from one person to the next. However, there were restrictions on the type of property that could be transferred in a will – normally only the personal estate (personalty) of the deceased, such as cash, possessions and leases of property, could be devised, and freehold land was thus excluded as realty, along with the buildings and houses constructed upon it. For a long time copyhold was also excluded on the grounds that it was not inheritable under the terms of tenure described in the previous chapter.

To bypass this handicap, the 'use' was employed by a landholder to establish trustees, who held the legal title to the land while permitting the landholder to enjoy the profits. As uses were considered personalty, the landholder could direct the trustees in his will to hold the land on behalf of another after his death, such as a widow, younger son or daughter.

The Statute of Uses in 1535 closed this loophole, but also prevented devises by wills. This proved so unpopular that in 1540 the Statute of Wills was passed to allow the limited devise of freehold land held in fee simple via a will. The abolition of military tenure by the Tenures Abolition Act in 1660 removed the last restrictions on what could be devised, and thereafter all freehold land held in fee simple could be devised. The 1677 Statute of Frauds stipulated that only written wills could devise real estate, and they had to be signed by the testator plus three or four witnesses.

People with copyhold property were still prevented from devising land until 1815, and before this date you will need to check for descent in manorial records instead. The Statute of Wills in 1837 permitted the devise of all realty in a will, although all wills were to be written and signed by the testator in the presence of two witnesses who did not benefit from the will.

7.2.2   The lack of a bequest in a will

There were many reasons why property was not mentioned in a will. One of the most important reasons is that not everyone left a will, and even if one had been made there is no guarantee that there was any need to specifically mention property.

As we have seen in Chapter 4, if land was held in fee simple and was not alienated during the lifetime of the holder, then it would automatically pass to his heir at law on his death. A similar restriction was placed on land held in fee tail. In other cases, property might have been disposed of beforehand through a private agreement within the family, perhaps as part of a marriage portion for a daughter or as part of a strict settlement. In any case, the ecclesiastical courts had no jurisdiction over realty, as this was the preserve of the common law and equity courts. In effect, what we know today as a will was in fact two separate bequests that were combined to form one document, with a testament covering the personalty and the will bequeathing realty.

Even if your property is mentioned within a will, it is rare to find street or house names specified; the usual format is to make a bequest of 'the house where I do dwell' to the relevant party. However, if you know the family was already in possession of a property, this can at least tell you who inherited the property next, and a new name can often prompt further searches in other areas. You may also find that names of occupiers are specified if a non-resident owner was bequeathing a leasehold property, and landowners with many houses can sometimes provide detailed specifications of where properties were situated and to whom they should next pass. Furthermore, if the occupier of a house was a leaseholder, the outstanding term of the lease could be bequeathed, and the name of the owner was sometimes included.

Until 1925, if a person died intestate, left an invalid will or failed to make provision for any realty in a will, the property passed to the heir at law, which was the nearest blood relative starting with descendants. Personalty was passed to the next of kin, starting with a spouse. After the 1925 Law of Property Act, both realty and personalty passed to the next of kin. If the deceased was of sufficient wealth, letters of administration were then granted. Administrations will be of only limited use to the house historian, as they did not contain details of the individual's realty. However, if you know that an individual owned a property and died intestate, you should be able to use the administrations to determine the place of residence of the deceased and the name of the next of kin to whom the letters of administration were granted. It is possible that a search of their records might provide additional information.

7.2.3   Probate jurisdictions before 1858

It is important to remember that wills were private documents and therefore can be difficult to locate and use. Where they have been deposited in the public domain, you are most likely to find them listed in local CROs, or diocesan record offices for the district that the property or owner was part of. They are often written in a difficult hand, and can be fragile. The PRO has a number of original wills in its collection and, aside from the probate records listed in section 7.3.3, they can usually be found in private papers or exhibit series.

Consequently, it might be easier to focus your attention on the process by which a deceased person's will was given official approval so that the executor or executrix of the will could begin honouring the bequests. This was known as the grant of probate, and until 1858 ecclesiastical courts were responsible for proving wills. However, there were various jurisdictions in operation, and the location and value of an individual's personal estate determined where probate was granted; a summary is provided below.

- Probate for property held solely within an archdeaconry was granted in the archdeacon's court.
- Probate for property held within more than one archdeaconry but within one diocese was granted within the bishop's (diocesan) court.
- Probate for property over £5, held within more than one diocese or jurisdiction, was granted within the archbishop's court, known as the Prerogative court.
- There were two Prerogative courts, one for the province of York and another for the province of Canterbury.
- Prerogative Court of York (PCY) covered the counties of Yorkshire (all ridings), Durham, Northumberland, Westmorland, Cumberland, Lancashire, Cheshire, Nottinghamshire and the Isle of Man.

- Prerogative Court of Canterbury (PCC) covered the rest of England and Wales.
- Probate for property held in both provinces was granted in both.
- Peculiars were also in existence that operated their own separate courts.

The records generated by archdeaconary, bishop (or diocesan) and peculiar courts were deposited at county or diocesan record offices, and those for the PCY are at the Borthwick Institute, York. Records created under the PCC are deposited at the PRO.

There are a number of books that can help you to identify the best place to begin your research for a will, and these are listed under **Useful publications.** By the nineteenth century, the PCC had become the main probate court for most wills in the southern province, as the £5 barrier (£10 in London) was rendered less of a restriction through inflation. However, you may well need to search in several different locations before you find an earlier will, if indeed one was made in the first place.

7.3   Searching for PCC wills and administrations

7.3.1   Will registers pre-1858

When a will was proved before the PCC, a copy was entered into a register. These survive for the period 1388–1858, in series **PROB 11**. The records for each year are arranged under the name of the principal registrar, and have been grouped in blocks of 16 pages. Each of these blocks is called a quire, and each quire was assigned a quire number. To provide a means of reference, basic initial alphabetical calendars of registered wills were created that assign quire numbers to wills. These are known as Register Books and serve as an index to **PROB 11**; they can be found in series **PROB 12**. However, the following finding aids have been produced based on information contained in **PROB 12** and are, unless indicated, available on open access at both the PRO and the FRC:

- 1383–1700 various printed indexes;
- 1701–49 printed/microfiche index (compiled by Friends of the PRO);
- 1750–1800 printed index (compiled by the Society of Genealogists);
- 1801–52 no indexes – consult the 'calendars' in **PROB 12** (printed volumes on open access at the FRC);
- 1853–8 alphabetically indexed calendars printed from microfiche, in **PROB 12**.

In most cases you will find a person's name under the year that probate was granted; this is then linked to the name of the registrar and the quire number in which the will is located. These can be matched in the series list for **PROB 11** to obtain a document reference, although some of the indexes listed above provide this too. If you are unable to find a registered will, try looking a year or so after the date of death, as it could take some time for the registration process to be completed, especially if the will was complicated or contested.

7.3.2 Administration Books pre-1858

Details of the letters of administration were recorded in Administration Act Books, which from 1559–1858 are in **PROB 6**. From 1796, the values of estates are also provided. These too can be searched by means of the Register Books in series **PROB 12** and, as with the will registers, a series of finding aids is available:

- 1559–1660 various printed indexes;
- 1661–4 typescript indexes;
- 1665–1700 no indexes – consult the calendars in **PROB 12**;
- 1701–49 printed/microfiche index (compiled by Friends of the PRO);
- 1751–1800 no indexes – consult the calendars in **PROB 12** (there is a card index at the Society of Genealogists, which they will search for a fee);
- 1801–52 no indexes – consult the 'calendars' in **PROB 12** (printed volumes on open access at the FRC);
- 1853–8 alphabetically indexed calendars printed from microfiche, in **PROB 12**.

7.3.3 Original wills

Original wills that were brought before the PCC have been deposited in series **PROB 1**, **PROB 10** and **PROB 20–23**. Where a probate act was granted and attached to the original will as evidence of probity, the grant was recorded in the Probate Act Book in series **PROB 8** (where estate values are provided from 1796) and **PROB 9**. However, these will provide no additional information to the entries in **PROB 11**.

7.3.4 Related probate material at the PRO

In addition to wills and administrations, a variety of other records generated by the probate courts will be of a passing interest to the house historian.

Probate inventories

Inventories were undertaken within a few days of death to protect the interests of any beneficiaries of the deceased, and the executors or administrators of the estate, against potential claims of fraud. Their purpose was to indicate the value

Table 7.1 Locating probate inventories

PROB 2 Inventories series I (1417–1660)	Index with series list
PROB 4 Parchment inventories (1661–1720)	Card index to names and places
PROB 5 Paper inventories (1661–1732)	Index with series list
PROB 32 Filed exhibits with inventories (1662–1720)	Index with series list
PROB 33 Indexes to exhibits (1683–1858)	Original indexes to exhibits in **PROB 31** and **PROB 37**
PROB 3 Inventories series II (1702, 1718–82)	Index with series list
PROB 31 Exhibits, main series (1722–1858)	Index of wills; card indexes of names and places to inventories and other exhibits

of the deceased's personal estate, to ensure that there were sufficient possessions that could be sold to honour any legacies once all debts had been paid off.
This process excluded realty, but the value of leases and mortgages would be
part of the assessment.

Inventories would often comprise a list of the deceased person's personal
effects, with a value assigned to each. The documents often took the form of a
survey of all household contents, and can give an impression of the interior of a
house, in terms of the number of inhabited rooms and the furniture, fixtures
and fittings in each. Inventories can be found in the series listed in Table 7.1.

You may also find inventories amongst the exhibit series in the law courts, as
they were occasionally produced as evidence in cases.

Contested wills

Records of wills that were contested were subject to the ecclesiastical courts
only if the material featured in the will related to personal effects, such as
goods, chattels, cash and leases; freehold property that was under dispute was

Table 7.2 Contested wills in ecclesiastical courts

Annotations of existence of a cause	
PROB 6	
PROB 7	
PROB 8	
PROB 9	
PROB 11	Indexes specified above
PROB 12	
Proceedings	
PROB 18	
PROB 25	Card indexes to causes, testators and intestates
PROB 28	Index to causes, testators and intestates
PROB 37	Index to testators and intestates – *List and Index Society, vol. 184*
Depositions	
PROB 24	
PROB 26	Index to causes, testators and intestates
Exhibits	
PROB 36	Card index to causes, testators and intestate
PROB 32	Indexed by name – *List and Index Society, vol. 204*
PROB 31	Index of wills, card index of names and places
Procedural records	
PROB 29	
PROB 30	Index to causes, testators and intestates – *List and Index Society, vol. 161*

referred to the courts of equity (Chancery, Exchequer etc.), where a suit would be filed. Therefore, the records generated by contested wills in ecclesiastical courts will be relevant to the house historian only if the property in question was leased to another party.

If this is the case, you will need to identify whether there was a dispute, or 'cause', presented to the PCC. The best place to begin your search will be with the card index to the proceedings in **PROB 18**, covering the period 1661–1858; you may also find information in the will register itself in **PROB 11**, and annotations that a sentence in a PCC court, or decree in an equity court, was passed can be found in the Act Books in **PROB 6–9** and the calendar to will registers in **PROB 12**. It is important to remember that the indexes will not be listed under the name of the deceased whose will was in dispute; as with the lay law courts, causes were filed and indexed under the name of the plaintiff, which you might not know. These annotations will give you the names of the contestants. The series listed in Table 7.2 will be worth examining for evidence.

7.3.5   Probate material after 1858

From 1858, the ecclesiastical courts ceased to register wills or grant administrations, and the civil Court of Probate took on this role. The Principal Probate Registry has copies of all wills and grants of administration that were made in England and Wales, and these can be viewed in central London at the Probate Search Room, First Avenue House (*see* **Useful addresses**). A national calendar, which acts as a name index for the period 1858–1943, is available on fiche at both the PRO and FRC.

7.3.6   Scotland and Ireland

The method of disposal of a deceased person's estates in Scotland was different. All documents connected with the process were known as testaments, and included an inventory of the deceased's possessions. Where a will was included, the document was called a 'testament testamentor' – the equivalent to the English probate; and when no will was attached, a 'testament dative' was produced, similar to letters of administration. From 1515–1823 commissary courts handled the procedures, and indexes to the registers of testaments produced by these courts have been published until 1801; other indexes are available at NAS from 1801–23. From 1824, all commissary courts, bar Edinburgh, were abolished and the sheriffs courts handled the process. Indexes are available at NAS, but from 1875 a calendar of confirmations is the main means of reference, and records after 1984 are consulted at the Edinburgh Commissary Court. It is important to bear in mind that property could not be inherited through testaments until 1868, although trust dispositions and settlements did allow people to make provision for heirs. These are usually to be found recorded in the Court of Sessions register of deeds.

PRONI holds original wills from 1900–94, and indexes to wills 1858–1984. Most original wills before 1900 were destroyed in Dublin in 1922, although local registries copied wills into bound books which can be accessed on microfilm in MIC.15C, and indexes to pre-1858 registers exist, as well as a card index to surviving original wills.

7.4   Death duty registers

From 1796 to 1805, death duty was payable on all legacies in a will worth over £20. After 1805, the liability was extended to include real estate, but until 1815 only if the terms of the will stipulated that the realty was to be sold to raise money to pay a legacy. Thereafter, all realty was assessed, which meant that a large number of house owners were liable for death duty and might be listed.

However, before you can search the death duty registers, you will need to know the name of the deceased and the rough date when he or she died.

There are two series of records that you will need to consult. The first is in PRO series **IR 27**, which contains annual initial indexes to the registers themselves and are arranged in date order by surname. Once you have located the relevant entry, make a note of the death duty reference number assigned to the individual, and then consult the series lists for the registers themselves in series **IR 26**. All indexes in **IR 27** are available on microfilm, as are the death duty records themselves from 1796–1857; from 1858–1903 you will need to order the originals, which are stored at Hayes and take three working days to be delivered to Kew.

Death duty registers can be confusing at first glance, as a lot of information was entered in a series of columns. A PRO leaflet helps you to interpret this data, but the house historian should be able to extract the name of the deceased and his or her address plus details of the next of kin; details of any contests in law courts that delayed probate; plus notes made up to 50 years after the original entry about the beneficiaries and how the estate was actually distributed. For example, if a will stipulated that a house was to be sold on the death or remarriage of a spouse, then you will find its sale value in the register, along with the date of the distribution of the money and the amount of duty this incurred.

Death duty registers also serve as a means of determining where a will was proved or grant of administration was issued, and can therefore assist the process of locating the correct probate court.

8 Legal disputes

8.1 Introduction

8.1.1 Property and the law

House owners have not always enjoyed undisputed possession of their land or property. The English legal system can be complicated at the best of times, and even more so when property or inheritance is concerned. Proof of ownership was vital if land was to be sold or passed on without challenge, and contested successions, sales or transfers were frequent, especially when families disagreed with the terms of an inheritance, settlement or will. Furthermore, there were many statutes in place that regulated and controlled the erection of new properties and the extension of old ones, and failure to comply often led to prosecution.

Fortunately for the modern house historian, if a little less fortunately for the contemporary house owner who was embroiled in a legal action, disputes and prosecutions have left a trail for us to follow. A great deal about property descent can be learnt from the deposited records of the various courts into which civil litigation could be taken, including the names of previous owners, dates of sales and even construction dates. This chapter describes the procedures and records of the popular courts that were used by litigants to register and settle property disputes, and how you can search the records they generated for information on your house. However, a cautionary note should be sounded before you think about using legal records. Unless you know that a property dispute ended up in court, legal records are not going to be the best place to start looking for clues about the history of your house; and you will probably need to have a rough date in mind, plus the names of the parties concerned. Without this information, to find your property via a random search of the surviving records would require an enormous quantity of luck, or patience, or probably both.

Table 8.1 The structure of civil law courts

Pre-1875

Common Law	Equity
King's Bench	Exchequer
Common Pleas	Chancery
Exchequer of Pleas	
Chancery (Plea side)	*Applied equity principles:*
	Star Chamber
	Requests
	Wards and Liveries

Post-1875
Supreme Court of Judicature
5 divisions:

King's/Queen's Bench	Common Pleas	Exchequer	Chancery	Probate, Admiralty and Divorce

Post-1881
Supreme Court of Judicature
3 divisions:

King's/Queen's Bench	Chancery	Probate, Admiralty and Divorce
Contracts	*Land, trusts, mortgages*	

8.1.2 The English legal system

Before 1875 there were two main branches of civil litigation that you will need to consider. Common law courts, such as King's Bench and the Court of Common Pleas, dispensed justice according to the 'common law' and ancient custom of the land, and as such awarded compensation or damages but were unable to enforce contracts that had been broken. This meant that they were less effective at solving property disputes that involved breach of trusts or wills. In comparison, the courts of equity, primarily Chancery and the Exchequer, were able to make judgments on the grounds of justice and conscience as opposed to 'law'. As such they could force remedial action to be taken, although they were not allowed to award damages.

In 1875, all these courts were abolished and a Supreme Court of Judicature was created with five divisions – Chancery, Common Pleas, Exchequer, King's (Queen's) Bench and Probate, Divorce and Admiralty. In 1881 the Common Pleas, King's (Queen's) Bench and Exchequer were amalgamated to form the King's (Queen's) Bench. Although cases could be heard in any division, and common law or equity rules applied whenever needed, the King's (Queen's) Bench heard most actions relating to contract, and Chancery usually dealt with land, trusts and mortgages. A brief summary is provided in Table 8.1.

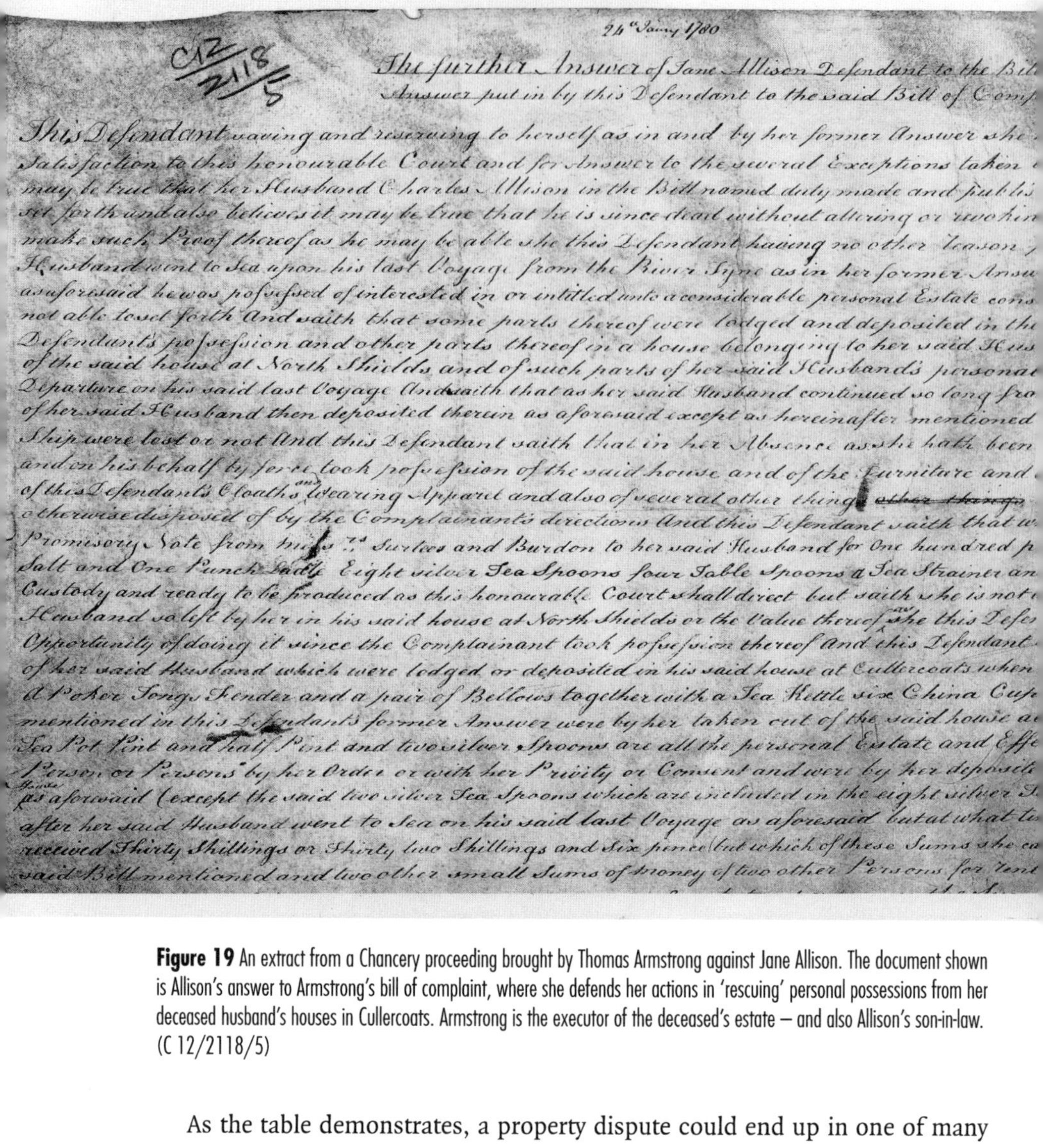
C12/2118/5

24th Jany 1780

The further Answer of Jane Allison Defendant to the Bill
Answer put in by this Defendant to the said Bill of Comp

This Defendant saving and reserving to herself as in and by her former Answer she
Satisfaction to this honourable Court and for Answer to the several Exceptions taken
may be true that her Husband Charles Allison in the Bill named duly made and publis
set forth and also believes it may be true that he is since dead without altering or revokin
make such Proof thereof as he may be able she this Defendant having no other Reason
Husband went to Sea upon his last Voyage from the River Tyne as in her former Answ
as aforesaid he was possessed of interested in or intitled unto a considerable personal Estate cons
not able to set forth And saith that some parts thereof were lodged and deposited in the
Defendant's possession and other parts thereof in a house belonging to her said Hus
of the said house at North Shields and of such parts of her said Husband's personal
Departure on his said last Voyage And saith that as her said Husband continued so long fro
of her said Husband then deposited therein as aforesaid except as hereinafter mentioned
Ship were lost or not And this Defendant saith that in her Absence as she hath been
and on his behalf by force took possession of the said house and of the Furniture and
of this Defendant's Cloaths and Wearing Apparel and also of several other things ~~other things~~
otherwise disposed of by the Complainant's directions And this Defendant saith that w
Promisory Note from Messrs Surtees and Burdon to her said Husband for One hundred p
Salt and One Punch Ladle Eight silver Tea Spoons four Table Spoons a Tea Strainer an
Custody and ready to be produced as this honourable Court shall direct but saith she is not
Husband so left by her in his said house at North Shields or the Value thereof she this Defen
Opportunity of doing it since the Complainant took possession thereof And this Defendant
of her said Husband which were lodged or deposited in his said house at Cullercoats when
A Poker Tongs Fender and a pair of Bellows together with a Tea Kettle six China Cup
mentioned in this Defendant's former Answer were by her taken out of the said house a
Tea Pot Pint and half Pint and two silver Spoons are all the personal Estate and Effe
Person or Persons by her Order or with her Privity or Consent and were by her deposite
House as aforesaid (except the said two silver Tea Spoons which are included in the eight silver T
after her said Husband went to Sea on his said last Voyage as aforesaid but at what ti
received Thirty Shillings or Thirty two Shillings and Six pence but which of these Sums she ca
said Bill mentioned and two other small Sums of money of two other Persons for Rent

Figure 19 An extract from a Chancery proceeding brought by Thomas Armstrong against Jane Allison. The document shown is Allison's answer to Armstrong's bill of complaint, where she defends her actions in 'rescuing' personal possessions from her deceased husband's houses in Cullercoats. Armstrong is the executor of the deceased's estate – and also Allison's son-in-law. (C 12/2118/5)

As the table demonstrates, a property dispute could end up in one of many places, and it was not unknown for a single dispute to move between courts during the course of the action, or indeed for a case to be started in more than one court. However, local newspapers can often provide clues as to which court heard a dispute, and legal papers in private hands can also give an indication of where to begin your research. Furthermore, many of the indexes to the equity courts are available online and can be searched for names via PROCAT.

8.2 Equity proceedings in Chancery

Thousands of equity cases were brought before the court of Chancery each year to resolve disputes between individuals or parties, covering a wide range of topics such as disputed wills, legacies, estate administration and property transfers (*see* **Figure 19**). During the course of a court case, many different types of documents were created, and the most useful are described in the following sections. However, it is important to remember that all documentation for a single case was not filed together, but rather in separate series determined by the type of document, making it difficult to accurately collate all material relating to a single case. Furthermore, documents were filed under the name of the first-listed plaintiff, so it will be very difficult to locate multi-party cases where the principal name is unknown. Party names also changed over time, especially in long cases where plaintiffs or defendants died and were succeeded by relatives.

Not all cases came to a conclusion, as they were often brought into Chancery in an attempt to force the defendant to settle out of court. Consequently, it can be difficult to locate a definite outcome for many cases.

8.2.1 Proceedings

When a plaintiff wished to start proceedings in the court of Chancery, he would instruct a lawyer to file an initial 'bill of complaint' with the Lord Chancellor, who technically presided over the court. The bill of complaint stated the charges that the plaintiff wanted the defendant to answer, and a justification for bringing an equity lawsuit as opposed to a case under common law. It would commonly include the name, occupation and residence of the plaintiff. The body of the bill would then provide specifics of the complaint, and this is where you will find information about property or disputed transfers.

Once a bill of complaint was filed, the defendant was required to provide a written 'answer' to the charges, and lay any counter charges against the plaintiff. The plaintiff might counter with a replication, and the defendant with a rejoinder. In essence this process, known as pleading, defined the limits of the case so that a recommendation could be made by one of the Masters of Chancery, who considered the case and reported back to the Lord Chancellor. Witness statements (depositions) were then taken and evidence (exhibits) brought into court to help the masters make a recommendation to the Lord Chancellor. When a verdict had been reached, a decree or order was issued settling the matter.

Chancery proceedings date from the late fourteenth century until 1875, when business was transferred to the Supreme Court of Judicature. The size, scope and detail of the documents varied throughout time, but you will find that, apart from the very earliest, they were written in English and should be legible. However, you may find that the repetitive nature of the legal language can be confusing at first, especially if the original bill was lost and you are left with later papers that contain unfathomable references to earlier documents.

The records are arranged chronologically and are located in several PRO series. From the mid seventeenth century there were six clerks working for the masters, and proceedings for a single case could have been filed with any of them. To ensure that you have not missed any paperwork, you should search for the case within all six divisions. A summary of PRO series is provided in Table 8.2.

Most of these indexes are arranged by the name of the plaintiff, or the first-listed plaintiff in a multi-party case, and unless you know this name it can be virtually impossible to determine from the indexes whether a case is relevant. The indexes to earlier series in **C 1–3** provide a brief outline of the case, but still

Table 8.2 Chancery proceedings and relevant indexes

c.1386–1558	
C 1 Early Chancery Proceedings	*List and Index, vols XII, XVI, XX, XXIX, XXXVIII, XLVIII, L, LI, LIV, LV,* searchable online.
1558–c.1640	
C 2 Chancery Proceedings Series I	Printed calendars for Elizabeth and Charles I, partial indexes for James I, all searchable online.
1558–c.1660	
C 3 Chancery Proceedings Series II	*List and Index, vols VII, XXIV, XXX,* searchable online.
Various dates	
C 4 Miscellaneous Proceedings	Index to first 46 bundles.
Six Cerks pre-1714	
C 5 Bridges (1613–1714)	*List and Index, vols XXIX, XLII, XLIV, XLV,* series searchable online.
C 6 Collins (1625–1714)	Indexes available, not searchable online.
C 7 Hamilton (1620–1714)	Indexes available, not searchable online.
C 8 Mitford (1570–1714)	Indexes available, not searchable online.
C 9 Reynardson (1649–1714)	Printed index, searchable online.
C 10 Whittington (1640–1714)	Indexes available, searchable online.
Various Six Clerks post-1714	
C 11 Series I (1714–58)	Indexes available for each, not searchable online.
C 12 Series II (1758–1800)	
C 13 Series III (1800–42)	
C 14 Modern (1842–52)	
C 15 Modern (1853–60)	
C 16 Modern (1861–75)	
C 18 Miscellaneous (1844—64)	
Court of Judicature 1875 onwards	
J 54 Chancery Division	Index for 1876–90 in **IND 1/2218–26**, not searchable online.

rely on names as a means of reference. However, some of the series are now fully listed online, and a key-word search of PROCAT can reveal the name of the principal plaintiff and defendant plus any places listed in the earlier series.

8.2.2   Depositions and affidavits

Once the pleadings had produced a final case to be answered, the Masters of Chancery collected evidence so that they could make an equitable decision. Depositions and affidavits played an important part of this process and are a good source of evidence about the background of the case and, in cases of property disputes, include detailed descriptions.

Depositions were written statements from deponents, namely individuals with knowledge of a dispute who were selected by both parties. A list of pertinent questions was compiled, known as an interrogatory. Sworn, signed and dated statements were then made in answer to the interrogatories and were used as evidence in the case. In comparison, affidavits were voluntary statements made on oath during the case. Table 8.3 provides a summary of PRO series, broken down in terms of Town Depositions (sworn in London) and Country Depositions (sworn elsewhere).

It is important to remember that the depositions were listed by the name of the plaintiff, rather than that of the deponent. If you know only the name of the deponent, then the Bernau Index is a good place to start looking. This is a composite index to the names of many parties in chancery equity cases, including deponents. It can be consulted on microfilm at the Latter Day Saints Family History Centres and at the Society of Genealogists, and publications that offer guidance on interpreting references obtained from Bernau are listed under **Useful publications**. However, you need to copy the Bernau reference accurately, in full, to assist conversion into a modern PRO reference.

8.2.3   Decree and Order Books

During a case the court might issue an order to one party or another, and when it reached a final decision it would issue a decree in favour of the victorious party. Before 1544, decrees and orders were sometimes enrolled on the back of the bill of complaint; between 1544 and 1875, they were recorded in Decree and Order Entry Books, in PRO series C 33, and thereafter in J 15. Decrees and Orders are usually written in English, and will tell you the outcome of the case; this will be of use to determine where the property ended up after the verdict. You should also be provided with the date that the hearing took place, plus information on when depositions or affidavits were recorded.

There are two sequences known as A and B books listing suits by plaintiff, and until Trinity term 1629, both A and B books list suits from A to Z. From 1629, entries for plaintiffs A–K are in the A books, and entries for plaintiffs L–Z are in the B books. In 1932 the A and B books were amalgamated. Indexes to these volumes, from 1546, are available on open access.

Decrees could be enrolled at extra cost, and are more likely to survive in cases involving property so that a permanent record was preserved. Decree rolls (1534–1903) are in C 78 and are indexed in **IND 1/16950–61B**; supplementary rolls are in C 79, with indexes in **IND 1/16960B**. A place-name index exists in **IND 1/16960A**. Appeals against enrolled decrees and orders take the form of petitions and are in C 36 (1774–1875, indexes **IND 1/15029–47**) and J 53 (1876–1925, indexes **IND 1/15048–51** and **1/15282**).

Table 8.3 Chancery depositions, affidavits and interrogatories and relevant indexes

Early depositions	
C 1 and **4** (1386–1534)	Indexes available (with proceedings).
Town depositions	
C 24 (1534–1853)	Indexes **IND 1/16759** and **1/9115–21**.
C 15–16, J 54 (1854–80)	Indexes available (with proceedings).
J 17 (1880–1925)	Indexes **IND 1/16748–52.**
Country depositions	
C 21 (1558–1649)	Indexes available, searchable online.
C 22 (1649–1714)	Indexes available, searchable online.
C 11–14 (1714–1880)	Indexes available, (with proceedings).
J 17 (1880–1925)	Indexes **IND 1/16748–52**.
Affidavits	
C 31 and **41** (1611–1875)	Indexes **IND 1/14545–67**; entry marked with a cross – original affidavit in **C 31**; no cross – copies in **C 41** (1615–1747).
J 4 (1876 onwards)	Various indexes in **IND 1**.
Interrogatories	
C 25 (1598–1852)	Mainly relating to Town examinations, and separated from the relevant depositions.

However, before starting a search of these records it is important to bear in mind that the majority of cases (approximately 90 per cent) never reached the stage where an order or decree might have been issued, and therefore the pleadings and depositions might be the only surviving evidence.

8.2.4 Arbitration and appeals

Occasionally, the Masters of Chancery acted as arbitrators, and you may find reports on such decisions in series **C 38** (1544–1875) and **J 57** (1875–1962). Indexes are available between 1606–1875 (**IND 1/1878–2028, 10700–41** and **14919–73**), with many other **IND 1** volumes for the post-1875 period. Awards were also enrolled in **C 33** (1544–1694), and un-enrolled awards are in **C 42** (1694–1844), although there are no indexes to this series.

8.3 Equity cases in the Court of Exchequer

Another court where property disputes could end up was the Exchequer, which dealt with equity cases from the mid sixteenth century until 1841, when such actions were transferred to Chancery. The procedures were the same as in

Chancery, namely that a process of pleading, based on bills and answers, created a simplified case that then required the presentation of evidence to allow a final decree to be made. In theory, the plaintiff was a debtor of the Crown, but this was usually a fiction designed to allow the action to be brought before the court.

Although the records of Exchequer equity cases are similar to those in Chancery, the means of reference are much harder to use. Fewer indexes exist, and very little material is available online for key word searching. If you suspect your property once formed part of a case in the Exchequer, the series described in this section might contain relevant material. However, one of the main ways of picking up information is through the country depositions in **E 134**, which were thoroughly listed and are available to search online.

Many PRO series contain information relating to equity cases and proceedings in the Court of Exchequer, but the most useful are listed in Table 8.4. You should consult the PRO leaflet for further information on the subject.

8.3.1   Proceedings

There are two series of bills and answers. **E III** mainly contains strays from other courts, and covers the reigns of Henry VII to Elizabeth I; but it is listed and available to search online.

E 112 contains the main series of bills and answers, and runs in date from Elizabeth's reign until the cessation of business in 1841 (4 Victoria). The documents are arranged by reign of the monarch in which the action was first filed, and grouped into counties. These are then indexed by means of contemporary bill books.

Replications and rejoinders that have strayed from **E 112** can be found in **E 193**; there is a partial index post-1700 in **OBS 1/752**.

8.3.2   Depositions and affidavits

Exchequer depositions taken in London (the equivalent of Chancery Town depositions) are stored in series **E 133**. There is an original calendar for pieces **E 133/1/1** to **E 133/10/1071** in **E 501/10**, which covers the period 2 Elizabeth I to 45 Elizabeth I and is arranged in chronological order. This is on open access, and will provide the county, date and legal term where the deposition was made, the suit number, the names of the plaintiff and defendant, and most importantly the subject of the deposition. The document reference is obtained by adding the bundle number and suit number to **E 133**. The period 1603–1841 is not so well served, as there is a list on open access that provides the bundle number, piece number and the names of the plaintiff and defendant for pieces **E 133/11/1** to

Table 8.4 Exchequer proceedings and relevant indexes

Bedford, Buckingham, Cambridge, Cheshire, Cornwall, Cumberland, Devon, Essex, Hampshire, Hereford, Hertford, Huntingdon, Kent, Lancashire, Lincoln, Middlesex, and all Welsh counties	Elizabeth I	1558–1603	**IND** 1/16820
	James I	1603–1625	**IND** 1/16822
	Charles I	1625–1649	**IND** 1/16824
	Interregnum	1649–1660	**IND** 1/16826
	Charles II	1660–1674	**IND** 1/16828
		1669–1685	**IND** 1/16830
	James II	1685–1688	**IND** 1/16832
	William & Mary	1688–1694	**IND** 1/16834
	William III	1694–1702	**IND** 1/16836
	Anne	1702–1714	**IND** 1/16836
	George I	1714–1727	**IND** 1/16838
	George II	1727–1760	**IND** 1/16840
	George III	1760–1801	**IND** 1/16842
		1776–1820	**IND** 1/16844
		1779–1820	**IND** 1/16846
	George IV	1820–1827	**IND** 1/16848
	William IV	1827–1837	**IND** 1/16850
	Victoria	1837–1841	**IND** 1/16852
Berkshire, Derby, Dorset, Durham, Leicester, Monmouth, Norfolk, Northampton, Northumberland, Nottingham, Oxford, Rutland, Shropshire, Somerset, Stafford, Suffolk, Surrey, Sussex, Warwick, Westmorland, Wiltshire, Worcester, York	Elizabeth I	1558–1603	**IND** 1/16821
	James I	1603–1625	**IND** 1/16823
	Charles I	1625–1649	**IND** 1/16825
	Interregnum	1649–1660	**IND** 1/16827
	Charles II	1660–1674	**IND** 1/16829
		1669–1685	**IND** 1/16831
	James II	1685–1688	**IND** 1/16833
	William & Mary	1688–1694	**IND** 1/16835
	William III	1694–1702	**IND** 1/16837
	Anne	1702–1714	**IND** 1/16837
	George I	1714–1727	**IND** 1/16839
	George II	1727–1760	**IND** 1/16841
	George III	1760–1801	**IND** 1/16843
		1776–1820	**IND** 1/16845
		1779–1820	**IND** 1/16847
	George IV	1820–1827	**IND** 1/16849
	William IV	1827–1837	**IND** 1/16851
	Victoria	1837–1841	**IND** 1/16853

E 133/164. The list is arranged alphabetically by name of plaintiff. However, the descriptions are available online, which will enable you to search for defendants as well as plaintiffs through PROCAT.

However, Exchequer country depositions are perhaps the most informative and easily accessible documents. They were taken by Exchequer commissioners, and are in series **E 134**. There are topographical calendars available on open access, which provide the names of the plaintiff and defendant, plus an outline of the case. The commissions themselves are in **E 178**, and can also be found via the indexed calendars for **E 134**; they provide the interrogatories on which the depositions were taken. Both series are available for searching online, and are probably the quickest way to find a case that might be relevant to your property.

Once you have identified a case, the documents will provide a list of statements in answer to the interrogatories. They often provide detailed descriptions of property, property boundaries, owners and occupiers; local events that impacted upon property; and disputed trusts, wills and property transfers.

E 111 is another area in which you should look, as it contains special commissions, interrogatories and depositions, and can be usefully searched via PROCAT. Affidavits can be found in **E 103** (1774–1841) and **E 218** (1695–1822). There are partial indexes for **E 103**, but none for **E 218**. Some affidavits relate to surveys requested by either party following an Exchequer commission, and can contain details of property boundaries.

8.3.3 Decrees and orders

At each stage of the case, an order was made so that the next stage could proceed. An order was entered in a minute book (**E 161**), written out (**E 128** and **131**) and registered (**E 123–5** and **127**). Sometimes the orders can provide additional information about the case.

Where a final judgment was reached, a decree was produced. As with orders, they were first entered in a minute book (**E 162**), written (**E 128** and **130**) and registered (**E 123–4** and **126**). A summary of surviving indexes to these series is provided in Table 8.5.

In 1819 Adam Martin published an alphabetical index to entry books from 1558 which covers some of the material contained in series **E 123–7**. The details of this publication can be found under **Useful publications**.

8.4   Other equity-based courts

In addition to Chancery and the Exchequer, other courts developed that followed the principle of equity when reaching decisions. The main two are described below; both the Court of Requests and Court of Star Chamber were offshoots of the King's Council. Furthermore, the Court of Wards and Liveries may contain some information about contested administrations of the estates of Crown tenants-in-chief.

8.4.1 Court of Requests

The court was established in 1483 with the aim of providing the poor with access to justice. Relevant cases heard by the court, from this date until its records end in 1642, cover disputes over title to property and contracts, includ-

Table 8.5 Exchequer decrees and orders and relevant indexes

E 111/56	Entry book, decrees and orders (Philip and Mary)	No index
E 123	Entry book, decrees and orders series I (1559–1605)	Manuscript index; also **IND 1/16897**
E 124	Entry book, decrees and orders series II (1603–25)	Manuscript index to 1610
E 125	Entry book, decrees and orders series III (1625–61)	**IND 1/16854–60**
E 126	Entry book, decrees and orders series IV (1604–1841)	**IND 1/16862–6**
E 127	Entry book, decrees and orders series V (1661–1841)	**IND 1/16860–1** and 16867–91
E 128	Decrees and orders files (1562–1662)	**OBS 1/424** (1634–42); thereafter use the indexes to the entry books.
E 130	Original decrees files (1660–1841)	**IND 1/16862–6**
E 131	Original orders files (1660–1842)	**IND 1/16860–1,** 16867–91

ing assignments of dower. The procedure of the court was very similar to Chancery, with a process of pleading producing a simplified case. Evidence in the form of depositions and affidavits was collected for the judges to consider; they determined an outcome on equitable grounds, and issued orders and decrees. Documents produced in this process were predominantly written in English.

Proceedings can be found in the series **REQ 2**, along with attached depositions. There are some indexes, usually by the name of the suitor and by place for the Elizabethan period, but a large number of documents after 1603 are unlisted, and trying to find relevant material can be time consuming and ultimately fruitless. A summary of the series is provided in Table 8.6.

All other relevant material will be in **REQ 1**, although it will be of limited use to a house historian. Decree and Order Books are in **REQ 1/1–38** and, **209**, with drafts in **REQ 1/39–103**. Affidavits are in **REQ 1/119–49**, with contemporary indexes in **REQ 1/118** and **1/150**.

8.4.2   Court of Star Chamber

The court was established in 1485 and abolished in 1641, and was named after the stars that decorated the ceiling of the room in which the court sat at Westminster. Aside from its judicial work, it heard cases that involved land

Table 8.6 Court of Requests proceedings and relevant indexes

1485–1547	**REQ 2/1–13**	Listed in *List and Index XXI*, index in *List and Index Supplementary, VII, vol. 1.*
1547–1553	**REQ 2/14–19**	Listed in *List and Index XXI*, index in *List and Index Supplementary, VII, vol. 1.*
1553–1558	**REQ 2/20–25**	Listed in *List and Index XXI*, index in *List and Index Supplementary, VII, vol. 1.*
1558–1603	**REQ 2/26–136**	Listed in *List and Index XXI*, index in *List and Index Supplementary, VII, vol. 1*
	REQ 2/137–156	Listed in *Aitkin's Calendar*, index in *List and Index Supplementary, VII, vol. 1*
	REQ 2/157–294	Manuscript list, index in *List and Index Supplementary, VII, vols 2 and 3.*
	REQ 2/269–386	None.
1603–1625	**REQ 2/295–311**	Manuscript list, index in *List and Index Supplementary, VII, vol. 4.*
	REQ 2/387–424	Manuscript list, index in *List and Index Supplementary, VII, vol. 4.*
	REQ 2/425–485	None.
1625–1649	**REQ 2/486–806**	None.
Various dates	**REQ 2/807–829**	None.

enclosures and contested property rights, in particular boundary disputes. As with the Court of Requests, it used the principle of equity to reach a decision, and therefore pleadings, evidence, orders and decrees were produced, mainly written in English.

Proceedings are arranged by the reign of the monarch in which they were first filed in court. They can be found in the series listed in Table 8.7.

A large amount of supplementary material has now been lost. For example, no Decree and Order Books survive, although very rare endorsements on the proceedings have been found. You may find some relevant items in court miscellanea in **STAC 10**, but this has not been listed and so can be difficult to use.

8.4.3   Court of Wards and Liveries

When a tenant-in-chief died, an inquisition post mortem was conducted to determine whether the Crown was entitled to feudal dues from the land, estate or property that the tenant held. When an heir was found to be under age, the Crown was legally entitled to administer the estate until majority was reached, which was usually 21, and enjoy the profits. The right to these profits could, and often were, sold by the Crown, and if they fell into private hands, disputes could

Table 8.7 Court of Star Chamber proceedings and relevant indexes

Henry VII Records: 1485–1509	**STAC 1**	Series list, index in *List and Indexes Supplementary series IV.*
Henry VIII Records: c.1450–1625	**STAC 2**	Series list, index in *List and Indexes Supplementary series IV.*
Edward VI Records: Hen VII–Eliz	**STAC 3**	Series list, index in *List and Indexes Supplementary series IV.*
Mary Records: Hen VII–Eliz	**STAC 4**	Series list, index in *List and Indexes Supplementary series IV.*
Elizabeth I Records: 1558–1601	**STAC 5** **STAC 7**	Four manuscript lists, index in *List and Indexes Supplementary series IV.* Manuscript list.
James I Records: 1601–25	**STAC 8**	Manuscript list, index in *Barnes index* (three coded volumes by party and place).
Charles I Records: 1625–41	**STAC 9**	Manuscript list.

arise. To settle issues, a Court of Wards and Liveries was set up, and operated between 1540–1660. Like the Court of Requests and Star Chamber, it operated under the rules of equity, and therefore documents were written in English. If your property once formed part of a large estate of a tenant-in-chief of the Crown, these records are worth investigating for evidence.

Pleadings are in **WARD 13**, and there are indexes in **IND 1/10218–21**; supplementary pleadings are in **WARD 22**; depositions can be found in **WARD 3**; and Decrees, Orders and affidavits are in **WARD 2**. Of particular value will be the surveys of tenants' lands in **WARD 5**. The miscellaneous books of the court are in **WARD 9**, and there are several published volumes relating to the miscellanea of the court available on open access.

8.5   Equity courts of semi-autonomous jurisdictions

The Palatinates of Chester, Durham and Lancaster and the Duchy of Lancaster operated their own equity courts where property disputes could be heard. The records are summarised in Table 8.8.

8.6   Equity court exhibits

In addition to the official records created to support each party's case – such as the depositions and affidavits described above – other evidence was often required, and was brought into court to help the officials reach a decision. In

Table 8.8 Equity records of semi-autonomous jurisdictions

Palatinate of Chester	Pleadings **CHES 15** Depositions **CHES 12** Decrees and Orders **CHES 14** and **13** (originals)
Palatinate of Durham	Pleadings **DURH 2** Depositions and Interrogatories **DURH 7** Decrees and Orders **DURH 5** and **6** (drafts)
Palatinate of Lancaster	Bills **PL 6** Answers **PL 7** Replications **PL 8** Depositions **PL 10** Decrees and Orders **PL 11**
Duchy of Lancaster	Pleadings **DL 49** Depositions **DL 3, 4** and **48** Decrees and Orders **DL 5** and **6** (drafts)

property disputes, this meant proof of title to land or evidence of prior legal agreements. However, at the conclusion of the case the litigants sometimes failed to retrieve this evidence, and the courts thus accumulated a vast collection of title deeds, legal papers, family trees, manorial records, maps, plans and other such material. These have been deposited at the PRO and are an amazing source for the house historian. Furthermore, they can (in theory) be linked to the cases that generated them, providing even more information about the litigants concerned.

8.6.1   Chancery Masters exhibits

Once the pleadings were complete, documentary evidence was presented to the Chancery Masters for consideration. During the eighteenth and nineteenth centuries the masters preserved a vast amount of this private material, and the documents themselves date from the twelfth century onwards. These are known collectively as the Chancery Masters Exhibits series (*see* **Figure 20**). The records are stored in **C 103–14**, and are primarily listed by the names of the parties concerned. A composite index to the parties exists in the **C 103** series list, although some supplementary indexes are also available; so it will be essential to have prior information before you start a search, such as the names of individuals involved in the case. However, you should also be able to pick up additional information, such as place names, occupants or previous owners, via a key word search of PROCAT, although some documents have perfunctory descriptions and may give only the names of the parties concerned. The Duchess of Norfolk's

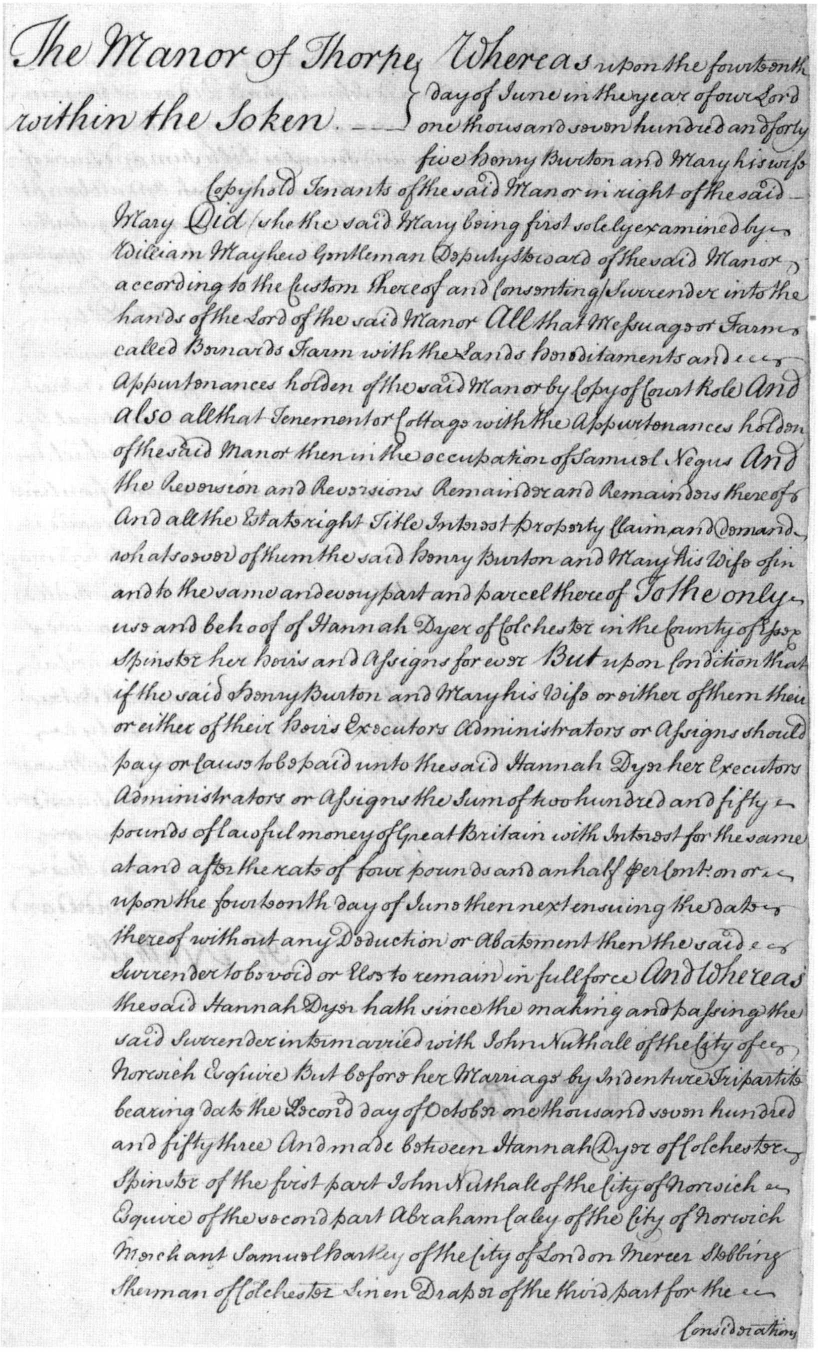

The Manor of Thorpe within the Soken. —— } Whereas upon the fourteenth day of June in the year of our Lord one thousand seven hundred and forty five Henry Burton and Mary his wife Copyhold Tenants of the said Manor or in right of the said Mary Did (she the said Mary being first solely examined by William Mayhew Gentleman Deputy Steward of the said Manor according to the custom thereof and consenting) Surrender into the hands of the Lord of the said Manor All that Messuage or Farm called Bonards Farm with the Lands Hereditaments and other Appurtenances holden of the said Manor by Copy of Court Roll And also all that Tenement or Cottage with the Appurtenances holden of the said Manor then in the occupation of Samuel Negus And the Reversion and Reversions Remainder and Remainders thereof And all the Estate right Title Interest property Claim and demand whatsoever of them the said Henry Burton and Mary his Wife of in and to the same and every part and parcel thereof To the only use and behoof of Hannah Dyer of Colchester in the County of Essex Spinster her heirs and Assigns for ever But upon Condition that if the said Henry Burton and Mary his Wife or either of them their or either of their heirs Executors Administrators or Assigns should pay or cause to be paid unto the said Hannah Dyer her Executors Administrators or Assigns the Sum of two hundred and fifty pounds of lawful money of Great Britain with Interest for the same at and after the rate of four pounds and an half per Cent: on or upon the fourteenth day of June then next ensuing the date thereof without any Deduction or Abatement then the said Surrender to be void or Else to remain in full force And Whereas the said Hannah Dyer hath since the making and passing the said Surrender intermarried with John Nuthall of the City of Norwich Esquire But before her Marriage by Indenture Tripartite bearing date the Second day of October one thousand seven hundred and fifty three And made between Hannah Dyer of Colchester Spinster of the first part John Nuthall of the City of Norwich Esquire of the second part Abraham Caley of the City of Norwich Merchant Samuel Barkley of the City of London Mercer Stebbing Sherman of Colchester Linen Draper of the third part for the Consideration

Figure 20 Part of the title deeds for a property in Thorpe-le-Soken, Essex, dated 14 June 1745, deposited as evidence in a Chancery case, Parsons v. Neville. The deeds produced as evidence range in date from 1644–1779, and other properties in the batch date from as early as 1573. (C 103/12/1)

Deeds are in **C 115**, and manor court rolls extracted from **C 103–14** are in **C 116**. Similar exhibits collected by the Six Clerks are stored in **C 171**.

Chancery Masters Documents are similar to exhibits, and they can be found in **C 117–29**. The records are arranged by the name of the Master who presided over the case, and so to search the records you will need to locate the relevant Master's name from an index in **C 103**.

Later exhibits and documents can be found in **J 90**, which has its own indexes with the series list. Most of the documents derive from the Chancery Division of the Supreme Court of Judicature, but there are also examples from the King's (Queen's) Bench Division, the Exchequer Division and the old Court of King's Bench. Records in **J 90** are stored at Hayes and currently require three working days' notice before they can be produced at Kew.

8.6.2 Exchequer exhibits

The Equity Court of Exchequer also required evidence to be collected, and there are a few areas where you can look for surviving exhibits. The best place to start is series **E 140**, which contains documents dating between 1319–1842; there are several manuscript calendars and indexes available, and the series is well listed and searchable online. Stray documents from Exchequer cases can be found in **C 106**, but you will also find other series such as **E 219** (Clerks Papers, 1625–1841), **E 163** (Miscellanea, 1154–1901) and **E 167** (Papers of the Clerk to the Deputy Remembrancer, 1689–1877) contain exhibits as well, many of which will be of use to the house historian. Later series from the Supreme Court that include Exchequer exhibits are **J 90** and **J 17**.

8.6.3 Exhibits for semi-autonomous jurisdictions

The equity courts of areas under semi-autonomous jurisdiction also retained exhibits. These can be found in **CHES 11** for the Palatinate of Chester, with cause papers in **CHES 9**; **DURH 21** (Palatinate of Durham); **PL 12** (Palatinate of Lancaster); and **DL 49** for the Duchy of Lancaster. Exhibits from the court of Wards and Liveries are in **WARD 2**.

8.7 Civil litigation in common law courts

8.7.1 Common law courts

Before 1875, there were four main central common law courts where litigants could enter a case. They are best summarised as in Table 8.9, although in reality all courts took cases between subjects.

Table 8.9 The common law courts pre-1875

Chancery	Cases between Crown and subject regarding royal rights
Common Pleas	Cases between subjects
Exchequer	Cases between Crown debtors
King's Bench	Cases between Crown and subjects

Property disputes between individuals that were settled under the auspices of the common law were less frequent than in the equity courts, unless the plaintiff was seeking compensation rather than restoration of land or enforcement of contract. However, cases can appear in any of the above areas, although many were dropped or a private agreement was reached before a judgment could be made. In these instances it will be difficult to extract much information about the process, as surviving records are difficult to use; the records of a single case can be scattered across many areas, and at present less is known about common law records compared to those of the equity courts. As such, it is easier to focus research on the main series of documents that were generated – the plea rolls – and then attempt to look in other areas, such as judgment books, for information. However, these tend to record the later stages of a case, and many disputes that were dropped at an early stage will simply be impossible to locate. It is also important to remember that the common law courts were used to record fictitious legal disputes as part of a conveyance, and it is necessary to distinguish between a genuine dispute and an enrolled deed or land transfer. In fact, the growth of conveyance in the court of Common Pleas by 'common recovery' led to a separate series of records, the recovery rolls, being created in 1538.

In theory, cases relating to property disputes might appear in any one of these courts; however, you are more likely to find pleas of cases between private individuals entered in the courts of Common Pleas or King's Bench. The Exchequer of Pleas was usually reserved for revenue cases, especially those that impinged on royal revenue-generating rights, although many land disputes found their way into this court. Chancery was also used primarily for cases that involved royal rights, but among the most important areas of litigation were the division of lands between joint heiresses, including assignment of dower, and challenges to inquisitions post mortem and feudal incidents payable on land and property.

8.7.2   Plea rolls of common law courts

Plea rolls record the formal processes in a common law court: until 1733 they were written in Latin, and were formulaic in the business they recorded. The

Table 8.10 Common law plea rolls and relevant indexes

Court	Date	Indexes
King's Bench		
KB 26	1194–1276	Various printed calendars.
KB 27	1273–1702	From 1390: docket rolls and books in **IND 1/1322–84** and **IND 1/6042–96**.
KB 122	1702–1875	Docket books in **IND 1/6097–372**.
Common Pleas		
CP 40	1273–1874	From 1509: prothonotaries docket books in **CP 60**, usually three books per term.
CP 43	1583–1837	Pleas of land; indexes in **IND 1/17183–216**.
Exchequer of Pleas		
E 13	1236–1875	Selective calendar in **IND 1**; for details consult *List and Index Society*, *vol. 232*. Index of places in **E 48/1–18**. Repertory rolls in **E 14** (only periods 1412–99, 1559–1669, 1822–30).
Chancery Pleas		
C 44	1272–1485	Series list.
C 43	1485–1625	Series list.
C 206	1558–1901	Series list.

details you would expect to find on a common law court plea roll include a description of the action concerned (where you will pick up details of the property or settlement under dispute); how the case proceeded within the court; and a final judgment, if one was actually made.

A summary of the plea rolls for the various courts, plus a list of finding aids and indexes, is provided in Table 8.10. You may need to look in a series of courts to find the records of a case.

8.7.3   Records of judgment

Judgments of cases were usually recorded on the plea rolls, but by the late eighteenth century many of the cases were not filed. To find out information about the names and dates involved in a case, plus a brief outline of the issues involved, various rolls exist that record judgments and orders. These can assist in filling in missing information for later cases, and various indexes to these records are set out in Table 8.11.

8.7.4   Supreme Court of Judicature (King's/Queen's Bench)

Following the reorganization of the judicial system in 1875, all courts were

Court	Series	Date/Indexes
Table 8.11 Common law records of judgment and relevant indexes		
King's Bench		
Entry Books of Judgment	**KB 168**	1699–1875; series includes indexes **KB 168/129–263.**
Specimens of destroyed documents	**J 89/13/286**	Index in **J 89/13/287.**
Common Pleas		
Entry Books of Judgment	**CP 64**	1859–74; series includes indexes.
Specimens of destroyed documents	**J 89**	
Exchequer		
Entry Books of Judgment	**E 45**	1830–75.
Chancery		
Remembrance Rolls	**C 221**	1565–1785.
	C 222	1638–1729.

amalgamated into the Supreme Court of Judicature, with five divisions. Each division could apply common law or equity according to the case it heard (*see* **Figure 21**), and it can therefore be difficult to locate papers of common law cases. The main place to look, though, will be among surviving King's (Queen's) Bench papers. Nethertheless, many of the records have been destroyed, and so you are likely to encounter great difficulty in finding information. Cause books are in **J 87** (Green Books, from 1875) and **J 168** (1879–1937), which provide the names of parties and a brief description of the cause; indexes to the Green Books from 1935 are in **J 88**. You may also find specimens of destroyed documents in series **J 89**.

8.7.5 Civil litigation in assize courts

Records of property disputes were heard in civil assize cases by itinerant justices if a writ *nisi prius* had been issued from one of the central common law courts in London. This enabled parties to transfer the case from the central court to a more convenient local assize court, which was held twice a year. The records generated by the assize courts were similar to those of the central courts, and are stored in a variety of PRO series; a leaflet summarises the best place to begin your research, as the records are arranged according to the relevant judicial circuits. Crown minute books will record the basic details of the case, such as the names of the parties, and are usually arranged chronologically. However, there are no indexes, so you will need to have some prior knowledge of when the case took place, perhaps from a local newspaper report.

The courts of King's Bench and Common Pleas kept note of cases that were

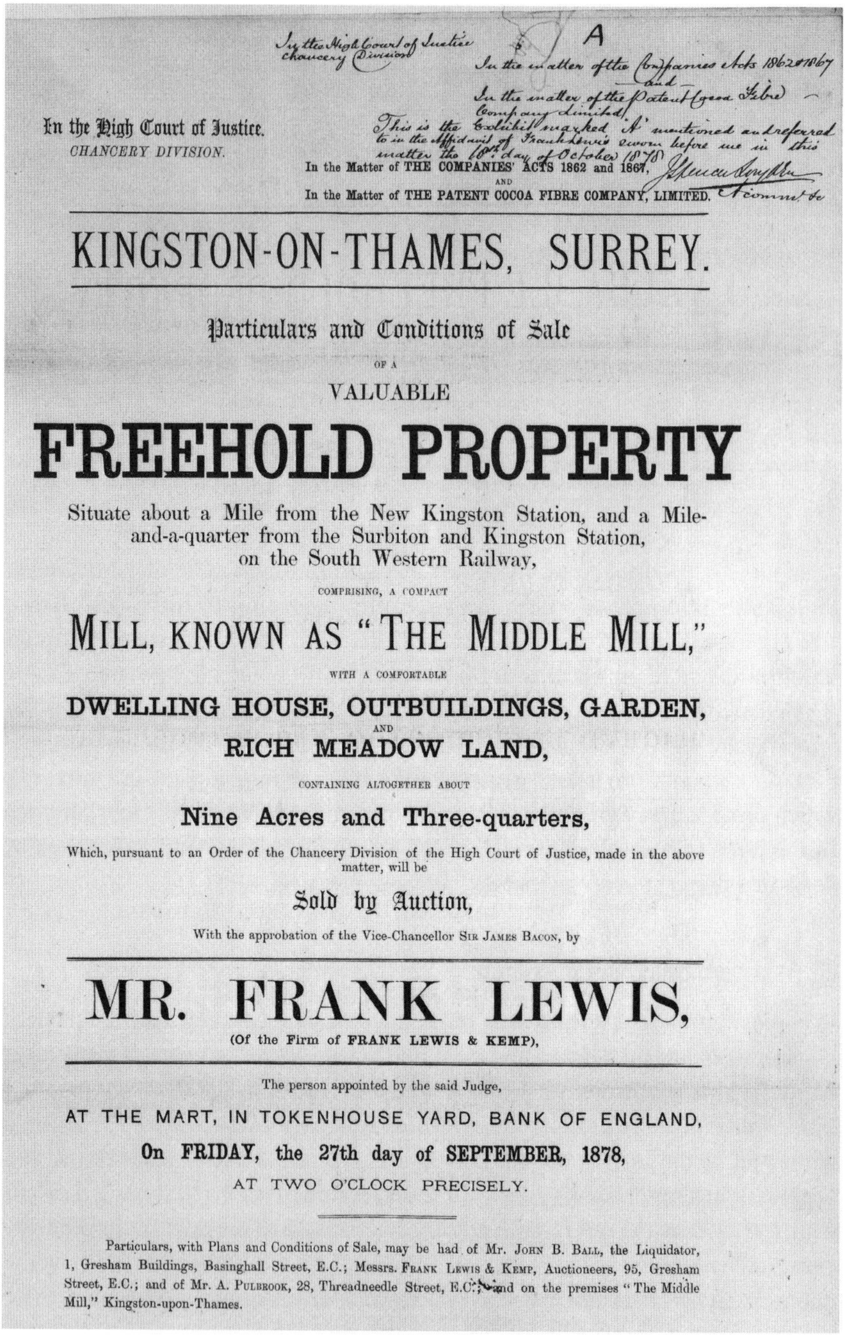

In the High Court of Justice.
CHANCERY DIVISION.

In the Matter of THE COMPANIES' ACTS 1862 and 1867,
AND
In the Matter of THE PATENT COCOA FIBRE COMPANY, LIMITED.

KINGSTON-ON-THAMES, SURREY.

Particulars and Conditions of Sale

OF A

VALUABLE

FREEHOLD PROPERTY

Situate about a Mile from the New Kingston Station, and a Mile-and-a-quarter from the Surbiton and Kingston Station, on the South Western Railway,

COMPRISING, A COMPACT

MILL, KNOWN AS "THE MIDDLE MILL,"

WITH A COMFORTABLE

DWELLING HOUSE, OUTBUILDINGS, GARDEN,
AND
RICH MEADOW LAND,

CONTAINING ALTOGETHER ABOUT

Nine Acres and Three-quarters,

Which, pursuant to an Order of the Chancery Division of the High Court of Justice, made in the above matter, will be

Sold by Auction,

With the approbation of the Vice-Chancellor SIR JAMES BACON, by

MR. FRANK LEWIS,

(Of the Firm of **FRANK LEWIS & KEMP**),

The person appointed by the said Judge,

AT THE MART, IN TOKENHOUSE YARD, BANK OF ENGLAND,

On FRIDAY, the 27th day of SEPTEMBER, 1878,

AT TWO O'CLOCK PRECISELY.

Particulars, with Plans and Conditions of Sale, may be had of Mr. JOHN B. BALL, the Liquidator, 1, Gresham Buildings, Basinghall Street, E.C.; Messrs. FRANK LEWIS & KEMP, Auctioneers, 95, Gresham Street, E.C.; and of Mr. A. PULBROOK, 28, Threadneedle Street, E.C.; and on the premises "The Middle Mill," Kingston-upon-Thames.

Figure 21 The sale particulars for Kingston Mill, to be sold by auction on 27 September 1878 by order of the Chancery Division of the Supreme Court. The case originally commenced in 1877, and related to the liquidation of the Patent Cocoa Fibre Company. (J 46/342A)

Table 8.12 Common law posteas

Court	Description	Date
Common Pleas		
CP36	Entry books of nisi prius	1644–1837
CP57	Early postea books	(unsorted)
CP41	Postea books	1689–1837
CP42	Postea books	1830–52
King's Bench		
KB146	Panella files (early posteas)	Pre-1522
KB20	Posteas	1664–1839
KB146	Notice of trial books (under nisi prius)	1698–1842

removed under nisi prius. These were known as posteas, and can be found in the PRO series listed in Table 8.12.

8.8   Quarter sessions records

It is important to make clear that the PRO holds no quarter sessions records at all. Where they survive, they will be found in the relevant CRO or amongst the deposited private papers of serving Justices of the Peace (JPs).

The quarter sessions were so named because they were held four times a year, and were courts presided over by JPs. Their remit was to undertake routine judicial and administrative functions in the shires, with the power to prosecute certain types of offence. More serious matters were referred to the itinerant assize judges, who toured on circuits twice a year.

Quarter sessions records tend to enjoy a mixed survival rate. As with all court records, prosecutions involved the creation of many different types of document, including personal working papers generated by the JPs. However, the main stages of a session that produced relevant records were indictments for an offence, recognizances to ensure appearance at a session, and summary convictions. The formal court sessions generated quarter-session rolls, which include writs to appear, lists of attendees, recognizances, indictments and jury lists; session and process books to record proceedings; order books to record court decisions; and session papers kept by the Clerk of the Peace, the main court official. Informal mediation and meetings to discuss routine administrative matters might be recorded in unofficial papers kept by individual JPs.

8.8.1   Records of prosecution

During the late sixteenth and early seventeenth centuries, overcrowding in or around towns and cities was a major concern, mainly due to the increased risk of fire or disease. Yet at the same time, population growth and urban expansion meant that there was pressure to provide sufficient accommodation for people who were drifting into urban areas. To prevent 'slums' appearing on the edges of towns, various statutes were passed that restricted new house building. The most important was 31 Elizabeth c.7 (1588–9), which stipulated that no new dwelling could be constructed without first assigning four acres of land to the site, thereby preventing overcrowding. One of the most important areas this affected was London and the surrounding counties. Punishment was potentially severe. An offender was liable to an initial £10 penalty, followed by 40 shillings per month for maintaining an illegal dwelling. Furthermore, if more than one family lived in the cottage there was an additional penalty of 10 shillings per month. Offences against this statute were usually prosecuted at the quarter sessions, and records can be found in surviving quarter-session rolls. These can be difficult to use as, like most formal courts, they are written in Latin until 1733; but a large number have been calendared and indexed, although the name and date of a case would make searching for evidence much easier.

8.8.2   Records of local administration

Other matters relating to the local community fell within the remit of the quarter sessions. Repairs to roads and highways were usually the responsibility of the relevant parish, unless covered by a private turnpike trust and so, if they were not maintained, the entire parish was liable to amercement. Surviving quarter sessions papers can often list stretches of road that needed repair, and used the names and addresses of residents as landmarks to identify the worst sections. However, the chances of finding such information about your house will be slim.

Records of other types of property can be found in the quarter sessions papers. For example, JPs were effectively responsible for granting licences to alehouses. They issued recognizances that were valid for one year, which bound over alehouse owners to keep the peace; if law and order had been maintained, a new recognizance was issued for the following year. You will often find the name of the alehouse keeper listed, plus the names of two others who would act as sureties for the original recognizance. Usually other alehouse keepers acted as a group and stood surety for each other, and where the records survive you can find a wealth of information about local hostelries in a community.

9 House occupancy

9.1 Introduction

You will find that one of the most important and interesting ways to trace the history of your house is through the life stories of the people that either owned the property, or who used to reside there. Furthermore, you will start to put flesh on the bones of your chronology by empathizing with the people who considered your house as their home as well; this process tends to personalize your findings and move your research beyond a simple history of the bricks and mortar. The people you uncover in the documents helped to shape the way your house looks today, and their experiences are a valid and important avenue to explore when trying to understand how your area evolved into the community that you now live in.

This chapter will outline ways in which you can utilize sources for genealogy to extract information about previous owners or occupants. The best place to start is with census returns because, unlike people who have a habit of moving around, houses stay fixed in one place and are easier to find in the records. You can create a research framework for your property by examining the valuation survey of 1910–15 and the tithe maps and apportionments of c.1836–58, both described in Chapter 3, and then use the existing census returns from 1841 to 1891 to fill in some of the gaps.

Records generated within the parish will often tell you about the community in which your house was situated, as well as recording the major events in an occupier's life – baptism, marriage and burial. In particular, marriages often acted as a catalyst for constructing extensions to existing property and undertaking rebuilding schemes or major redecorations. Other unusual architectural features can be explained by looking in trade directories – houses also doubled up as places of work, and may have retained some of the original layout.

Earlier sources for genealogy are also suggested, such as inquisitions post mortem for major estate owners, and assignment of dower. Although not all houses will be old enough for you to able to use these sources, they can provide a remarkably vivid insight into previous dwellings that perhaps existed on the site of your current home. You may even uncover the story of why an older house was demolished to make way for a more modern property.

9.2   Census returns

9.2.1   Census returns 1801–31

Since Roman times, assessments of population numbers have been made to assist governments with their work. The first nationwide census in the United Kingdom was undertaken in 1801, and thereafter repeated every ten years. Between 1801 and 1831 only very basic information was recorded; in essence, the number of people who resided in a parish or street, with perhaps the heads of household listed and statistics that refer to age or occupation. The number of inhabited and uninhabited houses was also compiled.

As such, these official returns will be of minimal use to the house historian, as they provide basic statistics for an area. However, partial assessment returns and the working papers of the enumerators do survive for some regions, and these can provide information that can be utilized in conjunction with additional sources. To cite two examples, there are census records in the Shropshire Record Office for 1821 that record heads of household on a street by street level for parts of Shrewsbury; and a notebook compiled by a census enumerator for Saxmundham, Suffolk, provides an insight into the 1831 assessment, linking names with a general survey of property occupancy dating from the 1790s.

9.2.2   Census returns 1841–91

It was with the 1841 census that the returns became an invaluable source for house history on a nationwide basis. For the first time, they record the names of all occupants for specific properties, as opposed to a general total by parish. Although street names are usually provided, house numbers are often omitted, and consequently the returns in isolation can be difficult to use. Nevertheless, you will obtain the names of all occupants, and where street numbers are not provided, the place where one property ends and another begins is marked on the return, usually with two dashes under the last name in the house. Households within a single property are also indicated, and are separated by a single slash. The full name, age, gender and occupation of all inhabitants are provided, although the ages of all over the age of 15 were rounded down to the nearest five years.

However, the subsequent census records from 1851 to 1891 provide far greater detail about the occupiers (*see* **Figure 22**) and should therefore allow you to positively identify your property with a greater degree of confidence. Each

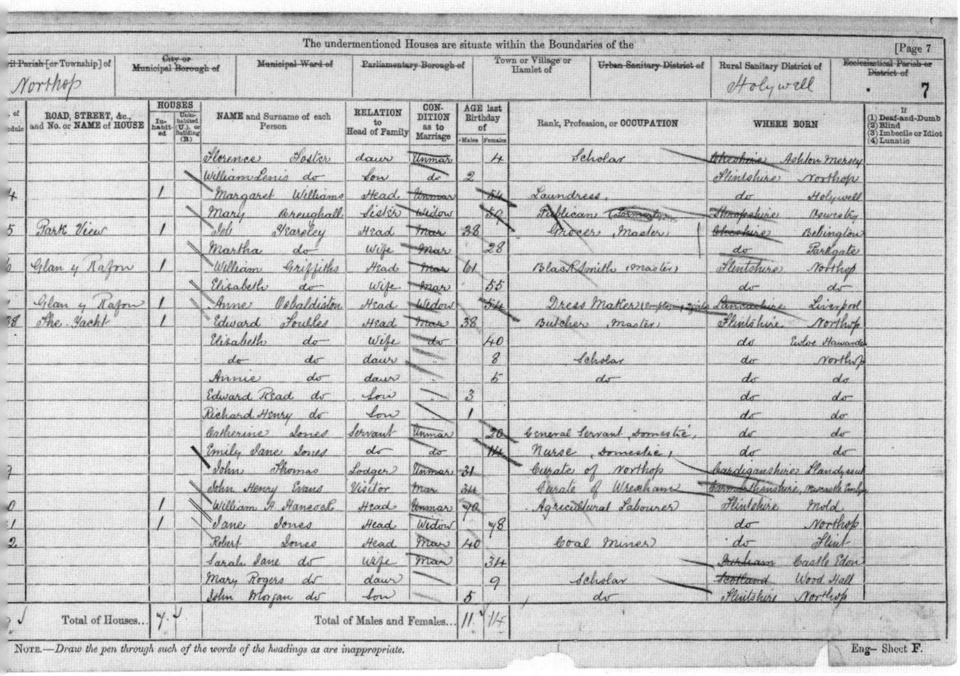

The undermentioned Houses are situate within the Boundaries of the [Page 7

Civil Parish [or Township] of	City or Municipal Borough of	Municipal Ward of	Parliamentary Borough of	Town or Village or Hamlet of	Urban Sanitary District of	Rural Sanitary District of	Ecclesiastical Parish or District of
Northop						Holywell	7

No. of Schedule	ROAD, STREET, &c., and No. or NAME of HOUSE	HOUSES In-habited	HOUSES Uninhabited (U.), or Building (B.)	NAME and Surname of each Person	RELATION to Head of Family	CONDITION as to Marriage	AGE last Birthday of Males	AGE last Birthday of Females	Rank, Profession, or OCCUPATION	WHERE BORN	If (1) Deaf-and-Dumb (2) Blind (3) Imbecile or Idiot (4) Lunatic
				Florence Foster	daur	Unmar		4	Scholar	Cheshire Ashton Mersey	
				William Lewis do	Son	do	2			Flintshire Northop	
4		1		Margaret Williams	Head	Unmar		54	Laundress	do Holywell	
				Mary Brougham	Sister	Widow		52	Publican Farmer	Shropshire Bronington	
5	Park View	1		Job Yearsley	Head	Mar	38		Grocer, Master	Cheshire Bebington	
				Martha do	Wife	Mar		28		do Parkgate	
6	Glan y Rafon	1		William Griffiths	Head	Mar	61		Blacksmith (master)	Flintshire Northop	
				Elisabeth do	Wife	Mar		55		do do	
	Glan y Rafon	1		Anne Oswaldiston	Head	Widow		54	Dress Maker (employing girls)	Lancashire Liverpool	
8	The Yacht	1		Edward Foulkes	Head	Mar	38		Butcher, master	Flintshire Northop	
				Elisabeth do	Wife	do		40		do Ewloe Hawarden	
				do do	daur			8	Scholar	do Northop	
				Annie do	daur			5	do	do do	
				Edward Read do	Son		3			do do	
				Richard Henry do	Son		1			do do	
				Catherine Jones	Servant	Unmar		20	General Servant, domestic	do do	
				Emily Jane Jones	do	do		14	Nurse, domestic	do do	
7				John Thomas	Lodger	Unmar	31		Curate of Northop	Cardiganshire Llandyssul	
				John Henry Evans	Visitor	Mar	34		Curate of Wrexham	Carmarthenshire, Newcastle Emlyn	
0		1		William H. Hancock	Head	Unmar	70		Agricultural Labourer	Flintshire Mold	
1		1		Jane Jones	Head	Widow		78		do Northop	
2				Robert Jones	Head	Mar	40		Coal miner	do Flint	
				Sarah Jane do	Wife	Mar		34		Durham Castle Eden	
				Mary Rogers do	daur			9	Scholar	Scotland Wood Hall	
				John Morgan do	Son		5		do	Flintshire Northop	
	Total of Houses...	7				Total of Males and Females...	11	14			

NOTE.—*Draw the pen through such of the words of the headings as are inappropriate.* Eng— Sheet F.

Figure 22 The 1881 census return for 'The Yacht', in Northop, Flintshire, formerly 'The Yacht Inn'. Its change in status is demonstrated by the occupation of Edward Foulkes, who is described as a master butcher. He resides there with his wife, four children and two house servants. Also listed is a lodger, the curate of Northop, and his visitor, the curate of Wrexham. (RG 11/5505)

person will be identified by his or her full name, exact age, marital status, relationship to the head of the household, gender, occupation, parish and county of birth and various medical disabilities. The later the records are, the easier they are to use; so if you are researching a property, it makes sense to start with the 1891 census and work backwards.

As a source for house history, the census returns are a rich series of records that will tell you about the people who dwelt in your house, with details of their families, their occupations or whether more than one household was resident in your property. This social and economic data will allow you to assess what the community was like, and therefore permit an evaluation of the status of your house. One of the main benefits of census returns is that they exist in a continuous series, and so you can work backwards decade by decade to build up a picture of change or continuity. This data can then act as a foundation for other areas of research, such as parish records, trade directories and electoral lists that are described later in this chapter.

However, it is important to beware of the pitfalls of using census returns to provide a picture of who lived in your house. For a start, they record occupation on only one given day of the year; it might be the case that your house was unoccupied and therefore will not appear in the records. Furthermore, house names and numbers, and even the name of the street it was built in, were subject to change over time, so it is important to check these details in advance to ensure you are researching the correct property. Even some of the later census returns do not always include street names or house numbers, making positive identification very difficult, and it is entirely possible that your house had not yet been constructed. One final point – census returns provide the names of house occupiers only, which is fine when the occupier was also the owner. However, non-resident owners will be important figures in your house history, as it was they who transferred property and influenced who occupied it; you will have to use other sources to obtain this information.

9.2.3   Locating later census records

The census returns from 1841 to 1891 for England and Wales have not been made available at the PRO; you will need to travel to the FRC in Myddleton Street, London, to view microfilm copies of the original returns. A summary of the record series is provided in Table 9.1.

For organizational purposes, the census adopted the registration districts and sub-districts established in 1837, which in turn were based on the Poor Law unions created in 1834. The FRC stocks place-name indexes for rural areas and street indexes for towns with a population in excess of 40,000 people. These provide the registration district and sub-district, and therefore allow you to locate the relevant document reference, having first consulted the appropriate volume in the search room. In turn, the reference corresponds to a microfilm that will contain the census returns.

Table 9.1 Census records

Available on microfilm at the FRC:

Date of census	Record series
1841	**HO 107/1–1465**
1851	**HO 107/1466–2531**
1861	**RG 9/1–4543**
1871	**RG 10/1–5785**
1881	**RG 11/1–5632**
1891	**RG 12/1–5643**

Available on microfiche at the PRO from January 2002:

1901	**RG 13**

As well as the official finding aids, there are separate name and place indexes available. The most comprehensive is for the 1881 census, now available on CD; and regional indexes for other years, most notably 1851, have also been compiled. Whilst these are a good place to begin looking for people, they will be of less use to a house historian as they are mainly designed for personal name searches. If travel to London is inconvenient, you will find that most CROs have microfiche or film copies for the relevant county. In addition, many local record societies have prepared separate indexes for census years other than 1851 and 1881. The Latter Day Saints maintain Family History Centres where you can hire in films for any county on request.

9.2.4   The 1901 census

In January 2002 the census returns for 1901 will be released in series **RG 13**. It is anticipated that this will be a vastly used resource, and plans are underway to digitize the census returns and make them available online, with a small charge to view or download data. Microfiche versions will also be produced, but if the project is successful, further census returns will be made available on the Internet. The PRO website carries information about this development.

9.2.5   Scotland and Ireland

The 1841–91 census returns for Scotland, stored by the Registrar General for Scotland, are available at New Register House, Edinburgh. A fee is currently charged for access to the microfilms. Alternatively, the entire 1881 census is available on CD-Rom, as is England and Wales. Digitized images of the 1891 census are available at New Register House, and indexes to both the 1881 and 1891 census can be obtained via the Internet at http://www.origins.net. Material for Ireland is held by the National Archives, Dublin. However, most of the nineteenth-century returns have been destroyed, although the returns for 1901 and 1911 are reasonably complete and are available for public inspection. Copies are also available at PRONI. Copies of Irish and Scottish films can also be hired at Latter Day Saints Family History Centres.

9.3   Electoral lists and registers

Electoral rights have not always been as inclusive as they are today. The right to vote has gradually been extended throughout the twentieth century to include all men and women over the age of 18, but before 1918 not all men and very few women were eligible. From the earliest times until the nineteenth century, the right to vote was based on the amount and type of land or property that a man held, and lists of voters were compiled. From the eighteenth century these were usually based on Land Tax returns, as the right to vote was linked to holding freehold property. Therefore, early lists, often known as poll books, provide a guide to freeholders in your area, and on occasion will provide a precise address. The Guildhall Library, Society of Genealogists Library, and the Institute of Historical Research, all have large collections of poll books.

From 1832, electoral registers were compiled that listed the names of all those entitled to vote, with a brief description of the property that provided eligibility. The right to vote was extended from 1867, and consequently the lists became more comprehensive and provided greater details of property. Modern electoral registers from 1928, when women over 21 were enfranchised, provided street names and house numbers, and can give a useful indication of who lived at your house.

The PRO does not hold any electoral lists in a distinct series, and the best place to begin your research will be the CRO or nearest branch library, where printed electoral registers are sometimes stored. However, a partial series of electoral registers for the early 1870s can be located in the PRO library.

9.4   Street and trade directories

Domestic dwellings were often used as places from which occupants also traded, and from the late eighteenth century street and trade directories were compiled to provide indexes to the whereabouts and occupation of tradespeople, and the private addresses of wealthier residents were often listed as well. The earliest lists will give only partial coverage for a town or parish, but those in the nineteenth and twentieth centuries can provide street indexes and maps that are more inclusive. Trade directories tended to cover a county or group of counties and list residents by parish, arranged under the types of occupation of the tradespeople. Street directories proliferate in urban areas, and usually give more detail. Rival directories may well give different information, so it is worth checking a variety if possible. Furthermore, they can contain incorrect data, as it was often down to the traders to inform the compilers that they had moved or ceased trading. Alternatively, the agents working for the compilers sometimes used information from earlier directories to prepare new versions. It is always sensible to corroborate your evidence from other sources. As you will see from the case study in Chapter 15, the proprietors of a public house continued to be listed in one directory for five years after they were buried in the local churchyard!

The PRO library has a selection of trade directories for the London area, but you should head for the relevant CRO or, in some cases, branch library for the best collection of local directories. The Guildhall Library in London has an excellent collection of London and provincial directories. In general you will find that there are many different directories, but the main publications to look for will be Kelly's and the Post Office Directory, as these developed nationwide editions.

9.5   Parish registers

If you are attempting to trace the history of a family in a local community, parish registers are an excellent place to begin. These are the records of baptisms, marriages and burials for a parish, and can date back as early as 1538 when the post-Reformation regime stipulated that they should be maintained. Although early parish registers are of little immediate use for locating details of property, by the nineteenth century places of residence were recorded alongside the individual's name, especially in parishes in or around cities. Parish registers are not stored at the PRO, but can usually be found in the relevant CRO. Various publications exist to help you locate their whereabouts.

In addition to parish registers, the parish chest may contain a variety of other useful documents. For example, assessments of parish rates were compiled that may record house names and property values, and these are considered in the next chapter. You might also find agreements among parishioners concerning rotas of duties for parish offices, such as parish constable or overseer of the poor; these are often arranged by house row.

9.6   Inquisitions post mortem

For earlier property or estates, you may find information contained in inquisitions post mortem (IPMs), particularly if you are tracing a substantial property or if your house was built on land that once formed part of a large estate. The records start in the thirteenth century and continue into the mid seventeenth, and were compiled by the Crown at the death of a tenant-in-chief to determine whether an heir at law was sane, or of age (21 years) to inherit. If he was, he would pay a relief to enter into his lands; if not, then the lands would default to the Crown until lucidity or majority was reached, and the heir would become a ward of the Crown; the estates would be administered on the heir's behalf, but the Crown would take the profits. Royal officials known as escheators conducted the inquisitions, and they filed the returns in Chancery, the Exchequer or, from the reign of Henry VIII, the Court of Wards.

At the very least, IPMs can confirm that the estate on which your house was built was passed to a descendant, thereby making a search for relevant archives that bit easier. However, the original documents are in Latin and can be difficult to interpret. A summary of the PRO series is provided in Table 9.2.

Table 9.2 Inquisitions Post Mortem and relevant indexes

1236–1418 **C 132** (Henry III), **C 133** (Edward I), **C 134** (Edward II),**C 135** (Edward III), **C 136** (Richard II), **C 137** (Henry IV), **C 138** (Henry V), **E 149**	Printed *Calendars of IPMs* (in English)
1418–85 **C 138** (Henry V), **C 139** (Henry VI), **C 140** (Edward IV), **C 141** (Richard III) **E 149**	Original Latin documents – Chancery files indexed in **C 138** series list, plus four volumes of calendars. Four manuscript indexes for Exchequer series.
1485–1509 **C 142** **E 150**	Printed *Calendar of IPMs* (in English)
1509–1640 **C 142** **E 150** **WARD 7**	Original Latin documents – published *Index of IPMs*

To order an original IPM from an entry in the calendar for the periods 1236–1418 and 1485–1509, you will need to convert it to a PRO reference.

Example

The IPM of Edmund Mussenden, taken 18 Richard II, includes a cottage and tenement at Guildford, Surrey. There are three calendar entries:
C.Ric.II file 84(10), E.Inq.PM File 64(5) and E.Enrolment etc. of Inq. no. 307

Copies of this IPM were deposited in both Chancery and Exchequer, with a separate copy being enrolled in the Exchequer. The regnal year is Richard II, so the Chancery series will be **C 136**. The entry also provides the PRO piece number, in this case 84, so you would need to order **C 136/84**. When the document arrives you will see that several IPMs were stitched into one file, and the number in brackets, in this case 10, provides the relevant IPM within the file. The Exchequer series will be **E 149**, and the same conversion principle applies – so the document reference will be **E 149/64** and the IPM will be the fifth in the file. The enrolment conversion is similar – the key sheet at the front of the calendar shows that the records are stored in **E 152**, and the relevant file is number 307, giving an ordering reference of **E 152/307**.

Later records for the Palatinates of Chester, Durham and Lancaster and the Duchy of Lancaster can be found in **CHES 3**, **DURH 3**, **PL 4** and **DL 7** respectively, and for the period 1509-1640 are included in the published *Index of IPMs*.

9.7 Assignments of dower

Since medieval times, a dower was assigned to the bride as part of the marriage agreement. Normally this took the form of money or goods, but the practice of including houses was common amongst wealthier classes. Furthermore, dower houses were often especially constructed for the bride, and would become her residence if her spouse pre-deceased her. Many high-status yet relatively small houses on the edge of large estates can be traced to this practice, and building accounts or personal papers in estate records can provide relevant information. Quite often such properties can contain salvage from higher-status houses that may provide misleading architectural clues. The PRO is not the best place to start looking for such material, and you should begin at the relevant CRO.

In some cases, assignments of dower that involved the legal transfer of property were enrolled to provide legal evidence of title. For example, the dower arrangement for Agnes Brown included a house near Billingsgate in London, and an indenture confirming this arrangement by the executors of her late husband's will was enrolled on the Hustings Roll in 1463, listing the layout of the property in great detail.

However, if a dower was disputed, you may find traces in one of the courts described in Chapter 8, in particular the Court of Requests. Furthermore, you may find inquisitions held into right of dower in lands or property that was part of a general IPM (known as an inquisition *de assignatione dotis*).

9.8 Diaries and personal correspondence

If you know the name of a house owner or occupier, you may be lucky enough to discover private correspondence or even a diary from the time that he or she lived in your property. These revealing insights are not only valuable for the light they throw on the way people used to live, but also for the evidence they contain about the house in which they lived. Not all diaries will be of use; but others have been known to include room by room descriptions of a house, even providing details about the room decorations.

As these are personal documents, the most logical place to begin a search is at the CRO. Diaries and correspondence occasionally turn up at the PRO in the various exhibit series, and in the **PRO** series there are non-public collections and family papers, accumulated through gift, purchase or deposit, that contain correspondence. Some of these are calendared, but others will provide no clues as to their contents. You will find them of use only if you know that your house once formed part of a large estate whose owners deposited material at the PRO.

10 Tax and rates records

10.1 Introduction

Taxation records may not sound the most fascinating area in which to look for information relating to your house, but throughout the centuries the Crown and its governments have found it expedient to raise levies that were assessed on land and property. We may grumble about paying taxes, but we should be thankful that previous occupiers of our houses have done so, as whenever assessments and payments have been made in the past, records were generated. It is therefore possible to obtain crucial information about houses and property from the assessments that were made upon them.

The most comprehensive and useful source for house historians was perhaps the valuation survey of 1910–15, described in Chapter 3, as it provided assessment data and maps that combine to give a nationwide snapshot of property at the start of the twentieth century. The sources described in this chapter are not as easy to use, widespread or comprehensive. However, in combination with other sources, plus a working knowledge of your local area, you will find that the forms of taxation listed below might yield some surprising results and take you a few decades further back in the documentary tale of your house's history. Some tax records might also help to explain any puzzling architectural anomalies in your house, as assessments were often based on the number of fixed features, such as hearths and windows. Evasion was widespread, and one of the simplest ways to reduce your tax bill was to remove these features by bricking them up. The data contained in these records should allow you to make a comparison between contemporary assessment data and the equivalent modern number of these features.

You will usually find that tax records list the names of the house owners and occupiers and are arranged by parish, rather than by house number in the modern sense. However, some will be arranged by street and maintain a continuous order or sequence of names from year to year, and by employing related sources, such as trade directories or electoral lists, you should be able to identify your property with a degree of confidence.

The PRO is a good place to start looking for some of the tax records listed in this chapter, but you will also need to undertake research at your CRO as well. Not only will you find tax records in 'official' sources, but also among the private papers of estate managers and assessors. Several guides on the location, use and interpretation of tax records have been written to assist you, and are listed under **Useful publications**.

10.2   Hearth Tax

10.2.1 History of the records

The earliest assessed tax on property was the Hearth Tax, introduced in 1662 to raise money for the recently restored monarchy of Charles II. Although the tax was continued until 1688, only the assessments for 1662–6 and 1669–74 provide useful data for the house historian. The rate of tax for the period 1662–74 was a half-yearly payment of one shilling for each hearth in all occupied property worth more than 20 shillings per year in terms of rent; the occupier also had to be a local ratepayer of church and poor rates.

10.2.2 Types of Hearth Tax returns

When the Hearth Tax was first introduced, various types of document were generated that related to the assessment and collection of the tax. The most relevant for the house historian will be liability assessments, which were compiled by local assessors. The assessor was usually the parish constable, who visited each property to obtain the number of hearths from the occupier. If he suspected that he had been provided with false information, he had powers of entry so that he could check for himself. The records can be difficult to use, as they list the name of the householder rather than provide a description of the property that was being assessed, and although not unknown, it is rare to find the name or location of properties specified. Therefore you will need to know either the number of hearths your property would have had, or the name of the householder who was being assessed. The problems associated with owner/occupier confusion were partially addressed in later assessments. Individuals who owned several properties were assessed where they were currently resident, and were issued with a certificate of residence as proof of payment. Earlier certificates of residence, which can be found in series **E 115**, list the place of abode where the person was assessed, and are arranged by the name of the individual.

To identify the potential number of hearths that would have been liable, you will need to do some basic arithmetic. First, identify the section or sections of your house that you think were contemporary at the time of the tax. Second, count the number of chimney stacks. Third, count the number of rooms that abut each chimney stack. The maximum number of hearths can be obtained by allowing for a hearth in all rooms on each floor for every chimney stack. For example, a two-storey house with a chimney stack at each end and a room on each floor should have four hearths.

In addition to assessment data, you may find certificates of exemption to be of some use, as these can provide more information about the householder or the house itself. They might be issued on grounds of poverty, or because a house was uninhabited or undergoing repairs. Bricks uncovered in a house in Sax-mundham, Suffolk, bore the date 1672, a Hearth Tax year, and it is tempting to imagine the occupier rebuilding sections of the property, leaving the hearths until last to avoid paying extra taxation. However, it is unlikely that he escaped for long, because periodical reassessments were conducted to pick up just this sort of evasion. Where reassessment or exemption records survive, they will be listed with the liability assessments at the PRO.

10.2.3 Locating the records

Hearth Tax returns can be found in PRO series **E 179** (*see* **Figure 23**). There are typed indexes, arranged by county, available on open access in the reading rooms that provide details of the tax, the area covered (usually a hundred or other county division), the type of Hearth Tax record, and whether names of individuals are recorded. In addition, there is a database of tax returns in **E 179** that allows you to search by place, type of tax, date of tax and type of tax record. The database does not cover all counties yet, but at present provides document references for Hearth Tax returns for the Home Counties. A basic summary of Hearth Tax returns is provided in Gibson's guide to the Hearth Tax (*see* **Useful publications**).

10.3   Land Tax

10.3.1 Historical background

An important method of taxation was the fixed quota, which had existed since 1334 and was frequently used by Henry VIII to raise subsidies. In 1696 this principle was adopted for the Land Tax. Instead of making assessments on individual properties based on an architectural feature such as the hearth, where widespread evasion was possible, a fixed sum of money was agreed that was to be levied from an entire county. The division of this tax burden fell to local assessors, who in turn created fixed quotas per parish to be paid by the

Figure 23 Hearth Tax return for Titchfield, Hampshire, c.1665. 'St Margarets' was formerly the property of the Earl of Southampton and in all probability had been constructed as a dower house, then later converted into a hunting lodge. (E 179/176/565)

proprietors of land. The tax was assessed on land units – although in principle these were restricted to landed property only – which were arranged in Land Tax parishes, the boundaries of which sometimes differed from ecclesiastical parishes. From 1780, an individual who paid Land Tax on freehold property worth £2 a year or more was entitled to vote, and so Land Tax returns were enrolled at the quarter sessions to provide lists of eligible voters. When a Parliamentary election was due, large landowners often sold plots of land that were just above this value in order to increase their voter numbers and thus secure the election of their favoured candidates, so it is always worth searching for related records prior to an election.

From 1798, Land Tax assessment forms were printed and contained the following information: rentals (yearly value of the property); name of proprietor or copyholder; name of occupier; name or description of property (usually from 1825). From 1832, there was less need to collect Land Tax assessments for electoral purposes, and so the forms were less frequently filed at the quarter sessions. Indeed, after 1798 it was possible to purchase redemption from the Land Tax, and once the compulsion to register names for electoral purposes was removed, the names of many who had purchased Land Tax redemption were thereafter omitted from the Land Tax lists. Returns will therefore be of less use after 1832. Indeed, compulsory redemption was introduced in 1949, and the tax was finally abolished in 1963.

Most of the surviving records will be found in CROs, either in the quarter sessions records or among the private papers of the assessors and collectors of the tax, and the majority of surviving records tend to date from the late eighteenth century. Many CROs maintain separate lists of Land Tax returns, and a Gibson guide (*see* **Useful publications**, under Taxation) outlines where you can locate surviving records for each county.

10.3.2 Land Tax records at the PRO

The PRO holds a few accounting documents relating to Land Tax, but only one set of comprehensive returns for the entire country. In 1798 changes were introduced to the system under the Land Tax Perpetuation Act (38 George III c.60), and a series of returns was compiled for all landholders so that the tax could be levied as a fixed annual charge. For each property these provide the name of the occupier, the name of the proprietor (if different), the amount assessed and the rate of redemption (if applicable). The PRO series **IR 23** contains these assessments, which are indexed by county via a series of four volumes on open access. From these you can obtain the folio number for the relevant tax parish, which can then be matched to a PRO reference in the series list.

From 1798 it became possible to purchase an exemption from paying the Land Tax. You may find data recorded in **IR 23**, such as the contract number and date of redemption. The records of such transactions are recorded in **IR 22** (Parish Books of Redemptions) and **IR 24** (Registers of Redemption Certificates), and are arranged by Land Tax parish. As well as providing details of individuals who were thus exempt, and will therefore disappear from future records in CROs, maps and plans of the properties in question can also be located.

In addition, material may be found in series **E 182**. The documents are arranged chronologically and by county, but the boxes are largely unsorted and there are no contemporary indexes. Therefore it can be a lengthy and frustrating process to wade through the material, with no guarantee of results at the end. However, many bundles seem to contain lists of people in arrears, changes in liability and those with double liability (such as Roman Catholics, aliens and denizens).

10.3.3 Using Land Tax data

The Gibson guide to Land Tax is the best place to start if you wish to locate Land

Tax returns. Surviving records can contain some useful data if viewed in conjunction with other contemporary sources. Where a sequence of Land Tax returns exist for a long period, it is possible to discern fixed patterns in the list of names that tend to reflect their respective positions in the street, which is particularly useful when no house names or numbers are provided. Parish rate books are particularly useful for this type of analysis. Although there will be a degree of uncertainty over the reliability of using sequential data of this nature, you can start to identify when occupiers came and went from your property by using known data about neighbouring properties as points of reference; this shows the benefit of researching the surrounding area. If possible, work backwards from the modern era, where house names and numbers survive in greater detail, or from the known to the unknown. For urban areas, trade directories are a good corroboratory source for this method of analysis, whilst manorial surveys and, from 1840, tithe and census returns can be of use in rural communities or villages. You may also find changes in the assessment level for your property, which can indicate a substantial rebuild or extension, thereby accruing a higher level of Land Tax.

10.4 Other assessed taxes

In addition to Hearth Tax and Land Tax, a variety of other features associated with houses and their contents were subject to assessment, and after 1784 they were all grouped together to be jointly described as 'assessed taxes'. In particular, Window Tax and Inhabited House Duty featured assessments based on property; but the problem with these records is that survival tends to be scarce.

10.4.1 Window Tax

The main component of the Window Tax was an assessment based on the number of windows in a property. The tax was introduced in 1696 and eventually repealed in 1851, and proved remarkably unpopular and difficult to collect. Properties were assessed in a series of bands, and a charge was levied on houses with over ten windows from 1696 to 1766, seven windows from 1766 to 1825 and eight windows from 1825 to 1851. There were many rules and regulations that permitted exemptions from the tax, which will affect whether your property was liable. However, you may still be able to use the data to identify periods when your property underwent rebuilding work or extensions, based on any changes in the Window Tax assessments from comparable returns over a series of years. Most assessments will provide the name of the taxpayer, plus the number of windows assessed and the amount of tax due. In most cases the taxpayer was also the occupier, and so you will not obtain much information on property owners unless they were the official resident. Furthermore, most of the individuals who were liable for the tax were already assessed for parish rates, which are described below. Another problem associated with Window Tax was evasion, as many people temporarily or permanently blocked up windows to avoid paying the duty. It was also possible to obtain an exemption by making the assessor believe that the property was a place of business.

Very few Window Tax returns now survive, as there was no compunction to enrol the material at the quarter sessions. Where they still exist, they are listed in Gibson's guide to Land Tax and assessed taxes. The PRO contains returns and particulars of assessed taxes in series **E 182**, but the records are largely unsorted. However, they do contain an enormous amount of material, although the qualifications in section 10.3.2 still apply, but if you have time to spare, you may be able to uncover a series of Window Tax returns for your particular area.

One of the places with the best Window Tax coverage is Scotland, as records were maintained by central government. These can be found at NAS in series **E 326**, and the returns also list properties with window numbers below the nominal tax liability.

10.4.2 House Tax and Inhabited House Duty

Although this was in theory a separate tax, returns for House Tax were usually made alongside those for Window Tax. It too was introduced from 1696, and assessed the number of actual occupiers of inhabited houses that were liable to church and poor rates. The vast majority of surviving records will be found at the relevant CRO, usually with the Window Tax returns, and are listed in the Gibson guide. The tax was repealed in 1834, despite the continuance of Window Tax, but Inhabited House Duty, one of the general 'assessed taxes', continued until 1924.

As with Window Tax, you will find material in **E 182**, although you will require time and patience if you want to extract any useful data of this unsorted series. The PRO also holds **IR 68** (precedent books and composition cases). These were compiled in cases where taxpayers were relieved from paying an annual assessment, and instead paid an agreed annual amount for three years. The series contains limited data for selected properties, but there are no indexes available to the two books.

To illustrate that all sorts of property were subject to Inhabited House Duty, the Brighton Aquarium was assessed for the tax in 1880 when a party of visiting Zulus slept in the aquarium during the course of an exhibition (PRO reference **IR 40/1157**).

10.4.3 The 1695 Marriage Assessment in the City of London

A tax peculiar to the City of London was in operation between 1694–5 and 1704, and is often referred to as the 1695 Marriage Assessment. It was liable on all births, marriages and burials, plus annual dues on bachelors over 25 and childless widowers. The records are stored in the Corporation of London Record Office and are arranged by parish, although the records for 17 parishes no longer survive. Furthermore, there are name indexes available for the assessment. The records can be used to identify the streets where people lived, although house names and numbers are rarely recorded.

10.5   Rates

'Rates' is an umbrella term that has been used to cover various forms of local taxation, all of which were designed to contribute to the community in which individuals lived. The levies took many shapes and forms, but can provide some basic information about property, as later documents for urban areas have been known to include assessment lists that denote house numbers.

The following are the most common sources that the house historian may find to be of some use. However, as the records were created or maintained at a parochial level, or were administered by local authorities, rate books and assessments are not stored at the PRO. Nevertheless, a brief outline of the material you may come across at your CRO is provided.

10.5.1 Poor, church and highway rates

Poor, church and highway rates were assessed on parishioners by the parochial church wardens to raise revenue for poor relief, to provide money to fund church repairs and ecclesiastical activity in each parish, or to maintain the highways within the parish. Where returns and assessments survive, they are to be found among the papers kept in the parish chest and subsequently deposited at the CRO. Alternatively, the private papers of individuals who acted as church wardens may also yield assessment records, as will quarter sessions records that relate to the failure of a parish to maintain a highway. They usually date from the eighteenth and early nineteenth centuries, although earlier returns from the sixteenth and seventeenth centuries can be found.

Parish rate books rarely list individuals by their place of abode, but will provide a list of eligible parishioners that can be cross-referenced with other sources. You will usually find a list of parishioners followed by the amounts they paid, and in some cases you may find an address attached. However, this can be a useful supplementary source for other records, such as Land Tax or Window

Tax; and where material on parish rates survives for the seventeenth century, it can also add to your knowledge of Hearth Tax. Data for towns and urban areas is often more detailed, and you will be more likely to find references to individual properties.

10.5.2 Local authority rate books

After the Poor Law Amendment Act of 1834, Poor Law unions replaced the parochial system for poor relief administration. In consequence, new ways of financing improvements to the local community were introduced, including rates that were levied and collected by the relevant Poor Law union. With changes to the administration of local affairs, the responsibility for raising and collecting rates gradually passed to the appropriate borough, rural, district, municipal or urban councils that were set up from the late nineteenth century onwards. The local authorities maintained rate books to record the details of the amounts levied, and these are now stored at the relevant CROs. Rate books normally recorded the name of the occupier, and sometimes included the name of the owner; an assessment of the value of the property in question; the amount to be collected; and, most important, the name or description of the property. They were often annotated to record changes of occupancy. As with Land Tax returns, it is sometimes easier to work from the modern era backwards, especially if there is a good sequence of books and you know the names of the householders. Even if you do not, you can use supplementary information such as trade directories, or a comparative analysis of neighbouring returns, to work backwards. Increases in assessment data can often indicate a rise in the value of the property, usually as a result of building work or other extensions to the property.

10.5.3 Sewer rate books

Sewer rate books are similar in format to local authority rate books, but exist for urban areas from the late eighteenth and nineteenth centuries where the construction and maintenance of sewers was necessary to maintain standards of public health. Local contributions were paid for sewers to be repaired and built, the terms of which were often specified in the original building lease; and where sewers were maintained by the local authority, sewer commissioners were appointed to assess and collect the revenue. Their records are known as sewer rate books, and will be found in the relevant CRO or municipal, urban or metropolitan record office. In addition to the name of the contributor, they can often contain street names and house numbers.

11 | Records of national events

11.1 Introduction

During the course of British history, there have been moments when national events have had a profound impact on local communities, and marked a turning point in the way our ancestors lived. Some of these events triggered large-scale house building or generated waves of property transactions, while others affected the way people thought about housing in general. The aim of this chapter is to present some examples of the records that these events have left behind. The house historian should always be aware that local history forms a crucial part of our understanding of national history. Indeed, the process of creating an empathy with previous owners or occupiers, and placing the house or property in its correct historical perspective, should form an important part of your research.

Events such as the dissolution of the monasteries and the English Civil War saw property and land change hands rapidly, and were often accompanied by enrolment of title deeds and law suits; in the case of the former, new buildings were created out of the fabric of the old monastic institutions. The development of railway networks also produced great social and economic change, with new towns developing around stations, and industrial expansion running hand in hand with population growth. Destructive events such as the Second World War meant that the landscape of Britain was radically altered, forcing large areas to be rebuilt and reconstructed following devastating bomb damage in the Blitz. Even today we see Green Belt land disappearing under 'new towns'.

Yet alongside these 'nationwide' issues will be events that had a particular impact on your own community. During the period of industrial and population expansion from the late eighteenth century onwards, local trades and industries would have had an enormous influence on the surrounding community. You will also have to consider why people began to build houses at a particular time. For example, Britain experienced a large share of global commerce in the eighteenth century that enabled merchants and traders to build grander houses from their profits; town houses were constructed and country estates underwent renovation during the Georgian period. These wider topics are briefly considered in this chapter, although relevant material is more likely to be found at a local level.

11.2 The dissolution of the monasteries

11.2.1 Historical background

For centuries, monasteries were an integral part of local communities, mainly because they had acquired large estates through private patronage. Hence, many people farmed land that was 'owned' by a monastery, paid their rents to the officials of the local abbot, inherited land through manorial courts presided over by the monks' representatives, and built property after obtaining the permission of the relevant institution. One of the most profound changes in English and Welsh social history occurred when Henry VIII broke away from the authority of the church in Rome and established himself as the Supreme Head of the Church of England. The process went hand in hand with the suppression of monastic institutions, mainly as a means of generating new revenue for the government from the extensive lands that they possessed.

The dissolution process had begun as early as 1524–8, when Cardinal Wolsey obtained papal authority to suppress about 30 small religious houses to create new places of learning; their lands and possessions were used to found colleges at Oxford and Ipswich. However, it was only when Thomas Cromwell rose to power that a full-scale suppression occurred. In 1534 Crown commissioners surveyed all ecclesiastical income, including monastic houses, and the returns were entered in the *Valor Ecclesiasticus* (literally, 'value of the church'). As part of the Act of Supremacy, all monasteries were required to swear an oath of allegiance to the Crown, and visitations were made to check on their spiritual condition. The first phase saw the suppression of small religious houses with incomes valued at less than £200 per annum; they were dissolved by Act of Parliament in 1536. Thereafter, larger houses were also persuaded to surrender, and the last monastery closed in 1540.

The dissolution process saw the Crown, as head of the Church of England and therefore the alleged founder of the monasteries, take possession of all lands and estates that the monastic institutions previously enjoyed. It was then free to sell, re-grant or take the profits of these lands. Furthermore, the government stipulated that the buildings themselves were to be destroyed, with the minimum requirement that the roof of an institution should be razed, so that the monks could not return. The implications of these measures for the house historian are considered below.

11.2.2 Disposing of the monastic estates

The dissolution effectively created an unprecedented flood of land into private hands, as the Crown disposed of a large number of the new estates through sales and leases. The business generated by this land movement was so immense that a new section of government was created to manage the process, known as the Court of Augmentations; this became the Augmentations Office in 1554. The records generated by this institution have largely been stored among the papers of the Exchequer, as the entire process was designed to raise revenue for the government.

With the new department came waves of documentation detailing the size, content and value of each parcel of land, and how and where it was reassigned. In addition, the title documents of the former monastic possessions fell into the Crown's hands, creating an impressive archive of title deeds. Furthermore, the sales themselves have left many records, not only in the papers of the Exchequer but also among the state papers of the era.

Locating monastic land

The first step is to determine whether dissolution documents are going to be of any use, and you should check whether your house was built on ex-monastic land. One of the best places to begin is with the various county histories that have been compiled, such as the VCH. This will outline the history of the monastery, but also describe the lands that formed its estate and what happened to them; alternatively, you can use manorial descents to establish if the manor within which your house is located was once owned by a monastic institution.

Evidences of title

If you suspect that there is a connection, then you can start to examine the many and varied monastic records that came to the Crown at the time of their suppression. Title deeds and cartularies were either presented to the new owners, or retained by the Crown. There is no single place of deposit at the PRO for these documents, and they are scattered across many record series, although the majority have been deposited with the Court of Augmentations.

Conventual leases record agreements made between religious houses (convents) and lay tenants who leased land from the monastic estates. The leases were then transferred to the Crown. Similarly, Crown commissioners and surveyors gathered title deeds and records of former grants to provide proof of title of the new estates, thus enabling the Crown to establish its rights. Many other documents appear in the miscellaneous books and papers collected by the Court

Table 11.1 Monastic evidence of title

Chancery	
C 109, 115	Chancery Masters Exhibits

Court of Augmentations	
E 303	Conventual leases
E 312	Leases and offices surrendered to the Crown
E 313	Original letters patent
E 314	Miscellanea
E 315	Miscellaneous books
E 326–30	Ancient deeds

Other Exchequer series	
E 118	King's Remembrancer: Conventual leases
E 135	Miscellaneous ecclesiastical documents

Land Revenue Office	
LR 1	Enrolment books

Duchy of Lancaster	
DL 25–7	Deeds
DL 36	Miscellaneous charters
DL 41	Miscellanea
DL 42	Enrolments, surveys and other books

of Augmentations, and land revenue enrolment books were also used to record copies of previous transactions conducted by the religious houses. The jurisdiction of the Duchy of Lancaster encompassed many monastic estates, and their deeds, leases and papers can be found amongst the Duchy's records.

Table 11.1 is a summary of some of the most important PRO series that contain the records described above. Most contain detailed descriptions of each item, and there is also a PRO leaflet that lists where the records of major institutions are to be found. Other areas of the Exchequer might also yield useful results, and the development of key word searches via PROCAT should enable you to locate the majority of relevant entries.

Sales, grants and leases

Disposal of monastic land began when commissioners surveyed the possessions of each institution, and the documents they produced often included an assessment of its value, goods, estates, major tenants, rents and buildings. Most of the rentals and surveys are now in PRO series SC 11 and 12, LR 1, 2, and 10, E 315, and DL 41 (for monasteries that form part of the Duchy of Lancaster). The PRO finding aid List and Index, vol. 25 will provide details of most surveys that have survived. Other surveys have turned up in Chancery Masters Exhibits series (C 103–15) among the private papers of individual surveyors.

One of the best places to begin looking for general information about ex-monastic lands are the printed *Letters and Papers Foreign and Domestic Henry VIII*, which cover the relevant period; later material can also be obtained from the *Calendars of State Papers* which exist for various chronological periods. All are indexed and on open access in the reading rooms, and there are separate manuscript keys that allow you to convert entries into PRO references.

Estates were initially taken into the hands of the Crown, and were administered by local officials. Their records can be found primarily among the ministers' and receivers' accounts in **SC 6**, **LR 6** and **DL 29** and are included in *List and Index, vol. 34*. A separate index lists surviving records for monastic estates. Although you are unlikely to find specific property listed, you may find references to expenditure on monastic buildings that were later converted into dwellings.

Records of lands that were granted to individuals can be found on the patent rolls. These are listed in the printed *Letters and Papers Foreign and Domestic Henry VIII*, on open access in the reading rooms. You will also find grants listed in land revenue enrolment books in **LR 1**. The details of the original grant appear in **E 318**, and a detailed index of grantees exists in the 9th and 10th DKRs. There is also a manuscript index to places, which might be of more use. Furthermore, the Court of Augmentations dealt with disputes that arose over the ex-monastic lands. Finally, leases of ex-monastic lands can be located in **E 307–12**. The series **E 321**, **314** and **315** will mainly contain sixteenth-century records, and thereafter you should search the records of the equity side of the Exchequer.

11.2.3 Monastic buildings

As well as providing rentals for lands, the surveys and inventories of monastic possessions compiled by the Crown commissioners can tell you a great deal about the monastic buildings themselves. They usually provide a room by room assessment of the goods and possessions of the houses that were to be offered for sale. Although most buildings were destroyed according to the directions of the government, many were either rebuilt to form large country houses, or converted into domestic dwellings. Some disputes arose about the dwellings themselves, and thus can appear in court cases. Ex-monastic buildings are frequently referred to in wills and legal transfers, and private papers of the purchasers can provide building accounts that shed light on the conversion process.

One of the best examples of a conversion comes from the papers of the Earl of Southampton, who purchased the estates and buildings of Titchfield Abbey. The Earl then built a large house on the site of the old monastery, converting many of the existing rooms into new accommodation. Letters which outline the conversion process exist in the state papers of Henry VIII, and can be located among the Wriothesley papers in **SP 7**.

In comparison, the fate of Blackladies nunnery (*see* **Figure 24**) in Brewood, Staffordshire, shows that the buildings themselves were sometimes sought as dwellings in their own right. In this instance, the Gifford family bought the site of the nunnery and then used the house to provide accommodation for a younger branch of the family. Not only do estate papers exist, but also there is official correspondence in *Letters and Papers Foreign and Domestic Henry VIII* and a supplementary survey in **C 115** to complement the official inventory in **E 315**.

However, the usual fate of the old monastic buildings was to be torn down and used as salvage for smaller dwellings in the neighbourhood. You may find stones in local houses, and architectural evidence should help you to determine monastic salvage.

11.3   The English Civil War

11.3.1 Historical background

The English Civil War was fought between supporters of King Charles I and those who backed the rule of Parliament. The first civil war raged from 1642 to 1645, and conflict broke out again between 1648 and 1649. The Parliamentary party was eventually victorious, and the execution of Charles I in 1649 enabled Parliament to establish the Commonwealth. An immediate problem facing the new regime was finance, and the lands of the Crown and the chief royalist supporters were an obvious source of income.

As a result of the sequestration of Crown and royalist lands, a land market was created between 1649 and 1660, with the profits initially used to pay for the wars and reward Parliamentary followers. However, the Commonwealth was dissolved and Cromwell was declared Lord Protector. No stable alternative to monarchy had been found, and on Cromwell's death Charles II was invited to return as King. In the aftermath of the Restoration, Crown lands and many Royalist estates were legally returned to their original owners (or their heirs). The resulting litigation, appeals and paperwork provided a convenient snapshot of property that was in dispute. Accordingly, there are various areas relating to the civil war period in which the house historian can look, although the best records survive for Crown lands and supporters of the Royalist cause.

11.3.2 Disposal of Crown lands

After the final defeat of the Royalists in 1648–9, the victorious Parliamentarians were faced with the task of raising revenue to pay war debts, and army arrears in

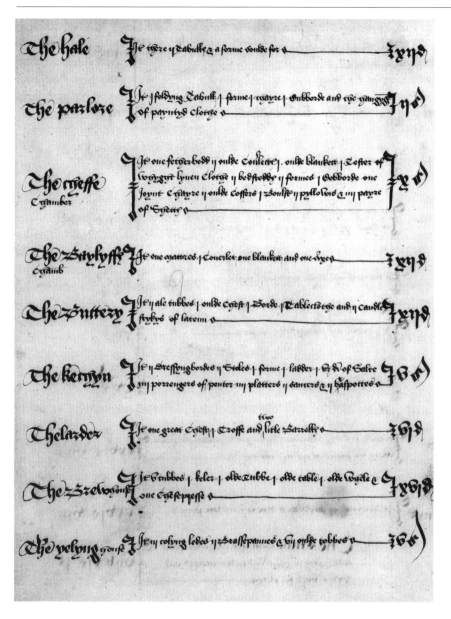

Figure 24 Detail from an inventory of the goods and possessions of Blackladies nunnery, Brewood, at the time of its dissolution in 1538. The survival of a later survey from 1650, with an identical room layout, suggests that, contrary to requirements, the original building was not demolished by its new owners but was converted into a domestic dwelling. (E 315/172)

particular. An Act of Parliament dated 16 July 1649 permitted the sale of Crown lands with this specific aim in mind, and an administrative machine was set up to facilitate the process. First, Crown lands were legally vested in trustees, who collected the revenues accruing to the lands. Next, contractors were appointed to act as sale agents, and negotiated sales with the prospective purchasers. Treasurers collected and accounted for the sale money, while a registry enrolled the transactions and provided title deeds for the purchasers.

Parliamentary surveys

To start the process, documents known as Parliamentary surveys (*see* **Figure 25**) were compiled from 1649to 1650. Local surveyors were appointed by the trustees to assess the revenue due from Crown manors and estates, and then to assign a sale value to the land. Two copies of each local survey were made, and the returns retained by the surveyor general are now in the PRO in series **E 317**. The surveys covered all land that was nominally part of the Crown's estates, and therefore any property that was built on Crown land was included. The most informative type of survey covered manors and other properties sold under the 1649 Act, as these gave detailed descriptions of buildings on the land, plus details of leases. Other surveys were conducted by hundred to permit the sale of fee-farm rents, and during the course of the process evidence was collected relating to title.

Where Parliamentary surveys survive, they can prove an excellent source of information for the house historian, including room by room descriptions of houses, with valuations attached. The series is arranged by county and lists manors and hundreds covered. The documents are included in *List and Index, vol.* 25 (Rentals and Surveys), and can also be searched by place-name via PROCAT. Duplicate copies are stored in **LR 2**, and material relating to the Duchy of Lancaster can be found in **DL 32**.

Other Crown properties are listed in great detail. For example, Richmond Palace was the subject of an individual survey, and it was demolished after the war to raise revenue from the sale of stones from the ruins. These were purchased for building purposes in the local community, and can still be seen in existing properties today.

Sale documents

In addition to the official surveys, the sales themselves generated swathes of documentation, including proofs of title; however, there is no overall composite index to the records, and so you may have to search through many series with little chance of finding particulars about your house. You should consider a

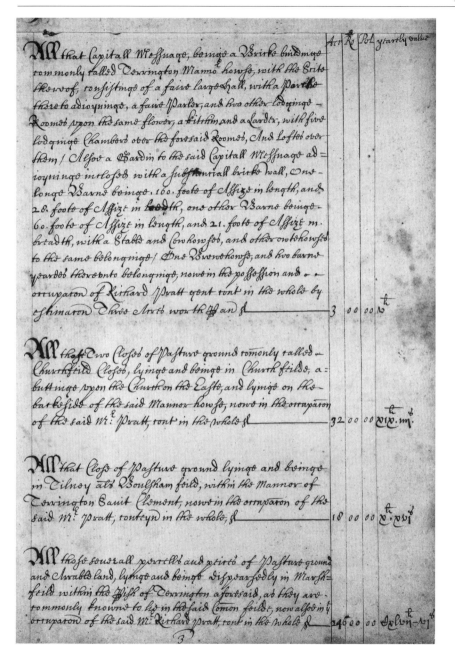

Figure 25 A survey made by Parliamentary commissioners in 1650 on the manor house at Terrington St Clements, Norfolk. It describes the house in great detail, even providing dimensions for the outbuildings attached to the property. The occupier's name (Richard Pratt) is given, and the site was valued at a yearly rent of £5. (E 317/norf/16)

search of these records only if you suspect your house was part of the sale process, or there is some evidence in the title deeds.

E 320 is a good place to begin looking for information, as it contains sale particulars drawn up by the registrar. You may also find various certificates that include details of purchaser and price, conveyance instructions and completion documents. There is a manuscript index to this series that is arranged by county. In addition, you can try the indexes to the close rolls to see if the title deeds were enrolled there. Other areas in which to start searching for certificates of sale include E 121 and 308/7 pt. II and SP 28/286 and 28/289.

In addition to the estates themselves, fee-farm rents were also sold to private individuals, and certificates of sale can be found in a variety of places. Particulars of sale will be of most use to the house historian, and are located in E 308 and among the particulars for leases in E 367; certificates of sale are in E 308/7 and 315/145, and enrolments can again be found on the close rolls in C 54. You may find references to individual property in requests made to sale contractors (SP 28/286), counterpart deeds (E 307) and entry contract books (E 308/7 pt. I, 315/141 and 315/144), whilst a chronological summary of purchases can be found in SP 28/288. Another useful series will be the books of the trustees in SP 26, including entry books of agreement to purchase.

11.3.3 Lands of Royalist supporters

From 1645, supporters of the Royalist cause faced severe repercussions under the Parliamentary regime. Technically they were viewed as traitors who had taken arms against the state, and therefore their lands were legally forfeited. However, the reality for most Royalist supporters was different, and they were allowed to pay a fine to retain their lands. This process, known as compounding, was administered by one of the new bodies created by the Parliamentary regime, entitled the Committee for Compounding with Delinquents. There are printed calendars available that enable you to locate the individuals who compounded, and properties are occasionally mentioned in detail. The records are in PRO series SP 23, and the most useful will be the lists of delinquents (the Royalists), as they often contain surveys of their estates. The committee compiled reports of individual compositions and sequestrations, and these can also contain particulars of the estates. Earlier records can be found in SP 20 (Sequestration Committee books and papers), for which a partial index survives in series ZBOX 1.

Royalists who refused to compound, or were not permitted to, found their estates sequestrated in a similar manner to Crown property. Property was transferred to the Treason Trustees, whose papers have largely disappeared. However, many lands were sold to private individuals, and you may find enrolments of deeds on the close rolls (**C 54**). New owners were required to notify the Committee for Compounding of each purchase, and you can once again track down the names of new owners, although some will be land agents acting on behalf of their clients, and others will be the names of those who sought to purchase property but were ultimately unsuccessful.

11.3.4 The Restoration

With the Restoration of the monarchy in 1660, the task of recovering Crown lands began in earnest. The 'late pretended sales' of Crown estates between 1649–60 were deemed to be illegal, and a new set of commissioners was appointed to assess the extent of the restitution payable to the purchasers of the land.

Commissions of enquiry survive among the records of the Exchequer, along with depositions taken from local witnesses who were questioned about the sales. These can be found in series **E 134** and **178**, and other references can be located among the state papers domestic (**SP 29**); these are calendared and on open access. Once the lands had been returned, the purchasers claimed restitution; information can be found in the Constat books that record details of Crown leases, in particular **CRES 6/1–8** that cover the period 1660–68. Local information can be traced through land revenue enrolment books in **LR 1**, which are grouped into counties and arranged chronologically.

Similarly, Royalist delinquents (or their heirs) whose lands had been sold after sequestration demanded a return of their possessions. As a result, many cases challenging the legality of the sales can be found in the equity courts after 1660. Compensation claims for war damage to property and houses were also filed in the courts, and the records generated by this procedure can provide great detail about houses and the damage they suffered, and this period can provide evidence of rebuilding programmes. Unfortunately the indexes for this period are usually by the names of the plaintiff, so you will need to know the name of the former owner.

11.4 Trade and commerce

From the late seventeenth century and throughout the eighteenth century, Britain started to expand its commercial activities overseas. Trading companies flourished, and on the back of the wealth that was generated in the face of competition with their French and Dutch rivals, many merchants were able to purchase land in cities and maintain country estates. The result was a major period of building that changed the face of towns and cities across Britain during the Georgian period.

Ports were the communities that benefited the most from these developments. Trade links with the colonies in the West Indies, North America and the East Indies stimulated rapid growth in places such as Bristol, Liverpool, Southampton and London, not only in terms of the volume of business they conducted, but also in the many new properties that were built by merchants from their profits. The PRO is not the best place to begin your research, as private records of the merchants are usually found in CROs where they are deposited, or at specialist institutions such as the India Office Library at the BL. For example, many of the papers of the former employees of the East India Company are deposited there. Before you begin searching, it is advisable to obtain clues about former merchant owners from existing title deeds, wills or later sales.

However, you might find records of properties built in the colonies themselves among the Colonial Office (CO) papers deposited at the PRO, as well as at institutions such as the India Office Library. If you wish to explore this line of research, there are publications to help you find the best place to look; but you ought to consider the historical background to this period before you begin, as many individuals became rich through their involvement with the slave trade. It is important to remember that, whilst such a practice may be abhorrent by today's standards, it was part of the fabric of life in the eighteenth century and funded the construction of many grand houses both in Britain and the colonies where the trade flourished.

It is sometimes easier to trace the records of the new urban areas that were developed in Britain during the eighteenth century. You will find many building leases assigned for individual properties and new 'estates' that date from this period. These were often specifically created for the rising merchant and gentry classes. High-status estates were often the work of local entrepreneurs who owned or purchased freehold land, but then sold the right to construct property to local builders. Once again you are more likely to find such material among private papers at CROs, but printed local histories will probably provide good background information with document references for you to follow up. Furthermore, many building leases can be located in local deed registries, for example London or Yorkshire.

11.5 Railways and the Industrial Revolution

11.5.1 Industrial expansion

With the development of large-scale industrial sites and factories during the late eighteenth and nineteenth centuries, new dwellings were required to house increasing numbers of workers who flocked to the embryonic industrial towns from the countryside in search of employment. In contrast to the commercial expansion of ports and existing cities throughout the eighteenth century that was largely stimulated by the merchant and gentry classes, the requirement for industrial towns was for lower status housing close to the emerging factories, in particular in the Midlands and north of England. Building programmes would have been a combination of private enterprise with commercial support, and you will often find rows of workers' cottages springing up on the outskirts of towns near to the factories to form industrial suburbs.

It is therefore important to consider what the local industry would have been and where it was located, as this can often explain patterns of housing construction and lead you to the archives of the companies concerned, regardless of whether they were running mines, mills, ship-building firms or ironworks. This material will be stored primarily at local archives, and you can use specialist publications and local histories to track down industrial and urban development in your area. Although records of individual houses within these developments can be difficult to locate, you can use a combination of maps, trade directories and census returns (in particular from 1851 when the enumerators included more information in their returns) to create a sense of when new areas of housing were constructed, as urban growth was usually linked to periods of industrial expansion.

Larger industries often ran housing associations to provide accommodation for their workers, and the PRO holds some material for nationalized industries, such as the papers of the National Coal Board. Correspondence and papers relating to housing for workers can be found in **COAL 48** and **66**. In addition, the Ministry of Housing maintained files in **HLG 40** on rural housing and tied houses, which were built by industrial companies. Information on housing associations can be gleaned from the papers in **HLG 101**, and many records in local archives will also be relevant.

11.5.2 Railways

In conjunction with the industrial revolution, one of the most significant changes in English social history was the widespread development of a railway network. Not only were communities joined together by a fast means of communication, but the network brought physical changes that left an indelible mark on the landscape. Townships underwent rapid expansion as new people settled or sought work, and property was often built around stations, which became the new focal point for communities. As part of this process, old houses were knocked down to make way for railroads, while railway companies often constructed new buildings to provide accommodation for their workers; these often took the form of housing associations.

Railway records were previously stored with the BTHR, and have now been transferred to the PRO along with records of the canal companies. The records are arranged by individual railway company, so you will need to identify which particular company operated along the line of track in your town or village. There are finding aids in the PRO to assist you, such as the general card index compiled by the BHTR.

The best place to begin your research will be with the maps and plans created by the companies. The main series can be found in **RAIL 1029–35**, and you will also find maps and plans scattered among company papers in other **RAIL** series as well. You should also consider examining **RAIL 1071**, which contains maps and plans produced with private Acts of Parliament for railway construction, and accordingly there will be more records deposited at the House of Lords Record Office, London, where large numbers of private Acts are now stored. Parliamentary papers in general (**RAIL 1062–79**) are worth consulting, as are collections of railway related material (**RAIL 1014–19**, **1038–60** and **1147–57**). For example, **RAIL 1189** holds files from the Surveyor and Estate Agent's branch of the Great Northern Railway, which contains correspondence dealing with the purchase of land required for new railways or the widening of existing railways, the disposal of surplus land, licensing of land and property to and by the company, enquiries from people and organizations outside the company concerning proposed purchases and sales of land and property, housing for staff and relocated residents, maintenance of property, and compensation paid to owners, lessees, tenants and residents affected by railway works. Similar material will be located with the records of the individual railway companies, in **RAIL 1–799**, and these are available for key word searches on PROCAT. Material on accommodation for persons made homeless by statutory instruments for railway construction can be found in **HLG 24**, whilst other relevant material can be located at CROs.

11.6 Twentieth-century warfare

The first half of the twentieth century was marked by two world wars, yet the records that were produced can provide information for the house historian. For example, many properties were requisitioned for military use during the Second World War, and the destruction caused to major cities during the Blitz stimulated post-war urban regeneration. These topics will be covered in more detail in the next chapter, but some of the series of documents that were used to detail the destruction caused by enemy bombing are described below.

11.6.1 Requisitioned property in the Second World War

There are no overall document series where requisitioned property is listed, but the following areas are worth investigating if you suspect that your house was once taken over for military purposes.

There are government property registers in **WORK 50** that include 'blue books' (**WORK 50/23–9**). These are requisition, compensation and settlement registers that record transfers of property out of government hands and derequisitioned property. However, these documents cover only Berkshire, Buckinghamshire, Hampshire and Oxfordshire, with limited details for Hertfordshire and Surrey. Some policy material on the disposal of requisitioned property and land after the war can be found in **HLG 102**, with related files in **HLG 101**.

Compensation claims for loss of earnings, and war damage to requisitioned property, can be traced through compensation claims handled by the Land Tribunal in **LT 6**, to which there are indexes and registers to general claims in **LT 7**. In addition, it might be worth investigating various series of records that were maintained by the Ministry of Home Security. You will find many references to requisitioned property in **HO 186** (Air Raid Precautions) under the headings Land and Accommodation, Finance, and Damage Reconstruction and Salvage, and there is similar material in **HO 187** (Fire Brigades Division) under the heading Buildings and Land. In addition, correspondence and papers in **HO 205** include several sections, with files on requisitioned property, and there are further documents in **HO 207** for each of the civil defence regions, particularly relating to compensation claims for damage. Other material relating to requisitions for emergency housing under special wartime functions of the Ministry of Health can be found in **HLG 7**.

11.6.2 Bomb damage in the Second World War

To assess the extent of the damage caused by German raids during the Blitz, and to attempt to find ways of minimizing damage caused by future raids, bomb census surveys were conducted; these can be a useful source of information about properties in cities affected by enemy action during the war. Maps, charts and plans were created that show the exact places where bombs were dropped, and can be found in **HO 193**. They are arranged by type of bomb (piloted and non-piloted aircraft), region and date. Documentation relating to the bomb census is in **HO 198**, although these will be of little use to the house historian.

The Ministry of Housing and Local Government created many files that relate to war damage and post-war reconstruction. Amongst the many series held by the PRO, **HLG 79** will be of most use as it is arranged by the name of each council authority; many files relate to proposals for reconstruction after war damage.

HLG 7 is another important series, as the Ministry of Health held special wartime responsibility for coordinating the Ministries of Works, Health and Labour and the War Damage Commission to effect repairs in London to relieve homelessness. This series contains papers of the London Repairs Executive, which was replaced by the London Housing Committee in 1945 to integrate war damage repairs with other housing work.

Records of the Central Land Board are in **HLG 98** (policy files), **HLG 99** (case files) and **HLG 112** (appeals files), which deal with cases that arose from the considerations of the War Damage Commission, whose papers are in **IR 33–9**. Papers relating to claims against damage caused by military personnel can be found in **WO 306**. Government papers on post-war rebuilding programmes and the control of building materials can be found in **WORK 45, 49** and **50**. All of these series are technical in nature, and will not give specific details about individual properties. However, they do provide a context for some of the building programmes that began in the post-war years.

In addition to the bomb census records at the PRO, an aerial survey was conducted after the war, whereby photographs were taken of various regions. These can be of some use to the house historian, and are stored at the Imperial War Museum.

11.6.3 Irish housing after the First World War

As a footnote to this section, there are records for houses and cottages constructed in Ireland after the conclusion of the First World War. A trust fund for Irish sailors and soldiers was set up to provide land for men who had served in the armed forces in the First World War. The trustees first met in 1924, and their headquarters were based in London. The records are stored in series **AP 1–8**, and can provide detailed information about the properties that were constructed, and who lived in them.

AP 5 contains a register of properties from 1923 to 1927 for Northern Ireland, whilst correspondence about the initial construction of the houses and cottages and tenancy affairs are in **AP 1** (London and Dublin) and **AP 2** (London and Belfast). Registers of documents sealed by the trust are to be found in **AP 8**, where names and addresses of tenants who opted into the trust's sell and buy scheme are listed, along with information on sub-letting and mortgages. Treasury files on the sale to tenants scheme can be found in **T 233/146**, while the financial aspects of the policy of substituting flats for cottages between 1930 and 1947 is addressed in **T 233/145**. **AP 7** contains other tenancy files, plus annotated OS maps, maps of building schemes and photographs of property; some of these can be matched with information in **AP 1** and **AP 2**, although you will need to sign an undertaking in order to view these records. **HO 351/199** also contains information on the requisition of land under the Irish Land (Provision of Sailors, Soldiers) Act 1919, and related material on land purchase is in **CAB 27/85**. Papers that describe the process of allocating housing to Northern Ireland from 1921 to 1924 are in **HO 45/11708**.

12 Sources for 'modern' houses

12.1 Introduction

Not every house can be traced very far back in time. However, there are plenty of excellent sources for late-nineteenth-century and twentieth-century houses that can tell you when your house was built, and perhaps what was there before it was constructed. The best place to begin will be with some of the sources already described, such as census returns (1841–91), the valuation survey (1910–15), the National Farm Survey (1940s), modern electoral lists, and trade and street directories. Furthermore, there is more chance that property transfers will be recorded in the Land Registry, and modern title deeds are going to be easier to track down. However, the twentieth century furnishes the house historian with many new sources that will reflect developments in housing policy to meet the needs of a growing population.

Some aspects of the Second World War have been considered in the previous chapter, but the long-term impact on urban regeneration and the immediate housing crisis that it produced can be traced through many important pieces of legislation that affected the remainder of the century. The Town and Country Planning Act of 1947 set out the guidelines for the post-war slum clearance, town planning and building techniques that shaped the landscape of the communities we live in today. Most of the records created by the central authorities are now at the PRO in archives deposited by the Housing and Local Government Department, the Local Government Board, the Ministry of Health and the Ministry of Town and Country Planning; however, there will be many more files, maps and plans generated by local authorities and stored at CROs.

To write in detail on the changing nature of houses and housing policy would be to write a social and economic history of the twentieth century, so this chapter will focus on only the most relevant and easily accessible sources at the PRO. In addition, files created by local authorities in response to specific housing matters are briefly considered, as are various sources that can provide additional information at a local level. Finally, advice about where to start research into building techniques and materials employed in twentieth-century housing is also provided.

12.2   Housing policy before the Second World War

12.2.1   Background information: tackling nineteenth-century poverty

During the nineteenth century, the rapid growth of towns and cities created problems of overcrowding, which in turn impacted upon public health. From the 1840s, the spread of epidemics, such as cholera, prompted numerous Royal Commissions to investigate how to tackle the combined health and housing crises. Much of the work fell upon newly created Poor Law unions, which had responsibility for implementing Poor Law legislation. Some of the records and correspondence of the Poor Law Commission and subsequent Poor Law Board, which coordinated the work of the unions, are in **MH 1** and **12**, but these will give only background information rather than specific references to houses; however, indexes in **MH 15** should allow you to locate relevant files in **MH 12** that relate to early housing policy. Plans of land and buildings used by local authorities under the terms of the Poor Laws can be found in **MH 14**, **HLG 6** and **MH 48**.

Of similar importance was the 1843 Royal Commission on the Health of Towns and Populous Places. Measures were drafted to prevent the spread of infectious disease, and a Board of Health was established. There are many records that deal with the problems caused by housing and overcrowding in correspondence located in **MH 13** and **HLG 1** and **46**, but – as with the records of the Poor Law Board – the records will provide only background information rather than specific property details.

You will find also information on the housing conditions that were prevalent in the works of Charles Booth and Edwin Chadwick, who compiled reports based on specific houses in the urban slum areas. These can be accessed via the index to the Parliamentary Sessional Papers, available on CD-Rom from the PRO Library. Copies of the papers themselves are stored on microfiche at Kew.

A publication that will provide further contemporary opinion on housing and sanitary conditions for the poor and working classes is *The Builder*, first published in 1842 and extensively developed under the editorship of George Godwin from 1844. It also focused on architecture and building debates of the age. Copies can be found at many main libraries, and there are annual indexes from 1842–79 and half-annual indexes from 1880 bound with the relevant volume.

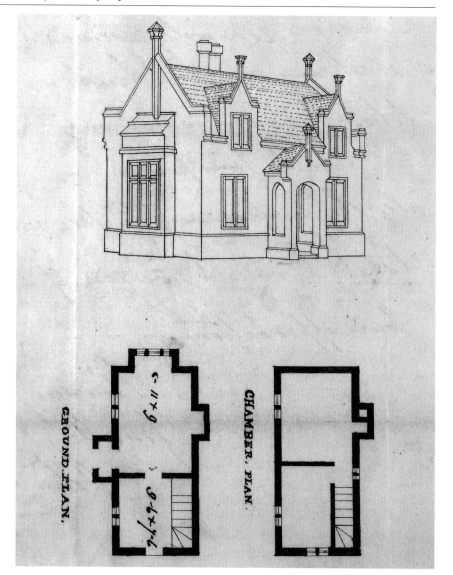

Figure 26 Plan for a worker's cottage in Delamere Forest, which cost £75 to construct in 1841. (CRES 2/132)

12.2.2 Slum clearance, redevelopment and planning schemes

The establishment of the Local Government Board by Act of Parliament in 1871 created an institution with powers to tackle housing problems at a local level, and the Board inherited many of the responsibilities of the Poor Law Board. Early responsibility for housing fell to the Sanitary Department, but by 1910 a separate Housing and Town Planning Department had been formed. In an effort to address the problem of housing for the working classes, from 1875 local authorities were permitted to purchase areas that were considered to be slums under the terms of the Artisans' and Labourers' Dwellings Act and submit redevelopment schemes to the Board for approval. After the First World War, the Ministry of Health inherited most of the housing work of the Local Government Board, and also developed an interest in building control in general. An important piece of legislation was the 1930 Housing Act, which enabled the Ministry of Health (Housing Department) to establish clearance and improvement areas and then demolish unfit houses whilst building new ones.

In consequence, there are many useful records now with the PRO that relate to urban regeneration in the late nineteenth and early twentieth centuries, housing for working classes and the creation of local authority housing estates. To make searching easier, you should begin by identifying which local authority your property falls within. Maps created by the Ministry of Health and previous departments that depict the boundaries of some of the Poor Law unions and district authorities can be found in **HLG 6** for the period 1800-1900, with similar and related material in **HLG 44**. These will at least afford some assistance if you are unsure, and can include properties that were affected by boundary changes.

If you are trying to track down slum clearance and redevelopment plans in your area that commenced before the Second World War, the place to begin should be the registered files for the planning schemes themselves. **HLG 4** contains the planning schemes developed by local authorities that were referred to the Local Government Board and its successors for approval under the Town and Country Planning Acts 1909–32. The records are arranged by the name of the local authority, and there is an introductory note in the series list to assist you. Alternatively, you can search for material in registers stored in **HLG 95**. Much of the material contained in the records will not be property specific, but you will obtain a general overview of the planning schemes and their extent. Extracted maps and plans that accompanied the schemes are in **HLG 5**, although you may find some material bound with the paperwork in **HLG 4**.

Local authorities were required to seek the permission of the relevant Government department before they could start to proceed with their plans. Consequently, the department's legal branch gained responsibility for drawing up the housing instruments for the erection of houses and new streets. These records are stored in **HLG 13**, and contain maps, instruments and consents for land sales, leases and purchases, construction of new streets and sewers, and general housing issues. Registers to the series exist in **HLG 14** and are arranged by date and type of local authority; the indexes will lead you to an instrument number, which is listed in **HLG 13**. Similar material will also be found in **HLG 95**.

Officially sealed orders made by the various institutions and departments that authorized permission for planning schemes to go ahead are to be found in

HLG 26, with sealed plans in HLG 23; later post-war material is in HLG 111. The records can contain great detail, in some instances describing a property and listing the current or former occupiers, but the level of information will vary according to the type of order and the date. The main drawback is that there are no internal indexes to the orders themselves, so you may need to undertake a great deal of searching. Registers and indexes that allow you to identify relevant documents in all three series are contained in HLG 66, although the series lists can usefully be searched on PROCAT.

In addition to the planning schemes, orders, instruments and consents listed above, other material can shed tremendous light on the actual proceedings themselves. For example, HLG 49 contains a wealth of information relating to detailed surveys of the conditions and needs of areas under local authority control, with proposals, plans, acquisition of land and surveyors' reports into the ensuing redevelopment work. The records are generally arranged by the name of the street, area or planning scheme, and are further grouped under the relevant council or local authority. You will also find some material on housing associations. Furthermore, registers of progress for some of these schemes can be found in HLG 96, and are arranged by county between 1934–41; however, they only provide basic statistical details of how many properties were demolished or built on given dates, and are not property-specific. HLG 47 (*see* **Figure 27**) will perhaps be of greater use, as it contains demolition and closing orders, papers relating to slum clearance, objections, compulsory purchase of property and correspondence, mainly relating to the period 1919–40, although earlier material can be identified. General correspondence on slum clearance, redevelopment and housing programmes can be found in HLG 118, although only a few places are listed by street or development scheme.

12.3   Post-war reconstruction and development

12.3.1 The 1947 Town and Country Planning Act

The need for regeneration of urban areas was brought into sharp focus by the devastation caused by bombing raids during the Blitz, a topic that has been considered in the previous chapter. Although planning for urban and rural redevelopment had long been a function of the various bodies described above, an Act of Parliament in 1943 established a separate Ministry of Town and Country Planning. Its remit was to regulate local authority wartime construction, and subsequently to redevelop areas that had been worst affected by damage or blight caused by the war. The result of the department's work was the 1947 Town and Country Planning Act, which made fresh provision for planning development and use of land. It also gave additional powers to local authorities to develop

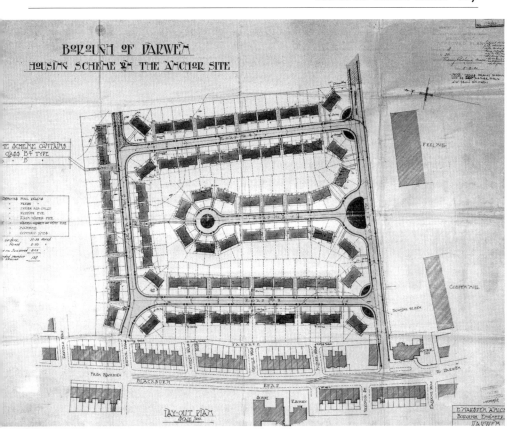

Figure 27 A plan attached to a new housing scheme proposed for the Borough of Darwin, Lancashire, dated 1920. The layout of the houses and new roads are referred to in the accompanying correspondence in the file. (HLG 47/323)

land for planning. A Central Land Board was established, and councils were directed to create development plans for their area of authority. From 1951, functions formerly under the Ministry of Health were added to create the Ministry of Local Government and Planning.

All local authorities were required to survey their area and prepare a development plan, which was to be submitted to the Ministry of Town and County Planning. Maps and written statements for each county are stored in series **HLG 119**, along with amendments to the plans made under later surveys. In addition, **HLG 79** contains the detailed submission of the proposals and plans by local authorities. The records are listed by the local authority, and cover a vast amount of material, such as housing programmes, war damage redevelopment, surveys, planning and reconstruction. Although the quality of information will vary from location to location, some records provide great detail, including maps and plans of the areas under consideration.

Other areas worth investigating include **HLG 71**, which contains general policy files. There is a subject index in the series list that displays the topics covered by the material, but the most important areas for property will include Planning, Land, Development Plans and Disposals. You will find many miscellaneous files, including planning appeals by local authority, aerial photographs, surveys, and even reports into 'moveable' dwellings such as caravan sites.

Many of the series listed in the previous section will also contain post-war information, in particular **HLG 47, 49** and **118**. In addition, **HLG 101** contains general material on government building programmes, housing associations, flats, and building research. A list of subject headings is provided at the front of the series list, including one on housing, and similar material and information on the disposal of land and property requisitioned during the war are found in **HLG 102**. You might also wish to browse **HLG 68** for general information on planning and development policy for the period, and background material on the Town and Country Planning Act is located in **HLG 104**.

12.3.2 New towns

In addition to the work on redeveloping existing towns and rural areas, and providing a national coordinating body, the Ministry of Town and Country Planning, and after 1951 the Ministry of Local Government and Planning, were responsible for developing new towns. The first piece of legislation to consider developing new urban areas was the New Town Act 1946, which was based on the experiences of the 'garden' cities of Letchworth and Welwyn. New Town Development Corporations were established to project-manage the creation of new towns, covering the acquisition of land, development of all services required by the new towns, and provision of adequate housing.

Consequently, there are numerous records of use to the house historian who lives in one of the post-war new town developments. General correspondence and files relating to planning policy and development of new towns can be found in **HLG 90**, which lists several specific proposals. The records of the New Town Development Corporations are in **HLG 91**, and there is an index to the corporations in the series list. There are maps, plans and papers on the entire planning process required to create a community from scratch, including references to specific houses and streets. Development proposals for the new towns, plus registered files, are in **HLG 115**, which is arranged by town with a key at the front of the series list. Topics are listed under each town corporation. You may also find Treasury files in **T 227** to be of interest, as the Social Services division contains files on housing, local government and new towns, and further background and policy information is in **HLG 116**.

12.3.3 Local authority rent control

In 1946, Rent Tribunals were established under the 1946 Furnished Houses (Rent Control) Act. Their work involved hearing applications from landlords, tenants and local authorities wishing to seek a decision on the level of reasonable rent for furnished property. The Tribunals therefore held hearings to decide the rent that should be paid, and in the course of their work they often visited the property in question. Once they had reached a decision, they then notified the local authority in which the property was located. Local authorities were then required by law to maintain a register of decisions made about fixing a reasonable level of rent between landlords and tenants. The PRO contains applications and Tribunal records for Devon, Cornwall and South Middlesex in **HLG 97**. This is an excellent source as it is arranged by district, and then by the address of the property in question, so it is easy to search for a specific property. You will find information on the name of the lessor, the name of the lessee, the dimensions of the property, details of rent, service provided by the lessor and general running costs of the property, such as rates, electricity and cleaning charges.

In addition, the 1965 Rent Act reintroduced rent control for unfurnished property, and rent officers decided an equitable level of rent that should be paid. Appeals by either landlords or tenants were made to Rent Assessment Committees, and selected cases are in series **HLG 121**. As with the Tribunal records, the assessment panel records are listed by the address of the property in question. **HLG 122** contains similarly listed cases produced by the rent officers themselves. Background material on rent control, plus subjects such as house building, slum clearance and the impact of building regulations on house design and construction, can be found in **HLG 118**.

12.3.4 Building research and byelaws

Most of the series at the PRO that have been listed in this chapter will be of relevance to individual properties, or housing development plans that affect properties in a particular area. However, there are numerous other files created by government departments that will provide information on house construction, plus the rules and regulations that affect buildings in general. These may be of interest if you wish to known more about how and why your house was built.

Background information on the planning process and building research can be found in **HLG 52**, which contains many files that complement those in **HLG 49**. Subjects such as planning and development, including research into building techniques, are covered and can provide much background information into the specific records contained in the series listed above. Other series holding similar details include **HLG 101** (housing policy and building research), which contains cross-references to many other series, and **HLG 118** (the impact of building regulations on house construction). In addition, **HLG 58** supplements this material as it contains files and papers on local authority byelaws that affect local planning and building. For those interested in Welsh local authority housing policy, case files, maps and plans, a search of **BD 11** might prove fruitful.

As well as permanent housing, there are many records at the PRO relating to the temporary housing that was introduced to ease the hardship caused by enemy bomb damage during the Second World War. The 1944 Housing (Temporary Accommodation) Act and the 1948 Local Government Act regulated the provision of post-war accommodation in the form of prefabricated houses. Records can be located in a variety of areas at the PRO, particularly in many of the series already listed above. In addition, files maintained by the Building Research Station on prefabricated house-building techniques, plus technical reports, are in **DSIR 4**, while general development papers can be found in **AVIA 65/230**. The impact of local building byelaws on prefabricated housing can be researched in **HLG 58**, and documentation on Treasury aid to the companies that constructed the houses is to be found in **T 227**. Series **BD 11** contains relevant material for Wales.

12.4 Records maintained by local authorities

The records described above relate to official files maintained by the relevant government departments and institutions in response to legislation regarding housing. This is only one side of the story, as the local authorities themselves created and maintained similar files that can provide even more detail on these topics, plus more specific information on council housing in general.

The PRO does not hold any records created by the various local authorities, and consequently CROs or city archives will be the logical place of deposit for the registered files that were created by these bodies. Most local authorities maintained departments with responsibility for housing, building contracts, architects, engineers, surveyors and urban development, and the records generated by these departments can be of great importance. Of particular use will be applications for planning permission to build or extend properties, as the relevant department would have to consider each application in turn before delivering a verdict; this process would create paperwork that lists names of owners and occupiers. Similar applications to council departments would have been made if a property were to be considered for listed buildings status, and records of surveys, assessments, judgments and justification of judgments will be of great use in determining the history of a property.

Similarly, local authorities had responsibility for all aspects of town planning, and in addition to the files listed above you will find reams of paperwork on decisions reached at a local level, plus deposited plans for the various schemes. The everyday administration of local towns and villages generated records that feature property in a number of surprising places. For example, sewers were fundamental in improving health conditions in the nineteenth century, and local authorities inherited the responsibility for maintaining them. They also inherited the maps and plans that accompanied the work, and these can be of great use to the urban house historian. Similarly, paving committees will list work in streets, often referring to particular houses or requests by house owners for work to be done.

Finally, the administration of council housing created under the various planning schemes and redevelopment plans listed above will contain a wealth of information on individual properties. Some archives will have a wider range of material than others, depending on the individual local authorities; and there may be restrictions on access depending on how recent the records are. However, if you suspect that your property was once maintained or owned by the local council, then you could find the names of previous tenants, rebuilding works and repairs, and even a construction or purchase date.

12.5   Records of utility companies

With the widespread introduction of water, electricity, gas and telephones from the late nineteenth century onwards, deposited records of pre-nationalization public utility companies can provide a useful guide to the location of properties from this period onwards. For example, when any of these services were installed in a street or community, maps and plans were usually created, and were amended as new connections were made. Similarly, papers relating to the installation of services within individual properties can provide the names of owners or occupiers. Some of the company records have been deposited at local archives, but others will still be with the companies themselves, so you may not automatically find records in the public domain.

13 How we used to live

13.1 Introduction

Most of this guide has been devoted to the documentary sources that are available to help you construct a chronology of your house's history, mainly by tracing the records generated by the owners and occupiers. However, it is easy to forget that these same individuals considered your house as their home too, and having established who these individuals were, your next step should be to find out more about how they would have lived, and in particular how they would have decorated or furnished your house to make it their home. You will come across a surprising amount of documentary evidence that can help you place the interior of your house in its original historical context, and many of the sources that have already been described can contain additional information about house interiors, furnishings and general layout. Although this guide is not the best place to undertake an analysis of period décor, this chapter will describe some areas in which to look if you would like to begin investigating how your house once appeared.

Frequent mention has been made already of the personal papers of past owners and occupants, and once again they will be useful if you wish to uncover more about how life would have been for former residents. These recollections can be supplemented by clues left behind in the internal architecture of your house. In addition to beams, doors, windows and stairs, which can be useful in helping you to date the construction of the house, you may find surviving fixtures or fittings that can be researched and assigned a rough date. From the mid nineteenth century onwards there are registers of designs and representations for patents and inventions, many of which relate to everyday household objects and decorations. Similarly, probate inventories and insurance records can shed light on how a house would have been furnished (*see* **Figure 28**), and sometimes provide detailed descriptions of the interior and layout of a property. You should not forget photographic evidence either.

Further reading on the subject of house interiors is provided under **Useful**

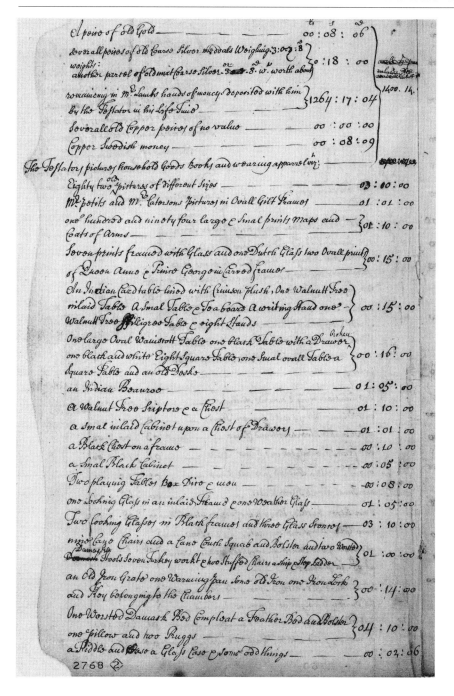

Figure 28 An extract from the inventory of personal effects found at the house of London lawyer Silvester Petyt. The inventory was made on 26 November 1723, and provides a vivid insight into the way a gentleman's early eighteenth century house would have been furnished. (PROB 5/2768)

publications, most of which will include tips about dating an interior from the surviving fixtures and fittings. If you are interested in restoring your house according to the manner in which it was once decorated, the addresses and websites of a few organizations are provided under **Useful addresses.**

13.2   Rediscovering previous interiors

13.2.1 Searching for clues

The best place to start is with the interior of your property. You can often use original fixtures and fittings to provide a date when the interior was constructed or decorated. Indeed, even original wallpaper can be used to date a property, and provide a feeling of how a property might once have looked. Various guides on dating techniques are listed under **Useful addresses**, and this is something that you should do in conjunction with your architectural analysis when first attempting to construct a chronological framework.

In addition, you will find that many old household objects can turn up under the soil in your garden. Clay pipes, tiles, even remnants of contemporary household 'technology' were thrown away, and these can offer a tantalising glimpse of the lifestyles of previous owners. Similarly, bags of dateable rubbish can be uncovered in attics or cellars. Some of the contents can be matched among the design registers and representations described below, and local museums can often provide advice about assigning a date to a particular object. Furthermore, the objects that you find may be linked to a previous use of the property, which might be reflected in the current or former name of the house.

13.2.2 Design registers and representations

If you have managed to locate old wallpaper, dateable objects, or perhaps a photograph showing how the house was decorated at a particular period, you can attempt to match some of this material with the original designs and sample representations that were registered by the proprietors who wished to protect their design from competitors. The records are now with the PRO as part of the holdings of the Board of Trade, and cover the period 1839–1964.

The records are arranged in various series, reflecting chronological periods and the type of design that was registered. There are also two areas in which to start your research – the registers, which contain the names and addresses of the design owner, the number of items registered, and the registered number; and the representations of each design, arranged by registered number. From 1842 to 1883 the documents were given separate registration numbers according to the type of material, although you may sometimes find items misfiled in the wrong series. There is a useful PRO leaflet that describes how to locate material. Furthermore, items from this period may possess a diamond mark, which contains information that should allow you to identify the relevant registration details. Another PRO leaflet explains the conversion process.

The representations are a wonderful source if you wish to discover period wallpaper designs and contemporary household inventions, and should allow you to paint a vivid picture of how your house might once have been furnished and decorated. Some of the sketches include illustrations on how household devices would have been installed, and can explain strange alcoves or other inexplicable anomalies in the internal structure of a property.

13.2.3 Patents and specifications

In addition to the registers and representations, applications by inventors for patents for new inventions up to 1853, with specifications from 1711 that provide detail of the invention, were enrolled in Chancery. Copies of the letter patent sent to the applicant were enrolled on the patent rolls in **C 66**, while the specifications of patents were enrolled in **C 54** (Close Rolls), **C 210** (Petty Bag Office, Specification and Surrender Rolls) or **C 73** (Rolls Chapel, Specification and Surrender Rolls). There is a series of publications available on open access that act as an index to patents and their specifications, and will allow you locate the relevant roll. Once you have found the date of a patent in the volume, you should then look this up in the respective patent roll calendar on open access, and then convert the entry into a PRO reference. Similarly, the volumes also list the relevant series in which you will find a specification.

Once you have matched an entry with the PRO reference and ordered the document, you should find that the enrolment contains a description of the item that has been granted a patent, which in theory protected the invention from other designers, or a transcript of the relevant specification for the item.

Early applications for patents can be found in various series. From 1661 there are entry books for patents in **SP 44**, continued from 1782 in series **HO 43**. After 1853, copies of patents are available from the Patent Office Sale Branch (*see* **Useful addresses**). Furthermore, printed transcripts of specifications enrolled before 1853 can be seen at the BL Science Reference Library.

13.2.4 Copyright files

You may also wish to examine the copyright entry forms maintained by the Stationers' Company at Stationers' Hall, London, under the various Copyright Acts from 1842, which have been deposited with the PRO and assigned the series **COPY 1**. A wide variety of items are covered in the records, some of which were used in domestic property. The records cover the period 1837–1912, and you can obtain the copyright number from the registers and indexes in **COPY 3**, which should correspond with the files in **COPY 1**. However, the entry forms are arranged by type of material and by date, so the copyright number will be of limited use for search purposes. The Stationers' Company has retained the registers for the period 1554–1842.

COPY 1 will also be of use if you are searching for images, as part of the series is devoted to copyright of photographs. Many of these relate to individual houses or properties. However, there is no place index available in the series list, and so the records are not easily accessible.

13.3   Inventories

Inventories are lists of possessions or property belonging to a particular person or persons. They were compiled for many reasons, and some of the best places to begin looking are listed below.

13.3.1 Probate inventories

Probate inventories were compiled to quantify a deceased person's estate, excluding realty, so that the executors knew the extent and value of the possessions that they were to distribute. These are described in detail in Chapter 7, but in summary you will find that they generally listed all possessions and belongings that were contained in relevant properties or dwellings, and usually a value was assigned to the goods so that they could be sold. Consequently, you will find a room by room list of personal possessions, furniture, clothes and paintings. For example, when the London lawyer Silvester Petyt died in 1720, the contents of his house were described in great detail; we are left with an impression of how an early-eighteenth-century gentleman would have furnished his lodgings, complete with furniture from India, Dutch glassware, Turkish carpets, four looking glasses, an eight-day clock, a musket, bayonet and sword, and nearly 200 prints and various pictures of family, royalty and judges (PRO reference **PROB 5/2768**).

13.3.2 Inventories in other series

You will find that many legal cases required inventories to be produced, particularly in the equity courts. A list of where to look for PRO series that contain exhibits is provided in Chapter 8.

In addition, there are a few distinct series that contain various inventories, such as **E 154** (goods and chattels, 1207–1721), which mainly covers premises and shops but also incorporates merchants' dwellings and private residences. Many of these refer to individuals who had been indicted for treason or other felonies, and this will lead you to other areas in which to look for inventories, as criminal cases heard by the Crown often resulted in the seizure of an indicted criminal's possessions. However, these can be notoriously difficult to track down, and are not the best place for the house historian to begin. Generally, inquisitions will be fruitful, as will accounts of forfeited property that usually take the form of an inventory. Series such as **E 101, 143, 163** and **199** and **FEC 1** contain such information, and inventories can also be found in **E 140, 219, 314** and **315; IR 59; LR 1, 2** and **5; and SP 28** and **46.**

13.4 Sale catalogues and prospectuses

To assist with the sale of a property, the estate or land agent who was handling the process often compiled a catalogue to provide information for the prospective purchaser. This is often listed among the business papers of the relevant firm of agents, who in the eighteenth and nineteenth centuries were usually solicitors. Occasionally you will find catalogues among the private papers of individuals who either bought the property or were involved in the sale process.

The format of the documents will vary from catalogue to catalogue, depending on what is being sold. The most useful records will be the sale of a deceased person's estate by an executor, as you will often find a room by room list of personal possessions that effectively forms an inventory, as well as serving as a guide to the layout of the house. Preliminary surveys to compile the official catalogue also survive among solicitors' or estate agents' papers, although these are quite rare. You will also need an idea of which firm of solicitors or estate agents handled the process. To identify contemporary local firms, you should examine relevant trade directories. If you are lucky, the firm may still be in operation, perhaps under a new name after previous mergers. There are a number of associations and societies that can be approached for further advice about tracking down company archives, and these are listed under **Useful addresses.**

Most sale catalogues will therefore be deposited at the relevant CRO, but the PRO holds a collection of catalogues dating from the late nineteenth century that were brought into the Supreme Court (Chancery Division) by solicitors. These related to forthcoming sales by auction by the order of the court, and are located in series **J 46**. The documents are arranged by county and thereafter by the name of the place that is listed in the sale catalogue.

You can also obtain useful information about the layout or interior of a property from sale notices in local newspapers. This is even more appropriate for properties that are advertised for rent, as a description of the fixtures and

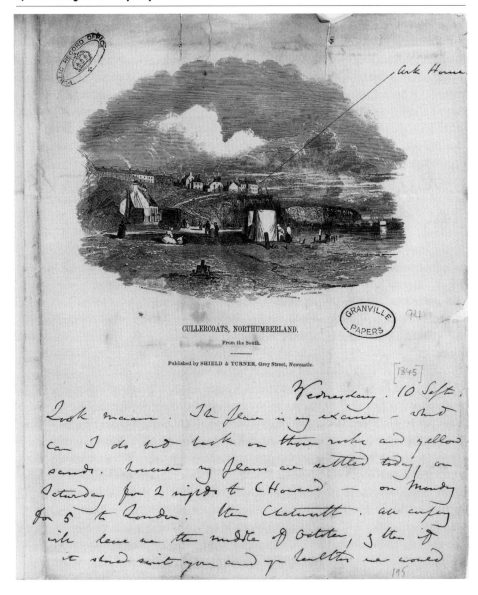

Figure 29 Found amongst the private correspondence of Lady Granville – a letter from her brother, the Duke of Devonshire, depicting the house at Cullercoats where he stayed during a visit. The Duke has marked the location of the property, Ark House, on the headed notepaper. The Duke's archives at Chatsworth House contain letters describing other visits to the house in more detail. (PRO 30/29/17/5)

fittings that accompany the property are sometimes listed. However, notices of either type can be difficult to locate unless you have obtained a potential sale date from other sources such as title deeds or private papers. Some CROs have compiled basic indexes for the more important publications, but these tend to list names, places and events, and as such do not cover these notices.

13.5 Correspondence and diaries

The thoughts and recollections of past occupants or visitors can provide an evocative window to the past, and can contain some quite revealing insights into the way people lived in your local community. Diaries and personal correspondence are a rich source – where they survive. You will be very fortunate to find anything that directly relates to your house, but you may well be able to find references to life in your village or street in the personal recollections of others.

The PRO has a limited range of diaries in its holdings. They are usually to be found amongst the exhibits brought to courts as evidence and never collected by the litigants. Other areas to begin looking will be among the private papers of owners, where far more personal correspondence can be found. However, at the PRO these tend to relate to major historical figures whose archives have been deposited or purchased due to their importance, and are mainly in the PRO series. Nevertheless some surprising evidence can be uncovered; for example, in the Granville papers, correspondence survives from the Duke of Devonshire to his sister, Lady Granville, that describes his stay at a private house high on the cliffs at Cullercoats (*see* **Figure 29**), a small village north of Tynemouth, Northumberland. The letter is written on headed paper that contains a printed depiction of the house in question. Further research in the Duke of Devonshire's own archives revealed similar correspondence from his sister, describing the interior of the same house in great detail during a stay of her own; she writes of the spectacular view from her bedroom, across the bay to the ruins of Tynemouth Priory in the distance.

13.6 Fire insurance records

Fire insurance offices were established in London from the late seventeenth century, with wider coverage throughout the eighteenth century onwards. Most provincial companies restricted their practice to the local area, but the major London firms, such as the Sun, Royal Exchange and Phoenix, expanded their business to set up provincial offices.

The companies insured all types of property against the risk of fire, and usually provided their own fire brigades as well. To identify an insured property, a fire mark was issued to the householder that was then fixed to the wall of the property; each company had a unique fire mark, which could also contain the policy number embossed in the corner.

The main type of record will be a policy register that details the policy number; name, status, occupation and address of the policyholder, plus the same data for tenants, if applicable; the location, type, nature of construction and value of the property to be insured; the premium paid to the company; the renewal date; and a brief outline of any endorsement. Entries in the registers were usually chronological, and each new entry was assigned a policy number. You may find that larger companies maintained concurrent registers, so the policies may not run in strict numerical order. The major companies also kept indexes to the registers, by name, place or policy number. Where contemporary indexes have failed to survive, limited indexing work has been undertaken for some companies.

The registers will give a rough indication of the layout of a property, and some individuals specified in great detail what was to be insured. However, these were usually much earlier policies, and the volume of business meant that the agents restricted the detail they recorded in the registers. Other records may be of use though. For example, endorsement books, claims records and surveyors' plans and reports exist for some companies, and these can provide great detail for any property covered.

Records for local companies will be deposited at the relevant CRO, either among the records of the company or in the personal papers of the individual agents that they employed. The Guildhall Library, London, has records of the Sun, Royal Exchange (both London and provincial business) and Hand-in-Hand (London only); the Phoenix records (London and provincial) are at Cambridge University Library, and the Westminster Fire Office (London and limited provincial) are at the Westminster Archives Centre. The PRO holds no fire insurance records.

14 Preparing a research plan

Some hints about beginning research have been provided in Chapter 2, but one of the most important 'first steps' is to sit down and sketch out a provisional research plan. Although every house will have a different research trail that reflects its own unique history, the majority of first-time house historians will find the following framework useful.

Furthermore, you should consider at the outset what you want to find out about your house. For some house historians, pinpointing a construction date will be sufficient reward for time spent in an archive; but for many others, the real excitement is provided by bringing the past back to life by finding out about the lives of the people who resided in your home, and how the local community evolved through the ages. Even if you live in a house built in the twentieth century, don't let this deter you from researching the previous history of the site.

14.1 First steps

(a) Work out what you want to find.

- Set your research parameters; these can change as you find out more, but you should try to limit yourself to one or two immediate goals.
- Do you want to concentrate solely on the chronology?
- Do you want to research previous owners?
- Do you want to research previous houses on the site?

(b) Make your goals realistic.

- How much research time do you have?
- Are you prepared to travel to distant archives?
- Research can be expensive – are you prepared to pay for photocopies (where available)?
- Do you require any additional skills (e.g. language, paleography)?

- Do you have access to research tools (e.g. personal computer, the Internet, Latin dictionaries, guides to local history)?

14.2 Background research

(a) Begin with the architecture of your house.

- Try to work out a rough date of construction for your house from the architectural clues that exist.
- You should also try to identify the dates of any major rebuilds or additions, as the cause of these might be important clues in your research.
- Compare your house to its neighbours – is it similar or different?
- Where is your house in relation to the village/town/city in which it is built? In general, if it is close to the centre it is probably older.

(b) Pinpoint the location of your house in the local area. This will probably involve a trip to the local studies centre. If possible:

- Locate the manor in which your house was once situated.
- Locate the parish it was in; this might be different from today.
- Locate the administrative district – county division (hundred, rape, riding, etc.); local authority (urban district council, rural district council, borough); Poor Law union; tax district; registration district.

(c) While you are at the local studies centre, read about your local area and its history in secondary sources.

- Local studies publications (e.g. VCH) may provide information and document references that you can follow up.
- Look for old photographs, newspaper clippings or any other items that can provide clues for your documentary research. It may be that some research has already been done on your property.

(d) Try to contact your mortgage provider.

- Ask to see your title deeds, as they give the names of previous owners.
- You may be charged a fee to view these documents.
- They may not go back that far, so don't be too disappointed if the information they contain is limited.

(e) Start your oral research.

- Talk to neighbours, local antiquarians, previous owners, estate agents and solicitors that handled the sale of the property – they might be able to provide you with evidence or stories for you to research.

- In particular, solicitors *may* have earlier title deeds, although they are most likely lost or with previous owners who paid off their mortgage.
- Remember to exercise diplomacy and courtesy when approaching any of these people.

(f) Start to locate relevant archives.

- Based on where parish, manorial, estate and relevant local records are located, you should start to plan where to continue your research.
- Consult the publications listed at the end of this book under **Useful publications**, or browse the HMC website.
- Contact potential archives and ask about opening times, entry requirements and document availability.

14.3 Archival research: creating a document framework

You can construct a document framework that in theory will provide names of owners and occupiers. The documents listed below mainly cover the period from 1840 to 1940. Although they are not appropriate for all houses and sometimes may not have survived, they cover the majority of properties in England and Wales and are recommended as the starting place for all house historians.

(a) PRO: Valuation survey

- Provides maps and names of owners/principal occupiers c.1910, plus a basic document description.

(b) PRO/CRO: Tithe apportionment

- Provides names of owners/principal occupiers c.1840s.

(c) FRC/CRO: Census returns

- Provides names of all occupiers 1841–91 (and 1901 from 2002).

(d) PRO/CRO: Enclosure awards

- Provides useful background information on local landowners and tenants, with maps; from 1780s, mainly nineteenth century.

(e) PRO: National Farm Survey

- Provides maps and names of owners of farm properties c.1940s.

14.4　Archival research: following up leads

Armed with the data from your document framework, plus information gleaned from your pre-research in step 2, you can start to plan your unique research trail. This will lead you to various archives, but it is usually best to start with the relevant CRO. The main documents you will probably use are listed below in descending order of potential value, although this will vary depending on the history of your house and what you find from your document framework.

(a) Relevant CRO

- Maps and plans of the local area (including OS).
- Manorial records (court rolls if copyhold).
- Other estate records (if copyhold, freehold or part of a larger estate).
- Deposited title deeds.
- Leases.
- Sale catalogues (among estate agents' papers).
- Wills (deposited, plus existing local consistory court registers).
- Electoral registers.
- Personal papers of known owners/occupiers.
- Trade directories.
- Land Tax (and other assessed taxes).
- Parochial material (for occupancy and local rates).
- Local newspapers (for listed sales).
- Local fire insurance registers.
- Records of local industries.
- Records of utility companies.
- Miscellaneous local records. (Be bold, be imaginative – you never know what you might uncover!)

Don't forget that you may need to visit other local record offices, such as borough or metropolitan archives. The local studies centre at your library may also have a collection of relevant documents.

(b) Public Record Office

- Maps and plans.
- PCC wills and administration pre-1858 (also at FRC).
- PCC inventories.
- Records of land transfer, conveyance and enrolled deeds.
- Legal disputes.
- Hearth Tax (and other assessed taxes).

- Records of national events.
- Records of modern houses.
- Private papers of known owners/occupiers.

(c) Other archives (in no particular order of relevance)

- FRC, Myddleton Street, London, for census, wills and registration of births, marriages and deaths.
- NRA, Chancery Lane, London, for Manorial Documents Register.
- LMA for property in Greater London.
- Corporation of London Record Office for property in the City of London.
- BL for maps, plans and records of private individuals.
- Guildhall Library for fire insurance registers for London companies (which will include records of provincial insurance).
- Borthwick Institute, York, for PCY wills, administrations and inventories pre-1858.
- First Avenue House, Holborn, London, for post-1858 probate material.
- NLW, Aberystwyth, for Welsh property not covered at the PRO.
- NAS, Edinburgh, for Scottish property.
- PRONI, Belfast, for property in Northern Ireland (some earlier material in Dublin).

You will find that your research takes you to any number of these archives, and you will use various combinations of the documents listed above. The next chapter uses a real case study to demonstrate how the history of your house can lead to some surprising discoveries.

15 Case study: Plymouth House

The following example is intended to provide a guide to the type of research you may have to undertake. The property in question is Plymouth House (*see* **Figures 30** and **31**), a guest house situated in the Welsh village of Northop, Flintshire.

15.1 First steps

The aim of the research was to find out as much as possible about the history of Plymouth House. The primary goal was to attempt to provide a construction date, but also to discover some of the social history associated with the property. There were various local stories about the history of the property, and one of the most important was the legend that it was once a coaching inn called 'the Yacht' that served the Holyhead to Chester mail-coach route in the eighteenth century.

There were also stories about a property in the village called Ty Mawr (translated as 'Great House'), which once had a plaque on the wall inscribed with the words 'Woe to Him That Buildeth in Unrighteousness, 1674'. No such house exists in Northop today, but given that Plymouth House is the largest property in the village, there is the intriguing possibility that it was once known by the name of Ty Mawr.

15.2 Background research

The first step was to place the house in the locality. The village of Northop is situated in the county of Flint, and the CRO is located at Hawarden; there is no main separate local study centre. The village also formed part of the parish of Northop; parish registers can be found at Hawarden or on microfilm at the National Library of Wales.

From the secondary sources at Hawarden it became apparent that the village of Northop once formed part of a manor with the same name, which itself was a component part of the estates of the Earl of Plymouth from 1706 until the early

Figure 30 Plymouth House, Northop, formerly a coaching inn called 'The Yacht'.

nineteenth century. A search of the NRA showed that records of the Plymouth estates were deposited at the NLW, Aberystwyth, with some rentals at the Glamorgan Record Office, Cardiff.

An article on Northop by the local antiquarian Thomas Edwards, published in the *Cambrian Quarterly Magazine*, suggests that The Yacht and Ty Mawr were separate buildings – Ty Mawr was situated in the centre of the village, and 'according to the style of building, entrance, garden, etc., would appear to be a dwelling of some significance'. However, The Yacht is listed separately as one of the six inns in Northop. So from this evidence it would appear that The Yacht was not Ty Mawr.

15.3 Archival research: creating a document framework

At the PRO, London

(a) Valuation survey

- From the finding aids, the relevant map (Flintshire IX.16) was identified as reference **IR 131/10/85** and ordered. The property is clearly depicted, set back from the road, with a marked path leading from the door to the road. This is unique in the village centre.

- On inspection, the hereditament number assigned to the property was 1685, which meant that the correct valuation book had the reference **IR 58/94483**.
- The Field Book recorded that the name of the owner was Edward Foulkes, who was also the freeholder and occupier. The name of the property was Plymouth House, 'an old property but substantially built', the outbuildings of which also contained 'an old coach house' (for storing coaches).

(b) Tithe apportionment

- Northop parish was identified in Kain and Oliver's publication, and the references were **IR 30/50/32** (map) and **IR 29/50/32** (apportionment).
- The plot number on the map was B38, and the apportionment for this plot showed that the owner was Benjamin Bellis and the occupant was Joseph Joynson; the property is described as a public house and yard called The Yacht. Bellis also rented 12 acres of land to Joynson.
- As with the valuation map, the house is clearly set back from the road, connected by a marked path.

At the FRC, London

(c) 1841–91 census returns

- The indexes were searched to find which district Northop was in, and document references for each census were obtained.
- 1841 (ref. **HO 107/1407/18**): 'Yacht Inn' not listed by name, but Joseph Joynson and family listed as an innkeeper in the village.
- 1851 (ref. **HO 107/2501**): 'Yacht Inn' listed in possession of Joseph Joynson, wife Catherine, 2 daughters Ann and Mary, and servant (Elizabeth Bellis).
- 1861 (ref. **RG 9/4272**): 'Yacht Inn' listed, in possession of John and Ann Whaley, 2 children and servant.
- 1871 (ref. **RG 10/5643**): 'Yacht Inn' no longer listed; 'Yacht House' in possession of Diana Davies.
- 1881 (ref. **RG 11/5505**): 'The Yacht' in possession of Edward Foulkes, master butcher, plus wife and 4 children, and 2 servants.
- 1891 (ref. **RG 12/4607**): 'Yacht House' in possession of Edward Foulkes and family.

In summary

- Plymouth House was formerly The Yacht, as its position on the tithe map and valuation map is the same.

- In 1840 it was owned by Thomas Bellis and was rented to Joseph Joynson.
- At some point between 1861 and 1871 it ceased trading as an inn and became a private residence.
- It was in the hands of Edward Foulkes and family by 1881, probably via Diana Davies.

15.4 Archival research: following up leads

Further research was continued at Hawarden based on the data found in the framework research.

(a) Local records confirmed some of the details.

- Trade directories periodically listed the innkeepers of The Yacht – Slater's directory in 1844, 1850 and 1856 list The Yacht in the possession of Joseph Joynson; in 1868 and 1874 Ann Whaley is listed as proprietor; Ann and Mary Joynson (daughters of Joseph) are running another inn nearby in Pentre, also called The Yacht.
- From 1876, The Yacht is not mentioned. However, parish registers show that John Whaley was buried in 1866 and Anne Whaley was buried in 1867, suggesting that the information in the trade directories is inaccurate; this also fits in with the census data for 1871.
- Church rates from 1826 list contributions from Mrs Bellis (owner) and Joseph Joynson (occupier), although the property concerned is not named.
- Quarter sessions records show that in 1823 four locals were bound over to keep the peace against Joseph Joynson, publican, following an affray in a local inn; it is likely that this is The Yacht.

(b) Other useful evidence was uncovered.

- An estate map created for the Earl of Plymouth in 1717 depicts a house on the site of the modern Plymouth House, partly drawn in profile. It appears to be the largest house in the village, and has land attached to it. As with the tithe and valuation maps, it is set back from the road and appears to have a strange entrance or path marked on it. Frustratingly, a survey book linking tenants with property has been lost, and all that survives is a list of names on the map with no means of reference. However, it would appear that this house, on the site of The Yacht and Plymouth House, once formed part of the Plymouth estates.
- A survey of the parish by Edward Llewyd c.1695 lists all the important property in the village. There is no mention of Ty Mawr, although a property named Kort Mawr is listed. 'Kort' translates as 'court', which refers to a court

or manor house (where the manorial court could also be heard if the lord of the manor lived elsewhere), so is this an early reference to Ty Mawr?

To follow up some of the leads about the Earl of Plymouth, the trail led to the NLW, which holds large sections of the Plymouth archives.

(c) Sale catalogue 1812.

- A crucial link between 'The Yacht Inn', the Earl of Plymouth and the Bellis family was uncovered among the Wigmore estate papers in a sale catalogue dated 1812. It listed all properties and land parcels to be sold from the Earl of Plymouth's estates, and notes that all properties to be sold were freehold estates of inheritance. This meant that they should (in theory) be listed among the estate papers of the Earls of Plymouth. However, court rolls would be of no use as they cover only copyhold property.
- Lot IX – 'The Yacht Inn, a substantial and commodious house, with excellent stabling, and every requisite for a respectable Inn, upon the much frequented road from Chester to Holyhead.' The inn included 9 acres of land. Lots XIII–XVII were in the tenancy of John Bellis 'of the Yacht'.

(d) With this clue, the Bellis family history was further investigated.

- Will of Edward Bellis, 1832 – son of Elizabeth Bellis, brother of John Hughes Bellis – leaves his share of property in Northop under the licence/occupation of Joseph Joynson to his wife for life, and then equally to his son John and daughter Elizabeth; if all were to die, then to his brother Benjamin.
- Will of John Hughes Bellis, 1830 (the innkeeper listed in 1812) – son of Elizabeth Bellis – described as gentleman, leaves his share of property in Northop to John Bellis, son of brother Edward.
- Will of Elizabeth Bellis, 1827 (listed in the Northop church rates) – widow of Benjamin Bellis – leaves all her property and possessions to her sons, Edward and Benjamin.
- The Northop parish registers provide dates for some of these events, plus the following entry – 'memorandum: the above correction and addition in the entry of John Bellis, christening 1825 was made by me this 14th day of May, Henry Jones, vicar, signed in the presence of us, Robert Jones parish clerk and Joseph Joynson, Yacht, Northop' – further evidence of ties between the Bellis family and Joseph Joynson, their tenant.

(e) A return to the Plymouth archives produced title deeds for their estates, and threw up some new names to track down.

- The descent of the manor of Northop was listed in great detail in the schedule of deeds for the Plymouth estate.

- 1706 marriage between Elizabeth Whitley, heiress of Roger Whitley, to Earl of Plymouth – marriage settlement includes the manor of Northop, previously held by the Whitley family. Various properties are listed as part of the manor, including 'The Courthouse'; The Yacht is not listed. Is this Kort Mawr alias Ty Mawr?
- Other deeds belonging to the Whitley family provide more detail about the Courthouse – 1703 Richard Lucas is the occupier; 1701 'formerly in the possession of Richard Sneade'; the earliest reference is in 1670, when Roger Whitley purchased Northop from the Earl of Bridgewater. The Courthouse and 12 acres of land is in the possession of Richard Sneade.
- Earlier descent of Northop: 1537 Thomas Billington esquire settles land in and title of Northop on his son Randall, who in 1578 sells it all to Thomas Egerton, later Lord Chancellor to James I; it then passes through the Egerton family (the Earls of Bridgewater) until 1670.

In summary

- The house was sold in 1812 to the Bellis family, who were tenants of the Earl of Plymouth before this date. Thereafter, and from at least 1823, it was let to Joseph Joynson.
- The inn was linked to the Chester–Holyhead coach route.
- No earlier references to The Yacht appear before this date.
- No mention is made of Ty Mawr, although the Courthouse is listed to c.1670.
- The descent of the manor of Northop is clear from 1537.

A search of the NRA showed that papers of Roger Whitley were held at various archives, including the Bodleian Library, Oxford; John Rylands University, Manchester; and the Post Office Archives, London. More research on Whitley showed that a history of his career had been compiled, and a copy deposited at Hawarden. From this, it appears he was a fervent Royalist who was rewarded at the Restoration with the position of Postmaster General, and used the wealth this generated to buy lands, including the manor of Northop.

However, this did not progress the story of the Yacht Inn before 1812. To change tactics, the history of the Chester–Holyhead mail-coach route was investigated, starting with the Chester Record Office, as the start venue of the route, and followed by the PRO, which held a report into the route c.1810.

(f) Coaching advertisements in local newspapers.

- The *Chester Chronicle* contained many notices about coach routes. Although searching was a time-consuming task, it was a worthwhile exercise.
- 16 May 1776 – Thomas Carter announced that he intended to address the

complaints about the lengthy and uncomfortable journey along the mail-coach route from Holyhead to Chester by funding a series of high-class inns along the route so that travellers could stop in comfort.

- 25 July 1776 – Thomas Carter proclaimed the first of his coaches, designed for the nobility and gentry travelling through North Wales, was ready to leave The Yacht, Chester, and make its way to the Walsh's Head, Holyhead, stopping at various inns along the way. The first stop out of Chester was the Yacht Inn, Northop, run by Thomas Bellis.

(g) Report into the Chester–Holyhead road at the PRO.

- A report into the Chester to Holyhead road in **MT 27/69** showed that the mail-coach route through Northop took longer than via a coastal route, and so the village was bypassed c.1810. The entire route was later dropped in favour of a new road that ran from Shrewsbury after 1812.

In summary

- These are crucial leads. First, it appears that Thomas Carter was creating a private coach route; and that from 1776 it included the Yacht Inn in Northop. If that is so, there is a possibility that the Earl of Plymouth was renting the property to either Carter or Bellis, and therefore it should appear in estate rentals.
- Second, the removal of the mail-coach route c.1810 meant a loss of business for Northop, and hence the coaching inn would have lost trade. This may explain why the Earl of Plymouth decided to sell the property in 1812.

Following up the lead on Thomas Carter, rentals for some of the Earl of Plymouth's lands were discovered at Glamorgan Record Office, Cardiff.

(h) Plymouth estate rentals at Glamorgan.

- No properties were assigned names in the rentals, but for the year ending March 1777, Thomas Carter is listed as renting two pieces of property from the Earl, valued at £16.10.0 and £4.10.0. They are described as 'late Edwards', meaning that they were previously rented to a tenant named Edwards.
- By tracking the rentals back, it is possible to determine who previously rented these properties.
- 1773–6 rented by Widow Davenport, late Edwards.
- 1772 Thomas Davenport.
- 1771 Samuel Crew now Thomas Davenport.
- 1770 Samuel Crew.
- 1768–9 Thomas Edwards.

- Another entry in 1771 provides crucial information. It lists 'repairs for the Courthouse and barn in Northop, Thomas Edwards late tenant thereof failed and now in gaol', and provides expenditure for renovating the property.

In summary

- Not only has the earliest recorded date of The Yacht been brought back to 1776, but it can also be linked to the Courthouse listed in the Plymouth deeds.
- The repairs listed in 1776 show that the tenant, Thomas Edwards, let the house fall into a state of disrepair, yet provided the first stage of renovation from a private high-status dwelling to a coaching inn under Thomas Carter.
- The link between The Yacht, the Courthouse and Kort Mawr is now very strong. The trail therefore leads back to Roger Whitley, as it was his purchase of Northop in 1670 that provided the first documentary proof of the Courthouse.

Roger Whitley was postmaster general under Charles II, and some of his personal papers were deposited in the Post Office Archives in London. This is also an excellent source for records of the Chester–Holyhead post route.

(i) Whitley's post office letter-books.

- These record correspondence with his deputy postmasters about postal affairs. Records show that from 1667 the postmaster for Northop was Richard Sneade, who was also listed in the Plymouth deeds as the tenant in the Courthouse in 1670.
- **POST 94/13**: 14 June 1673, letter from Whitley to Sneade, Northop – 'I pray present my service to my cousin Evans and family, tell him I will speedily send the length of the timber I would have cut for your house, as for slates, I would have the best and most useful, resolving to make it handsome. Remember Midsummer is at hand, make your rent ready also which is due to the office.'
- **POST 94/15**: 23 January 1674/5, letter from Whitley to Sneade, Northop – 'Let me advise you (once more) to send me an exact account of what money you have paid my brother and also give me a full assurance, that I shall be speedily and punctually paid for the remainder. If you fail herein I am resolved to get another postmaster for Northop, and also a new tenant for my house.'
- **POST 94/15**: 13 April 1675, letter from Whitley to Sneade, Northop – 'My brother informs me, he can get no money from you, I wonder, you use me so ill, let me prevail with you, to pay him what is due, immediately upon receipt

Figure 31 The doorway of Plymouth House.

of this letter (and before the next post returns on Saturday next) or I will give direction to put you out of employment, and place a more careful and just man in it.'

- Further correspondence shows that Mrs Sneade acts as postmaster for Northop from 1676.

In summary

- We now have a potential explanation for the cryptic plaque on Ty Mawr, if it is the same as Kort Mawr. 'Woe to Him That Buildeth in Unrighteousness' could refer to Richard Sneade, the non-payment of funds, and his presumed death by 1676; the date of a major reconstruction of the Courthouse/Ty Mawr is c.1673–4.
- This ties in with the purchase date for the manor of Northop in 1670, and perhaps represents an attempt by a non-resident lord of the manor to renovate the manor (court) house.

Tying up the loose ends, we find from the parish records in Hawarden that Richard Sneade was buried in Northop parish churchyard on 25 September 1675 – perhaps another chilling reference to the inscription on the plaque?

In 1670 Roger Whitley purchased Northop from the Egerton family. Having checked the NRA, it would appear that records of the Egerton family before 1670 were largely with the Ellesmere papers, which are stored in the Huntington Library, San Marino, California, USA. After an email research request, it was confirmed that rentals for Northop did exist but no names linked to the Court-house were found.

Final summary/chronology

- Plymouth House from c.1900 onwards.
- Private residence, known as Yacht House, from c.1870–c.1900.
- The 'Yacht Inn' from 1776 to 1870; part of private high-class coaching chain run by Thomas Carter and sub-let to the Bellis family, yet owned by the Earl of Plymouth until its sale to the Bellis family in 1812.
- The 'Courthouse' from 1670 to 1775; residence of the Northop postmaster Richard Sneade from c.1667–95, and thereafter his widow. Underwent an extensive rebuild c.1673–4 on the orders of the Lord of the Manor, Roger Whitley; thereafter passed to private hands until the fall from grace of Thomas Edwards in 1769–70, and renovated c.1771.
- The house was probably known as Ty Mawr, a derivation of Kort Mawr (1695).
- Records before 1670 may exist, but are in the USA.

Conclusion

This case study demonstrates that you will have to employ some lateral thinking in your research, as well as educated guesses and a great deal of searching. You may also be left with an inconclusive answer – in this example, it is highly likely that Plymouth House *was* Ty Mawr, but it is not possible to prove this through the documents as a certain *fact*. You should also note that the research led back-wards and forwards between archives, following clues as and when they became relevant. You may find that some evidence initially seems inconsequential, but then becomes vital in the wake of later discoveries. You should never assume that you have 'finished' with an archive, as you may have to return to re-check sources you thought you had discarded. Hopefully you will achieve an end result as satisfactory as this one!

PRO series that contain title deeds

1. Private deeds

Collection	Finding aids
Chancery	
C 146 Ancient Deeds Series C c.1100–1695 11,087 deeds	Pieces 1–8060 in *Descriptive Catalogue of Ancient Deeds*;* pieces 8061–11087 in transcript with index.
C 147 Ancient Deeds Series CC c.1100–16 1,310 deeds	Series list, pieces 1–373; card index to persons and places, pieces 1–315.
C 148 Ancient Deeds Series CS 1256–1603 171 boxes	Typescript list, pieces 1–169, manuscript list pieces 170–171; card index (with **C 147**).
C 149 Modern Deeds Series C c.1600–c.1800 65 boxes	Unlisted and unsorted.
Exchequer of Receipt	
E 40 Ancient Deeds Series A c.1100–1603 15,912 deeds	Pieces 1–13672 in *Descriptive Catalogue of Ancient Deeds*; pieces 13673–15068 and 15069–15910 in *List and Index Society*, *vols 151* and *152* respectively.
E 41 Ancient Deeds Series AA c.1100–1642 533 deeds	Pieces 461 and 464 printed in *The Pipe Roll Society*, X (1888).
E 42 Ancient Deeds Series AS c.1100–1590 549 deeds	Pieces 1–549 in *List and Index Society, vol. 158.*
E 44 Modern Deeds Series A 20 Hen VII–4 Geo III 535 deeds	Series list.

* *A Descriptive Catalogue of Ancient Deeds in the Public Record Office*, 6 volumes (HMSO, 1890–1906).

Collection	Finding aids
Exchequer: King's Remembrancer **E 132** Transcript of Deeds Edward 1–James 1 66 files and rolls	Series list.
E 210 Ancient Deeds Series D 1120–1609 11,325 deeds	Pieces 1–1330 in *Descriptive Catalogue of Ancient Deeds.*
E 211 Ancient Deeds Series DD c.1101–1645 724 boxes	Pieces 1–724 in *List and Index Society, vol. 200.*
E 212 Ancient Deeds Series DS 1228–1582 139 deeds	Series list.
E 214 Modern Deeds Series D 1603–1851 1,679 deeds	Series list, indexed for persons and places.
Exchequer Augmentation Office **E 326** Ancient Deeds Series B c.1200–1592 *101, 113* and *124*	Pieces 1–4232 in *Descriptive Catalogue of Ancient Deeds;* pieces 4233–4827, 4838–9000 and 9001–12950, plus index to 13,677 deeds　　　4233–12950, in *List and Index Society,* vols 95, respectively.
E 327 Ancient Deeds Series BX Hen I–1543 783 deeds	All deeds published in Thomas Madox, *Formulare Anglicanum* (London, 1702).
E 328 Ancient Deeds Series BB 1225–1667 441 boxes, files	Index to pieces 1–433 in *List and Index Society, vol. 137.*
E 329 Ancient Deeds Series BS 1148–1560 484 deeds	Series list.
E 330 Modern Deeds Series B 1548–1803 50 deeds	Series list.
Exchequer Pipe Office **E 354** Ancient Deeds Series P 1524-1608 50 deeds	Series list.
E 355 Ancient Deeds Series PP c.1500–c.1600 7 boxes	Unsorted, restricted access.

2. Private deeds for semi-autonomous jurisdictions

Collection	Finding aids
Duchy of Lancaster **DL 25** Deeds Series L c.1100–34 Chas II 3,652 documents	Various pieces are published in several sources – see series list for details.
DL 26 Deeds Series LL 6 Edw I–10 Geo III 106 deeds	Pieces 1–7 in introduction to series list.
DL 27 Deeds Series LS to 12 Jas I 332 documents	Various pieces are published in several sources – see series list for details.
DL 36 Cartae Miscellanae c.1125–17th century 3 volumes	PRO Lists and Indexes, Supplementary Series, vol.3.
Palatinate of Durham **DURH 21** Chancery Deeds Series G 1557–1799 9 bundles	Unsorted, with restricted access.
Palatinate of Lancaster **PL 29** Deeds, etc. Series H 1501–1844 63 papers	Series list.
Palatinate of Chester **WALE 29** Ancient Deeds Series F c.1270–1602 516 deeds	Series list.
WALE 30 Ancient Deeds Series FF 1508–1634 53 deeds	Typescript list available on open access, indexed by person and place.
WALE 31 Modern Deeds Series F 1297-1830 11 boxes of deeds	Transferred to National Library of Wales (NLW).

3. Deeds for Crown properties

Collection	Finding aids
Crown Estate Commissioners **CRES 38** Title deeds: property acquired, sold or leased by the Crown Edward 1–1967 2,219 pieces	Series list.

Collection	Finding aids
Office of Auditors of Land Revenue **LR 14** Ancient Deeds Series E 1223–1730 1,178 deeds	Pieces 1–1178 in *List and Index Society, vol. 181.*
LR 15 Ancient Deeds Series EE 1349–1731 322 deeds	Typescript calendar, indexed by people and places on open access.
LR 16 Modern Deeds Series E Jas I–c.1800 14 deeds	Unsorted, with restricted access.
Office of Land Revenue **LRRO 5** Deposited Documents Henry VIII–1917 69 volumes, rolls and bundles	Series list.
LRRO 37 Miscellaneous Records 1629–1921 137 rolls, volumes, etc.	Series list.
Office of Works **WORK 7** Deeds Series I c.1700–1915 84 boxes	Series list.
WORK 8 Deeds Series II 1710–1904 82 boxes	Ancient monuments, historic buildings; series list.
WORK 13 Deeds Series III 1844–1951 1,395 rolls	Public offices and buildings; series list.
WORK 24 Deeds Series IV 1614–1929 8 boxes	Property in Westminster; series list.

Glossary

Affidavit – a voluntary statement made on oath.

Alienate – to transfer property away from the normal line of inheritance.

Amercement – a financial penalty.

Ancient Lights – the light that falls on the windows of a house from the heavens, and which the owner claims to enjoy unobscured by obstructions erected by his neighbours.

Assize – a biennial court presided over by itinerant royal justices who toured a circuit of neighbouring counties.

Bar (an entail) – to destroy the normal line of descent.

Bequeath – to leave possessions to another by will.

Calendar – a summary of the contents of a document, usually in printed form.

Capital messuage – the main property in a manor, commonly referred to as the manor house.

Common law – the laws developed from the common customs of England.

Common socage – agricultural service owed to a lord.

Compounding – a payment made by Royalists to retain their forfeited lands after the English Civil War.

Contingent remainder – a remainder (in an entail) that might happen but was not certain.

Conveyancing – the legal transfer of title to property from one party to another.

Copyhold land – 'unfree' land, held according to the custom of the manor and transferred through the manorial court.

Customary tenant – a manorial tenant who held land according to the custom of the manor; also referred to as copyholder.

Demesne – land reserved by the lord of the manor for his own use.

Demise – to lease land for a given period.

Deposition – a sworn statement made in response to a specific interrogatory.

Devise – to leave by will, usually with reference to realty.

Dower – property or income settled on a woman at marriage by her husband's family that she enjoyed on her husband's death.

Enclosure – a wide-ranging term that describes changes in land use or status (*see also* encroaching and engrossing).

Encroaching – amalgamation of smaller plots of land.

Enfranchisement – with regard to land, the term applied to the conversion of copyhold into freehold.

Engrossing – amalgamation of two farms.

Entail – *see* fee tail.

Equity – a body of law based on judgments according to the merits of the case rather than the confines of common law.

Escheat – the return of land to the original grantor, either through the death of the last heir or default.

Essoin – a payment made to excuse a tenant's attendance at the manorial court.

Estate – with regard to land, the type of interest in the land is called the 'estate' (fee simple, fee tail, life interest, or term of years).

Fee farm – an alternate name for a lease.

Fee simple – an interest in property limited to a man and his heirs.

Fee tail – an interest in property limited to a man and the heirs of his body.

Fine – with regard to land, a legal document that ended a fictitious lawsuit.

Freehold land – land held from the lord of the manor on fixed terms.

Gavelkind – inheritance where property is divided equally between sons, a practice prevalent in Kent.

Hereditament number – a number assigned to a plot of land, used as part of the 1910 Valuation survey.

Impartible inheritance – property that could not be divided on death, and therefore passed intact.

Interrogatory – a list of specific questions relevant to a legal case.

Lease – an interest in land fixed for a set period known as a term of years.

Legacy – personal property left to another in a will.

Life interest – an interest in property limited to the life of the tenant.

Majority – the age at which an heir was entitled to inherit, traditionally 21 years until 1969.

Memorial – an abstract of a deed.

Messuage – a term used in manorial documents for a house.

Mortgage – conveyance of real estate as security for a loan.

Palaeography – the term used to describe handwriting and abbreviations used in documents.

Partible inheritance – a form of inheritance where land could be divided between several parties according to the customs of the manor.

Personalty – personal property that can be devised by will; this can include leases and uses.

Possession – the legal holder of land was deemed to be in possession.

Primogeniture – inheritance through the first-born male.

Probate – notification that a will had been proved in the relevant court.

Pur autre vie – a lease or grant that could be held for only as long as the lessor or grantor lived; literally 'for the life of another'.

Quarter sessions – a quarterly local court presided over by JPs that dealt with administrative matters and minor offences.

Quit rent – the conversion of agricultural services to monetary payments.

Realty – land, also defined as real estate.

Regnal year – a method of dating using the first day of the monarch's reign as the first day of the year. Hence the regnal year '1 Henry VIII' ran from 22 April 1509 to 21 April 1510.

Remainder – a future interest in land beginning at the end of another interest.

Rentcharge – rent that was charged on a plot of land, as opposed to rent service that was owed to a feudal lord as a condition of holding the land.

Repertory roll – a roll fulfilling the task of a list, index, catalogue or calendar.

Reversion – land that would revert to the original grantor at the end of the term was held 'in reversion'.

Rotulus – the Latin name for a roll, used to describe the individual sheets of parchment in a document.

Settlement – a land grant that involved the creation of a succession of interests in the land.

Strict settlement – a settlement that restricted inheritance to certain persons.

Tenant-in-chief – one who holds land direct from the Crown.

Tenement – a term used in manorial documents for a house.

Tenure – the terms by which land was held.

Term of years – *see* lease.

Tithe – payments in kind of a tenth of the annual produce of land by way of crops and animals.

Tithe apportionment – a formal agreement that set a monetary value to commuted tithes for a parish, and then divided it amongst liable individuals.

Title deeds – the collected legal documentation for past transfers of a particular piece of land or property that conveys legal possession.

Turnpike trust – a body responsible for the finance and administration of the roads (turnpikes) in its jurisdiction.

Trust – the interest of a person who is invested with property for the benefit of another.

Trustee – the person to whom an estate was conveyed in trust for another.

Use – the older name for trust.

Wardship – the control of the land of an under-age heir by his lord.

List of abbreviations

BL	British Library
BTHR	British Transport Historical Records
CARN	County Archive Research Network
CRO	County Record Office
DKR	Deputy Keeper's Report
FRC	Family Records Centre
HMC	Royal Commission for Historical Manuscripts
IPM	Inquisition post mortem
ITP	Income Tax Parish
JP	Justice of the Peace
LMA	London Metropolitan Archives
MAF	Ministry of Agriculture and Fisheries
MDR	Manorial Documents Register
NAS	National Archives of Scotland
NLW	National Library of Wales
NRA	National Register of Archives
OS	Ordnance Survey
PCC	Prerogative Court of Canterbury
PCY	Prerogative Court of York
PRO	Public Record Office
PRONI	Public Record Office of Northern Ireland
VCH	*Victoria County Histories*

Useful addresses

Association of Genealogists and Record Agents, 29 Badgers Close, Horsham, West Sussex RH12 5RU.

Bodleian Library, Broad Street, Oxford OX1 3BG. Tel: 01865 277158.

Borthwick Institute of Historical Research, St Anthony's Hall, Peasholme Green, York YO1 2PW. Tel: 01904 642315.

British Association for Local History, PO Box 1576, Salisbury, Wiltshire SP2 8SY.

British Geological Survey, Keyworth, Nottingham NG12 5GG.

British Library, 96 Euston Road, London NW1 2DB. Tel: 020 7412 7676. Also houses the **Science Reference Library, Oriental and India Office Library** and **Map Library**.

British Library Newspaper Library, Colindale Avenue, London NW9 5HE. Tel: 020 7412 7356.

British Records Association, 40 Northampton Road, London EC1R OHB. Tel: 020 7833 0428.

Cambridge University Library, West Road, Cambridge CB3 9DR. Tel: 01223 333000.

City of Westminster Archive Centre, 10 St Ann's Buildings, London SW1P 2DE. Tel: 020 7641 5180.

College of Arms, Queen Victoria Street, London EC4V 4BT. Tel: 020 7248 2762.

Corporation of London Record Office, PO Box 270, Guildhall, London EC2P 2EJ. Tel: 020 7332 1251.

EARL: The Consortium for Public Library Networking, Fourth Floor, Gun Court, 70 Wapping Lane, London E1W 2RS. Tel: 020 7702 2020.

English Heritage, Customer Services Department, PO Box 569, Swindon SN2 2YP. Tel: 01793 414910.

Family Records Centre, 1 Myddleton Street, London EC1R 1UW. Tel: 020 8392 5300.

General Register Office (Northern Ireland), Oxford House, 49–55 Chichester Street, Belfast BT1 4HL. Tel: 01232 252020.

General Register Office (Scotland), New Register House, Edinburgh EH1 3YT. Tel: 0131 334 0380.

Geologists' Association, Burlington House, Piccadilly, London WC1V 0JU. Tel: 020 7734 2356.

Guildhall Library, Aldermanbury, London EC2P 2EJ. Tel: 020 7332 1863.

House of Lords Record Office, House of Lords, London SW1A 0PW Tel: 020 7219 5316.

Imperial War Museum, Department of Documents, Lambeth Road, London SE1 6HZ
Tel: 020 74165221.

India Office Library *see* British Library.

Institute of Historical Research, University of London, Senate House,
London WC1E 7HU. Tel: 020 7862 8740.

Land Registry, HM, Lincoln's Inn Fields, London WC2A 3PH. Tel: 020 7917 8888.

Law Society Archives, Ipsley Court, Redditch, Hereford and Worcester.
Tel: 020 7242 1222.

Law Society, Chancery Lane, London WC2A 1PL. Tel: 020 7320 5946.

London Metropolitan Archives, 40 Northampton Road, London EC1R 0HB.
Tel: 020 7332 3820.

Manorial Documents Register *see* National Register of Archives.

Ministry of Agriculture, Fisheries and Food, Records Review Section, Lion House,
Willowburn Trading Estate, Alnwick, Northumberland NE66 2PF.

Ministry of Defence, Military Survey, Acquisitions and Library Group,
Block A, Government Buildings, Hook Rise South, Tolworth, Surrey KT6 7NB.
Tel: 020 8330 7959.

National Archives of Scotland, HM General Register House, Edinburgh EH1 3YY.

National Archives of Scotland (West Register House), Charlotte Square,
Edinburgh EH2 4DF. Tel: 0131 535 1314.

National Library of Scotland, George IV Bridge, Edinburgh EH1 1EW. Tel: 0131 226 4351.

National Library of Wales, Aberystwyth, Dyfed SY23 3BU. Tel: 01970 623816.

National Monuments Record (England), Great Western Village, Kemble Drive,
Swindon SN2 2GZ.

National Monuments Record of Scotland, John Sinclair House, 16 Bernard Terrace,
Edinburgh EH8 9NX.

National Monuments Record of Wales, Plas Crug, Aberystwyth, Dyfed SY23 1NJ.

National Railway Museum Library, Leeman Road, York YO2 4XJ. Tel: 01904 621261.

National Register of Archives, Royal Commission for Historical Manuscripts,
Quality House, Quality Court, Chancery Lane, London WC2A 1HP. Tel: 020 7242 1198.

Patent Office Sale Branch, St Mary Cray, Orpington, Kent BR5 3RD.

Principal Registry of the Family Division, First Avenue House, 42–49 High Holborn,
London WC1V 6NP. Tel: 020 7936 7000.

Public Record Office, Ruskin Avenue, Kew, Richmond, Surrey TW9 4DU.
Tel: 020 8876 3444.

Public Record Office of Northern Ireland, 66 Balmoral Avenue, Belfast BT9 6NY.
Tel: 01232 251318.

Registry of Deeds, King's Inn, Henrietta Street, Dublin, Republic of Ireland.
Tel: 003531 6707500.

Royal Institute of British Architects Library, 66 Portland Place, London W1N 4AD.

Rural History Centre and Museum of English Rural Life, The University of Reading,
Whiteknights, PO Box 229, Reading RG6 2AG.

Society of Genealogists, 14 Charterhouse Buildings, Goswell Road, London EC1M 7BA.
Tel: 020 7251 8799.

Stationers' Hall, Stationers' Hall Court, London EC4.
Victoria and Albert Museum, Cromwell Road, South Kensington, London SW7 2RL.
   Tel: 020 7942 2000.

Useful websites

Archives and other institutions
PRO and FRC   http://www.pro.gov.uk
National Archives of Scotland   http://www.nas.gov.uk
PRONI   http://proni.nics.gov.uk
British Library   http://www.bl.gov.uk
National Register of Archives   http://www.hmc.gov.uk/nra
ARCHON   http://www.hmc.gov.uk/archon
English Heritage   http://www.english-heritage.co.uk
Land Registry   http://www.landreg.gov.uk
British Records Association   http://www.hmc.dov.uk/bra
College of Arms   http://www.college-of-arms.gov.uk
EARL – Public Library Networking   http://www.earl.gov.uk
Law Society   http://lawsoc.org.uk
Bodleian Library, Oxford   http://www.bodley.ox.ac.uk
Getting started   http://www.arts-scheme.co.uk (*from Autumn 2001*)

Genealogy
Family History Portal   http://www.familyrecords.gov.uk
Society of Genealogists   http://www.socgen.co.uk
Genealogy in UK and Ireland   http://www.genuki.com
Familia   http://www.familia.com
Origins   http://www.origins.net

House history
House history   http://www.house-detectives.co.uk (*from Autumn 2001*)

Local history
Victoria County Histories   http://www.ihrinfo.ac.uk/vch
British Association for Local History   http://www.balh.co.uk
Gazetteer of British Place Names   http://www.gazetteer.co.uk

Maps
Online access to aerial and street maps   http://www.getmapping.com
                                           http://www.multimap.com
                                           http://www.streetmap.co.uk

Period properties
Period properties   http://www.periodproperty.co.uk
Society for the Protection of Ancient Buildings   http://www.spab.org.uk
Britannia (histories of country houses)   http://www.britannia.com

Useful publications

House history (general)

D. Austin, M. Dowdy, J. Miller, *Be Your Own House Detective* (BBC Books, 1997)

J. H. Harvey, *Sources for the History of Houses* (British Records Association, 1968)

B. Breckon and J. Parker, *Tracing the History of Houses* (Countryside Books, 1998)

M. W. Bailey, *The English Farmhouse and Cottage* (Sutton, 1987)

R. W. Brunskill, *Illustrated Handbook of Vernacular Architecture* (Faber, 1970)

D. Iredale and J. Barrett, *Discovering Your Old House* (Shire Publications, 1991)

P. Bushell, *Tracing the History of Your House* (Pavilion Books, 1989)

N. Currer-Briggs, *Debrett's Guide to Your House* (Headline, 1993)

N. Pevsner *et al.*, *The Buildings of England* (Penguin, 1951–)

M. Wood, *The English Medieval House* (Ferndale, 1981)

C. L. Kingsford, 'A London Merchant's House and its Owners', *Archaelogica* 74 (1923–4), pp. 137–58

D. Cruickshank and P. Wyld, *Georgian Town Houses and Their Details* (Butterworth, 1990)

H. M. Colvin, *A Biographical Dictionary of British Architects 1600–1840*, 3rd edn (Yale University Press, 1995)

A. Felstead, J. Franklin, L. Pinfield, *Directory of British Architects 1834–1900* (Mansell, 1993)

Local history guides and publications

Alphabetical List of Parishes and Places in England and Wales, 2 vols (HMSO, 1897)

English Place Name Society series (published by county)

Victoria History of the Counties of England series (published by county)

J. S. W. Gibson, *Local Newspapers 1750–1920* (FFHS, 1987)

M. D. Herber, *Ancestral Trails* (Sutton, 1997)

D. Hey, *Oxford Companion to Local and Family History* (Oxford University Press, 1996)

S. Lewis, *Topographical Dictionary of England* (London, 1840)

S. Lewis, *Topographical Dictionary of Ireland* (London, 1846)

S. Lewis, *Topographical Dictionary of Scotland* (London, 1846)

S. Lewis, *Topographical Dictionary of Wales* (London, 1840)

A. Macfarlane, *A Guide to English Historical Records* (Cambridge University Press, 1983)

L. Munby, Rev. K. M Thompson, *Short Guides to Records, 2 series* (Historical Association, 1994, 1997)

P. Riden, *Local History: a Handbook for Beginners*, 2nd edn (Batsford, 1998)

C. D. Rogers and J. H. Smith, *Local Family History in England, 1538–1914* (Manchester University Press, 1991)

W. B. Stephens, *Sources for English Local History* (Phillimore, 1994)

F. A. Youngs Jr, *Guide to the Administrative Units of England, 2 vols* (Royal Historical Society, 1980, 1991)

Guides to the PRO and FRC

A. Bevan (ed.), *Tracing Your Ancestors at the PRO*, 5th edn (PRO, 1999)

J. Cox, *New to Kew?* (PRO, 1997)

J. Cox and S. Colwell, *Never Been Here Before? A Genealogist's Guide to the FRC* (PRO, 1998)

Guides to record offices

Royal Commission on Historical Manuscripts, *Record Repositories in Great Britain*, 11th edn (PRO, 1999)

J. Foster and J. Sheppard, *British Archives: A Guide to Archive Resources in the United Kingdom* (Macmillan, 1995)

J. S. W. Gibson and P. Peskett, *Record Offices and How to Find Them* (FFHS, 1998)

S. Guy, *English Local Studies Handbook: A Guide to Resources for Each County including Libraries, Record Societies, Journals and Museums* (University of Exeter Press, 1992)

Guides to document interpretation

C. Trice-Martin, *The Record Interpreter* (Phillimore, 1982)

C. T. Lewis and C. Short, *A Latin Dictionary* Clarendon Press, 1886)

R. E. Latham, *Revised Medieval Latin Word List* (Oxford University Press, 1989)

E. Gooder, *Latin for Local History*, 2nd edn (Longman, 1978)

D. Stuart, *Latin for local and county historians: A Beginner's Guide* (Phillimore, 1995)

B. H. Kennedy, rev. Sir J. Mountford, *Shorter Latin Primer* (Longman, 1974)

C. R. Cheney, rev. M. Jones, *Handbook of Dates for Students of British History* (Cambridge University Press, 2000)

W. S. B. Buck, *Examples of Handwriting 1550–1650* (Society of Genealogists, 1996).

Maps, plans and land surveys

General

Maps and Plans in the British Isles 1410–1860 (PRO, 1967)

W. Foot, *Maps for Family History* (PRO, 1994)

Royal Historical Society Guides and Handbooks No. 18, 'Historians' Guide to British Maps' (London, 1994)

B. P. Hindle, *Maps for Local History* (Batsford, 1988)

P. D. A. Harvey, *Maps in Tudor England* (British Library, 1993)

J. B. Harley, *Maps for the Local Historian: A Guide to British Sources* (National Council for Social Service, 1972).

O. Mason (ed.), *Bartholomew Gazetteer of Places in Britain* (Bartholomew, 1986)

Valuation survey

B. Short and M. Reed, 'An Edwardian Land Survey: the Finance (1909–1910) Act 1910 Records', *Journal of the Society of Archivists*, VIII (1) and VIII (2) (1986)

B. Short and M. Reed, *Landownership and Society in Edwardian England and Wales: the Finance (1909–10) Act 1910 Records* (University of Sussex, 1987)

Tithe apportionments

R. J. P. Kain and R. R. Oliver, *The Tithe Maps and Apportionments of England and Wales* (Cambridge University Press, 1994)

R. J. P. Kain and H. C. Prince, *The Tithe Surveys of England and Wales* (Cambridge University Press, 1985)

E. J. Evans, *The Contentious Tithe* (Routledge & Keegan Paul, 1976)

National Farm Survey

P. S. Barnwell, 'The National Farm Survey 1941–43', *Journal of the Historic Farm Buildings Group*, VII (1994)

J. A. Edwards, *Historical Farm Records* (University of Reading, 1973)

P. Edwards, *Farming: Sources for Local Historians* (Batsford, 1992)

Enclosure

W. E.Tate, *A Domesday of Enclosure Acts and Awards* (University of Reading, 1978)

W. E. Tate, *The English Village Community and the Enclosure Movements* (Gollancz, 1967)

W. E. Tate, 'Some unexplored records of the English Enclosure Movement', *English Historical Review*, LVII (1942)

M. W. Beresford, 'Habitiation versus Improvement: the debate on enclosure by agreement' in F. J. Fisher (ed.), *Essays in the Economic and Social History of Tudor and Stuart England in Honour of R.H. Tawney* (Cambridge University Press, 1961)

Land law and conveyancing

J. G. Riddall, *Introduction to Land Law*, 5th edn (Butterworth, 1993)

B. English and J. Saville, *Strict Settlement: A Guide for Historians* (University of Hull, 1983)

A. W. B. Simpson, *A History of the Land Law* (Clarendon Press, 1986)

R. E. Latham, 'Feet of Fines', *The Amateur Historian*, I (1) (1952)

J. Kissock, 'Medieval Feet of Fines: a study of their uses', *The Local Historian*, XXIV (2) (1994)

Title deeds

A Descriptive Catalogue of Ancient Deeds in the Public Record Office, 6 volumes (HMSO, 1890–1906)

N. W. Alcock, *Old Title Deeds* (Phillimore, 1986)

A. A. Dibben, *Title Deeds* (Historical Association, 1971)

F. Sheppard and V. Belcher, 'The Deed Registries of Yorkshire and Middlesex', *Journal of the Society of Archivists* VI (1978–81), pp. 274–286

K. T. Ward, 'Pre-Registration Title Deeds: The Legal Issues of Ownership, Custody and Abandonment', *Journal of the Society of Archivists* XVI (1995), pp. 27–39

Manorial and estate records

M. Ellis, *Using Manorial Records* (PRO, 1997)

P. D. A. Harvey, *Manorial Records* (British Records Association, 1984)

D. Stuart, *Manorial Records* (Phillimore, 1992)

R. Hoyle, *The Estates of the English Crown, 1558–1640* (Cambridge University Press, 1992)

A. Travers, 'Manorial Documents', *Genealogists' Magazine* XXI (1983)

Records of property inheritance

M. Scott, *Prerogative Court of Canterbury: Wills and Other Probate Records* (PRO, 1997)

J. Cox, *Hatred Pursued Beyond the Grave* (HMSO, 1993)

A. J. Camp, *Wills and their Whereabouts*, 4th edn (British Records Association, 1974)

E. McLaughlin, *Wills before 1858* (FFHS, 1994)

E. McLaughlin, *Wills from 1858* (FFHS, 1995)

B. English, 'Inheritance and Succession in Landed Families 1660–1925', *Genealogists' Magazine*, XXIV, pp. 433–8

Legal disputes

J. H. Baker, *An Introduction to English Legal History* (Butterworth, 1990)

R. E. F. Garrett, *Chancery and other Legal Proceedings* (Pinhorns, 1968)

H. Horwitz, *Chancery Equity Records and Proceedings 1600–1800*, a guide to documents in the PRO, rev. edn (PRO, 1998)

H. Horwitz, *Exchequer Equity Records and Proceedings 1649–1841*, a guide to documents in the PRO (PRO, 2001)

A. Martin, *Index to various Repertories, Books of Orders, and Decrees, and other Records preserved in the Court of Exchequer* (Society of the Inner Temple, 1819)

W. H. Bryson, *The Equity side of the Exchequer* (Cambridge University Press, 1975)

H. Sharp, *How to Use the Bernau Index* (Society of Genealogists, 1996)

J. S. W. Gibson, *Quarter Session Records for Family Historians: A Select List* (FFHS, 1995)

Sir Julius Caesar, *The Ancient State, Authority and Proceedings of the Court of Requests* L. M. Hill (ed.) (Cambridge University Press, 1975)

J. A. Guy, *The Court of Star Chamber and its Records to the Reign of Elizabeth I* (PRO, 1984)

Genealogy

General

S. Colwell, *Dictionary of Genealogical Sources in the PRO* (Weidenfeld & Nicolson, 1992)

S. Raymond, *County Genealogical Bibliographies*, published by county

J. S. W. Gibson and M. Walcot, *Where to find the International Genealogical Index* (FFHS, 1985)

Census

E. Higgs, *A clearer sense of the census* (HMSO, 1996)
S. Lumas, *Making sense of the census* (PRO, 1992)
J. S. W. Gibson and E. Hampson, *Census Returns 1841–1891 on Microform: a Directory to Local Holdings* (FFHS, 1997)
C. Chapman, *Pre-1841 Census and Population Listings* (Lochin Publishing, 1994)

Electoral material

J. S. W. Gibson and C. Rogers, *Electoral Registers since 1832 and Burgers Rolls* (FFHS, 1990)
J. S. W. Gibson and C. Rogers, *Poll Books c.1696–1872* (FFHS, 1994)
J. Sims, *A Handlist of British Parliamentary Poll Books* (University of Leicester History Department, 1984)

Parish registers

C. Humphrey-Smith, *The Phillimore Atlas and Index of Parish Registers* (Phillimore, 1984)
National Index of Parish Registers (Society of Genealogists, 1968 continuing)
W. Tate, *The Parish Chest* (Cambridge University Press, 1969)

Trade directories

G. Shaw and A. Tipper, *British Directories: A Bibliography and Guide* (Leicester University Press, 1989)
P. J. Atkins, *The Directories of London 1677–1977* (Mansell Publishing, 1990)

Taxation

J. Gibson, *Hearth Tax Returns and other later Stuart Tax Lists and the Association Oath Rolls* (FFHS, 1996)
J. Gibson, M. Medlycott and D. Mills, *Land and Window Tax Assessments 1690–1950* (FFHS, 1997)
M. Jurkowski, C. L. Smith and D. Crook, *Lay Taxes in England and Wales* (PRO, 1998)
D. V. Glass, *London Inhabitants Within the Walls 1695*, vol.2 (London Record Society Publications, 1966); Corporation of London Record Office has a typescript index of *London Inhabitants Without the Walls*

'A Supplement to the London Inhabitants List of 1695 Compiled by Staff at Guildhall Library', *Guildhall Studies in London History*, vol. 2, no. 2 (Part 1: surnames beginning A–M) and no. 3 (Part 2: surnames beginning N–Z, plus index of trades) (April and October 1976)

National events

J. Youings, *The Dissolution of the Monasteries* (Allen & Unwin, 1971)

W. C. Richardson, *History of the Court of Augmentations, 1536–1640* (Baton Rouge, 1961)

G. E. Aylmer and J. S. Morrill, *The Civil War and Interregnum, Sources for Local Historians* (Bedford Square Press, 1979)

E. Carter, *An Historical Geography of the Railways of the British Isles* (Cassell, 1959)

Modern housing

A. Cole, *An Introduction to Poor Law Documents before 1834* (FFHS, 1993)

For background information on the Poor Law reforms and housing conditions in the mid nineteenth century, consult *Index to Parliamentary Papers* (also available on CD-Rom).

J. D. Cantwell, *The Second World War: A Guide to Documents in the PRO*, 3rd edn (PRO, 1998)

How we used to live

H. A. L. Cockerell and E. Green, *The British Insurance Business, 1547–1970*, 2nd edn (Sheffield Academic Press, 1994)

M. W. Beresford, 'Building History from Fire Insurance Records', *Urban History Yearbook* (Leicester University Press, 1976)

E. Arber (ed.), *A Transcript of the Registers of the Company of Stationers of London 1554–1640* (London, 1875–94)

B. Eyre (ed.), *A Transcript of the Registers of the Worshipful Company of Stationers 1640–1708* (London, 1913–14)

J. S. Batts, *British Manuscripts Diaries of the 19th Century: An Annotated Listing* (Totawa, NJ, 1976)

J. Miller, *Period Details Sourcebook* (Mitchell Beazley, 1999)

Index

Bold page numbers refer to illustrations, captions or examples